305.4
SKAINE

Skaine, Rosemarie
   The women of
Afghanistan under
the Taliban

## DATE DUE

| | | | |
|---|---|---|---|
| SEP 2 5 2004 | | | |
| SEP 1 2 2006 | | | |
| | | | |
| | | | |
| | | | |
| | | | |
| | | | |
| | | | |
| | | | |
| | | | |
| | | | |
| | | | |
| | | | |
| | | | |
| | | | |

Demco, Inc. 38-293

# THE WOMEN
# OF AFGHANISTAN
# UNDER THE TALIBAN

*by*
*Rosemarie Skaine*

McFarland & Company, Inc., Publishers
*olina, and London*

To our Afghan sisters

ISBN 0-7864-1090-6 (softcover : 50# alkaline paper) ∞

Library of Congress cataloguing data are available

British Library cataloguing data are available

Manufactured in the United States of America

*Cover photograph ©2000 Luke Powell/globalphoto.com*

*McFarland & Company, Inc., Publishers
Box 611, Jefferson, North Carolina 28640
www.mcfarlandpub.com*

# Acknowledgments

I thank the people I interviewed. Through them I gained perspective and focus. Haron Amin, Afghan diplomat (first secretary), Islamic State of Afghanistan, United Nations, provided the critical first interview. His insightful, inspirational and informative remarks gave me a sense of direction for this very complex topic.

The Revolutionary Association of the Women of Afghanistan (RAWA) provided interviews with Afghan women and with Shabana, an activist and member of the Cultural Committee. I am grateful to Salma, coordinator of the Foreign Relations Committee; Farid, translator; and Huma and Selay for their assistance. To the women who bared their souls in interviews so that I could record their stories, I am deeply grateful. For the risks they take each day I thank all of these women.

Nasarine Abou-Bakre Gross gave a most helpful interview and has written insightfully on Afghan women. Mora Hashimi and Rahman Hashimi of Springfield, Virginia, provided personal accounts of their lives in Afghanistan.

Peter Tomsen, ambassador-in-residence, University of Nebraska at Omaha and former special envoy to the Afghan Resistance, 1989–1992, enabled me to understand better the role of the United States in Afghanistan's wars. Abdul Raheem Yaseer, coordinator of International Exchange Programs and deputy director of the Center for Afghanistan Studies at the University of Nebraska at Omaha, shared his heritage and understanding and his ongoing work for Afghanistan. Catherine Daly of the Department of Textiles, Clothing and Design and the Research Association for the Center of Afghanistan Studies, University of Nebraska at Omaha, shared with me her expertise on Afghan women and their dress. Mavis Leno, chair of the Feminist Majority Foundation's Campaign on Gender Apartheid, and the members of the Feminist Majority have worked tirelessly on behalf of Afghan women.

I am grateful to Susie Gilligan, Feminist Majority, for her facilitation of the interview with Mavis Leno, and to Midhat Abraham, Ph.D., Middle East librarian, University of Arizona Library, Tucson, Arizona, for assistance with transliteration.

Many organizations added to the knowledge base of this book. Angela E.V. King, special adviser to the secretary-general on gender issues and advancement of women, United Nations, Department of Economic and Social Affairs, provided a most helpful official report. Dr. Amir S. Hassanyar, director, Cooperation Centre for Afghanistan, sent informative reports and newsletters. Sima Wali, president, Refugee Women in Development, Inc., Washington, D.C., made published works available. Daoud Yaqub, Afghanistan Foundation, Washington, D.C., emailed current accounts of events as they occurred. In the critical early stages of the book, Janice Eisenhauer, Women for Women in Afghanistan, Calgary, Canada, provided information and a sense of direction.

Senator Charles Grassley (R-Iowa) and Fred Schuster, Northeast Iowa Regional Director, I thank for their ongoing willingness to make my government a meaningful and participatory democracy for me, their constituent. I appreciate their helping me wend my way through the maze of governmental departments.

RADM D.M. "Mac" Williams, Jr., U.S. Navy (ret.), former Naval Investigative Service Commander, provided much appreciated support and assistance.

James C. Skaine edited and assisted in the research. My late, beloved father, Warren V. Keller, gave a lasting gift of love. Other family members provided encouragement: Richard L. and Nancy L. Craft Kuehner, William V. and Carolyn E. Guenther Kuehner, and Paulette, George and Sarah Mouchet.

My friend Robert Kramer, professor emeritus, Center for Social and Behavioral Research and Department of Sociology, Anthropology, and Criminology, University of Northern Iowa, provided invaluable expertise in cyber technology.

My friend of yesteryear, Cass Paley, I thank for his gift of truth that can set anyone free into an invincible summer.

# Contents

# Tables

# Abbreviations

In the interests of clarity and consistency, I have used the abbreviations and spellings indicated below, unless a direct citation spells something otherwise.

| | |
|---|---|
| AI | Amnesty International |
| AWN | Afghan Women's Network |
| AWC | Afghan Women's Council |
| CCA | Co-operation Centre for Afghanistan |
| DRA | Democratic Republic of Afghanistan |
| ICHRDD | International Centre for Human Rights and Democratic Development |
| ICRC | International Committee of the Red Cross |
| ISI | Inter-Services Intelligence Agency of Pakistan |
| KOAW | Khalq Organization of Afghan Women |
| NEGAR | Defense of Afghan Women's Rights |
| NGO | non-governmental organization |
| NIFA | National Islamic Front of Afghanistan |
| PDPA | People's Democratic Party of Afghanistan |
| PHR | Physicians for Human Rights |
| RAWA | Revolutionary Association of the Women of Afghanistan |
| RefWID | Refugee Women in Development |
| UFA | United Front for Afghanistan (Northern Alliance) |
| UNHCR | United Nations High Commissioner for Refugees |
| UNICEF | United Nations International Children's Emergency Fund |
| UNOCHA | United Nations Office for the Coordination of Humanitarian Assistance in Afghanistan |

| | |
|---|---|
| UNSMA | United Nations Special Mission for Peace in Afghanistan |
| WAPHA | Women's Alliance for Peace and Human Rights in Afghanistan |
| WDOA | Women's Democratic Organization of Afghanistan |
| WLUML | The Women Living Under Muslim Laws |
| WORFA | Women on the Road for Afghanistan |

# Preface

*I'm the woman who has awoken*
*I've arisen and become a tempest through the ashes of my burnt*
*    children*
*I've arisen from the rivulets of my brother's blood*
*My nation's wrath has empowered me*
*My ruined and burnt villages fill me with hatred against the enemy...*
*Oh compatriot, oh brother, no longer regard me weak and incapable*
*With all my strength I'm with you on the path of my land's liberation.*
*My voice has mingled with thousands of arisen women*
*My fists are clenched with the fists of thousands of compatriots*
*Along with you I've stepped up to the path of my nation,*
*To break all these sufferings all these fetters of slavery.*
*Oh compatriot, Oh brother, I'm not what I was*
*I'm the woman who has awoken*
*I've found my path and will never return.*

Meena[1]

   This book addresses the lives of Afghan women in their geopolitical, social, religious, national identity, and historical roles in order to understand their courage and achievements. Since 1979, they have lived in a country torn by war and have been subjected to violence, killing and imprisonment. The hope of rebuilding Afghanistan lies in the courage of all Afghans, especially the women.

   That the most unbelievable atrocities have been committed against the Afghan people—women, men and children alike—cannot be denied. For over 20 years, constant war has exacted a huge toll. Before 1979, Afghanistan was a nation moving toward greater freedoms for its people and toward a peaceful society. When the current warfare ends, the people will rebuild as they have done in the past.

   As this book goes to press, the Taliban's future is uncertain. Under heavy attack by the United States and its allies in response to the terrorist actions of September 11, 2001, the Taliban may soon fall. Once free, Afghanistan will need help from strong global leadership in building a new government.

Important cogs in rebuilding Afghan society are the women. Afghan women are strong and courageous. They pass Afghan culture from generation to generation and play a critical role in their society. Peter Marsden says that where nationalist or religious identity has been involved, women have often taken on a symbolic importance as the reproducers of that identity.[2]

It is important to view Afghan women within their cultural context and to realize that Afghan society is not any more homogeneous than Western society. The law of the Taliban is not Afghan or Islam, but a law unto itself and driven by forces outside Afghanistan.

The fierce and spirited lives of Afghan women are reflected in studies and collections of their stories. Valiant voices of the living tell us of their enduring strength in the face of the ravages of war. The forever silenced voices must also be heard as the powerful legacy of ancient Afghanistan continues. Meena, a martyred founder of the Revolutionary Association of the Women of Afghanistan (RAWA), said it best in the poem quoted above: her voice, she says, has mingled with those of thousands of women to break the sufferings and the fetters of slavery.

The purpose of this book is twofold: to demonstrate the politicization of Afghan women, and to preserve their voices.

# Introduction

*In the second round of colonization the women can develop a mission of eating away at the power of the Taliban in the same guerrilla way that the men did in the first round. Maybe not with stinger missiles, but with other means.*

Nasrine Abou-Bakre Gross[1]

Afghanistan has been ruled by many conquerors since its beginning. In the early period, Darius ruled in 500 B.C. Alexander the Great conquered Afghanistan in 329–327 B.C. when it was the "Gateway to India."[2] The Islamic period began around the 7th century A.D. and lasted until the 18th century. This period included such rulers as Genghis Khan in c. 1220 and Timure Lung in the 14th century. The Afghan Empire period lasted from 1709 to 1826.[3]

The "Great Game," as the European imperial period was called, took place from 1826 to 1919. Britain and Russia tried to control Afghanistan as part of the effort to gain control of northern access to India. The Afghans battled the British army from 1839 to 1842. The "Great Game" is defined by Peter Hopkirk as "maneuvering for long-term advantage" by rival outside powers competing to fill political and economic voids.[4] The second Afghan War with Britain occurred from 1878 to 1881. Britain received governance concessions in the treaty that ended this war.

Amir Habibullah Khan was king from 1901 to 1919. Under the rule of King Amanullah, Afghanistan won its independence from Britain and in 1926 established a monarchy that granted rights to women. Afghanistan had a period of independent monarchy from 1919 to 1973. Close ties with Russia developed under Zahir Shah from 1933 to 1973. Under Sardar Mohammad Daoud Khan from 1973 to 1978, Afghanistan was proclaimed a republic. From 1978 to 1979 under Nur Mohammad Taraki it was a Marxist state and a dictatorship. The Soviet Union invaded Afghanistan in 1979.

From 1980 to 1986 Russia supported President Babrak Karmal. The Soviets were forced to withdraw from Afghanistan in 1989.

Factional fighting broke out after the Russian withdrawal. The Mujahedin and strict Islam prevailed from 1992 to 1996. In 1994, the Taliban militia and its brand of harsh fundamentalist Islam began to dominate. The Taliban captured Kandahar in November 1994, Herat in September 1995, and Jalalabad in 1996. The Taliban's dominance reached a peak when they took control of Kabul in September 1996.[5]

Much Taliban activity is extreme and brutal. Haron Amin explains that the Taliban are taking their harshness out on the women, but when one looks beyond women, and focuses on other ethnic and religious groups, one sees an "extremely dangerous and powerful concoction."[6] The Muslim Women's League adds its voice to the philosophies of government officials and scholars: "Taliban's stand on the seclusion of women is not derived from Islam, but, rather, from a cultural bias found in suppressive movements throughout the region."[7]

The current plight of the Afghan people, however, is part of larger, global problems that do not begin or end with the Taliban. Some Afghan activists believe their country's straits are global in nature. In 1990, Peter Hopkirk predicted a new struggle was under way as Central Asia's position in "the new Great Game" took center stage. Some of the players are new, the stakes are higher, but it is the "continuation of the age-old struggle," and one of the "most powerful players in today's Great Game is the last of the superpowers, the United States of America." Hopkirk believed it impossible to guess how "things would work out."[8] As the superpowers struggle with nuclear power, what Louis Dupree reminded us of in 1980 remains true today: Afghanistan, "created partly as a result of imperialism, but never a colony," may find achieving stability not impossible, but challenging.[9]

Afghanistan is mostly a rugged, mountainous country. It is slightly smaller than the state of Texas and has a population estimated to be about 26 million.[10] Jan Goodwin calls Afghanistan a country of savage beauty. Its mountains are some of the highest in the world, and while the landscape is harsh, trees and streams dot the terrain.[11] Economically, it is very poor and depends on farming and raising sheep and goats. Vigorous opium poppy cultivation is the mainstay of the economy. In 1999, Afghanistan became the largest opium producer in the world. Yet, agriculture is threatened by the lack of resources to rebuild roads, reconstruct irrigation, and replant orchards, and by the presence of landmines.

The country is one of the world's most mine-laden, with an estimated 500,000 to 800,000 antitank and antipersonnel mines that were buried during the war with the Soviets from 1979 to 1989.[12] Landmines prevent refugees from returning to rebuild, as does the continuous fighting among factions, some of which are materially aided by external forces. The U.S. Department of State reported that the continued fighting has discouraged many refugees from returning. In 1999, about 96,700 returned voluntarily with assistance from the U.N. High Commissioner for Refugees.

Estimates of life expectancy range from 45.47 years for women to 46.97 for men. A woman can expect to have about six children. Afghanistan's infant mortality rate is about one in seven.[13] About half of the males and only 15 percent of the women age 15 and over can read and write. International assistance of $280 per capita per year may not be adequate, the World Bank observes.

Rural Afghans are thought to be better off because they can live off

## TABLE 1.1
## THE AFGHAN PEOPLE AT A GLANCE
2001 Estimates Except Where Otherwise Noted

|  | Number | Percent of Population |
|---|---|---|
| Population | 26,813,057 |  |
| 0–14 years | 11,314,757 | 42.2 |
| male | 5,775,921 | 21.5 |
| female | 5,538,836 | 20.7 |
| 15–64 years | 14,750,810 | 55.01 |
| male | 7,644,242 | 28.51 |
| female | 7,106,568 | 26.5 |
| 65 years and over | 747,490 | 2.79 |
| male | 394,444 | 1.47 |
| female | 353,046 | 1.32 |
| Life expectancy in years |  |  |
| population | 46.24 |  |
| male | 46.97 |  |
| female | 45.47 |  |
| Birth rate/1,000 | 41.42 |  |
| Death rate/1,000 | 17.72 |  |
| Infant mortality rate/1,000 live births | 147.02 |  |
| Total fertility rate/children born/woman | 5.79 |  |
| Population growth rate (includes the continued return of refugees) |  | 3.48 |
| Net migration rate/1,000 population | 11.11 |  |
| Literacy rate(persons aged 15 and over who can read and write) (1999) |  | 31.5 |
| male (1999) |  | 47.2 |
| female (1999) |  | 15 |

*Source:* CIA, "The World Factbook 1999 and 2001—Afghanistan," Jan. 1, 1999 and Jan. 1, 2001. Available: http://www.cia.gov/cia/publications/factbook/geos/af.html, Jan. 28, 2000 and Oct. 6, 2001.

the land, but 70 percent of the working age population in Kabul are job-less. People sell their belongings on the street and women beg at dusk. Water is in short supply and electricity is nearly nil.[14] Many who beg, according to Pam Constable of the *Washington Post*, are missing limbs because they have stepped on a landmine.

The four major ethnic groups in Afghanistan are the Pushtun who comprise 38 percent; Tajik, 25 percent; Hazara, 19 percent; and Uzbek, 6 percent. Aimaks, Turkmen, and Baloch are among the minor ethnic groups. Eighty-four percent of Afghans practice the Sunni Muslim religion. Fifteen percent are Shi'a Muslim. The remaining 1 percent consists of small groups of Sikhs, Hindus and Jews. The desire of the factions to promote Islam as a state religion is reflected in the official names they have chosen for Afghanistan. The Taliban chose the Islamic Emirate of Afghanistan, and the Northern Alliance chose the Islamic State of Afghanistan.

Currently, Afghanistan has no constitution and no legal system. It is more or less an unspoken agreement among the various factions that Shari'a (Islamic law) will prevail. There is no legislative or judicial branch of government, and the executive branch is divided among the fighting factions of the country.

On September 27, 1996, the ruling members of the Afghan government were displaced by members of the Islamic Taliban movement. The Islamic State of Afghanistan has no functioning government at this time. The country remains divided as factional fighting continues. Although the Taliban have declared themselves the legitimate government of Afghanistan, the U.N. has deferred a decision on credentials.[15]

The Organization of the Islamic Conference has left the Afghan seat vacant until the question of legitimacy can be resolved through negotiations among the warring factions. The country is essentially divided along ethnic lines: the Taliban control the capital of Kabul and approximately two-thirds of the country, including the predominately ethnic Pushtun areas in Southern Afghanistan. The opposing factions have their stronghold in the ethnically diverse North, which includes the Islamic Taliban, the Islamic State of Afghanistan and others.[16]

Ahmed Rashid describes the Taliban as dangerous to ignore. Their interpretation of Islam has elements of black humor regarding human rights, he says. As rulers over a criminal economy, they profit from 80 percent of the European trade of heroin. They receive support from Saudi Arabia and Pakistan. Robin Banerji says, "The prospect of a similar regime seizing power in nuclear-armed Pakistan is horrifying."[17]

While much of the Afghan population suffers under the Taliban, women bear specific, unrelenting and often violent adversity, including the denial of basic human rights, veiling, seclusion and segregation. Haron Amin says the way women are being treated by the Taliban is "not Afghan."

Some of the questions and issues this book examines are: Who are the Taliban? What is their world status? Is there too much focus on the Taliban, and not enough on the Afghans? Who comprises the internal factions and to what extent are outsiders controlling the wars? Is the war really a civil war? Or does the war have the character of proxy wars by

## TABLE 1.2
## CHRONOLOGY OF RECENT WAR IN AFGHANISTAN

| Date | Event |
| --- | --- |
| 1979 December | Soviet invasion |
| 1989 February | Soviet troops withdraw |
| 1992 April | Mujahedin government in Kabul |
| 1994 November | Taliban capture Kandahar |
| 1995 September | Taliban capture Herat |
| 1996 September | Taliban capture Jalalabad and Kabul |
| | Soon after, imposition of Shari'a law forbidding women from working outside the home, banning their education, and restricting attire. |
| 1997 July | Taliban issue new restrictions on women such as forbidding them to create noise while walking; to wear white socks; to speak to men who are not blood relatives; to travel alongside men who are not members of their family; and to be visible through the windows of their homes. Couples caught in adultery are to be stoned to death. |
| 1998 August | U.S. fires missiles in Afghanistan at alleged terrorist networks |
| 1998 August | Massacre, Mazar-i-Sharif |
| 1998 October | Iranian diplomats found dead in Afghanistan |
| 2000 June | Taliban demands U.N. Security Council support for Afghans after United States and Russia form a "Working Group" against international terrorists' network |
| 2001 October | U.S. and allies launch massive attack in Afghanistan at alleged terrorist networks |

*Sources:* "Country: Afghanistan." "Events," *Kaleidoscope*, ABC-CLIO, Inc., 1999; "Taliban Appeal to UNSC Not to Slap More Curbs on Afghanistan," *Afghan News*, Jun. 12, 2000. Accessed at *Afghan News* website, Jun. 12, 2000; Peter Marsden, *The Taliban: War, Religion and the New Order in Afghanistan*, (Karachi, Lahore, Islamabad: Oxford University Press; London and New York: Zed Books Ltd., 1998), vi–vii.

outsiders using Afghan groups inside Pakistan, as Ambassador Peter Tomsen believes?[18] What great strengths are the women exhibiting during the Taliban rule? Is it only a matter of time until movements in Afghanistan optimize women's strengths and talents?

It is necessary to view Afghan women in the context of their culture in order to understand their journey. Chapter One of this book offers an overview of Afghanistan's progress and setbacks during the 20th century in giving its women political and social rights. Afghan women have long participated in Afghan society. Although scholars differ on the emphasis that should be given to Afghan women's social roles, this chapter addresses these roles as they intertwine with tribal customs. Sima Wali says that the Afghan culture and the values that she grew up with had inherent richness and profound depth, characteristics that have been stolen from the Afghans during over 20 years of war. Hafizullah Emadi writes that the plight of women remains a neglected issue in the literature addressing women and development, and the works that have been written examine women's movements in isolation from international development and the class struggle within the country.[19]

Chapter Two presents the interpretation of Islam and the treatment of women in relationship to the war. Provocative issues surface. Do the Taliban practice true Islam, or are their actions taking Islam to an extreme? Although their policies are harsh for men, the Taliban are extremely cruel to women and girls. A conflict has existed between modernists and Islamic fundamentalists since the 1920s. The Islamic fundamentalists' conception of the role of women has been always conservative. In 1996, the fundamentalists diminished women's power once again by denying them their human rights.[20]

Chapter Three analyzes the complexity of the Afghanistan situation, internally and externally. Over two decades of war have exacted a tremendous toll on all Afghans. Robin Banerji reports that 1.5 million Afghans have died in war since 1979.[21] Geopolitical forces have historically influenced what happens in Afghanistan and continue to do so.

Chapter Four describes the hardships and atrocities imposed on women. Under the rule of the Taliban, women have been abducted, raped, sold into prostitution, taken as wives against their will, stoned, and killed. Women face an uncertain fate when they simply step into the street. Afghan women are denied formal education. They are restricted in the work they are allowed to do and in their freedom to move about in the country. Health care for women has all but ceased. The far-reaching effects of refugee life pose difficult problems for women who are dislocated as they develop new notions of home, and handle the balancing act of family and the new outside world. Unfortunately, some women did not live beyond their experiences with Taliban-supported or other recent governments and cannot tell their stories. One of the most destructive effects of the Taliban's restrictions on women working is that a generation of children are growing up uneducated because most of Afghanistan's teachers were women.

Against all odds, however, Afghan women are finding ways to prevail.

Some women, for example, have not accepted being denied an education. In March 2000, Barry Bearak reported in the *New York Times* that a few women had opened a school for girls. One of the women who opened the school goes about with her face uncovered, a practice also forbidden.[22] Perhaps she will be one of many Afghan women to reclaim basic rights such as education, work, and health care. Sima Wali says that the Afghan conflict has remained hidden to the West and the Afghan women and men whose voices have been silenced should be heard.

Chapter Five, which profiles individual Afghan women, is not for the faint of heart. Some of these profiles include stories of great suffering. Yet the Afghan women's suffering is not a sign of weakness. Their courage in dealing with their crisis is inspiring. Interviews conducted by and translated by the Revolutionary Association of the Women of Afghanistan (RAWA) tell the stories of 30 Afghan women and their families.

Chapter Six examines the possibility of positive change in the future. Such change is sorely needed. Eclipsed by political and military turmoil, humanitarian and economic problems have not received the attention that Afghanistan needs. Afghanistan has indeed a massive human rights problem. Many have fled their country and now face new definitions of home. Many countries and the United Nations continue efforts to restore the rights of women. Angela E.V. King, U.N. Office of the Special Advisor on Gender Issues and Advancement of Women, says, "Further progress was likely to be as slow as the modest progress achieved over the past two years, unless there was a strong negotiated peace."[23]

As Chapter Six shows, however, many organizations are working with and for Afghan women to make a difference. These include Women's Alliance for Peace and Human Rights in Afghanistan (WAPHA); the Revolutionary Association of the Women of Afghanistan (RAWA); the Physicians for Human Rights (PHR); Women's Alliance for Peace and Human Rights in Afghanistan; Afghan Women's Network (AWN); Amnesty International (AI); Co-operation Centre for Afghanistan (CCA); Defense of Afghan Women's Rights (NEGAR); Doctors Without Borders; Human Rights Commission in Pakistan; the Feminist Majority Foundation; International Centre for Human Rights and Democratic Development (ICHRDD); Physicians Human Rights Educators; Relief Organization for Afghan Orphans and Widows (ROAOW); Refugee Women in Development (RefWID); and Women on the Road for Afghanistan (WORFA). Individuals and organizations are helping to create a milieu for change and are influencing policy makers. Mavis Leno, wife of *Tonight* show host Jay Leno, is chair of the Feminist Majority Foundation's campaign on gender apartheid. She has worked intensively to bring the crisis of Afghan women to public attention.

Those Afghan women fortunate enough to have escaped with their lives, whether inside or outside Afghanistan, will provide the strength and continuity of a culture that has not known peace for over 20 years. The return of a once beautiful life will depend on the efforts of Afghan women and those people and organizations who advocate a better existence for them. Afghanistan is a country in dire difficulty. Foreign assistance is not without problems for all countries involved. The international community must help Afghanistan to become an independent country, but it is difficult to determine how best to give that help so that its infrastructure can be rebuilt and its people can choose a representative government.

In the response to the terrorist attacks of September 11, 2001, the United States and its allies attacked the Taliban and Osama bin Laden in Afghanistan. When that campaign is concluded, the world powers must exert leadership to help the Afghans establish a government of their choice. The Afghan women, who deserve a better life, must be included in the process.

# Modern Political and Social Roles of Afghan Women

*Every day I bear a burden, and I bear this calamity for a purpose:*
*I bear the discomfort of cold and December's snow in hope of spring.*
*—Rumi[1]*

## Politics and the Rights of Women

Haron Amin, Afghan diplomat, says that the current treatment of women in Afghanistan is "not Afghan." He goes on to say:

> If you look at the history of Afghanistan, you see that Afghan women were never beaten publicly because there was always a very, very high degree of respect provided or given toward women. In the 1860s, Ayisha Durrani a forward intellectual woman poet, in fact, wrote on political issues. We had women like that. In the civil composition in a civil society in Afghanistan, women have always played a very, very important role. Throughout the 20th century, you had a progressive movement or governments in Afghanistan that wanted to copy and move along with what was happening in the rest of the world.[2]

When we put a few dates in perspective as Amin suggests, history demonstrates that the Afghans have held women in high esteem. In fact, Queen Gawhar Shad from her throne in Herat ruled an empire from the Tigris River to China. Her husband, Shah Rukh, was weak, and the Queen was the ruling force. When he died in 1447, she ruled for 10 more years.[3]

During Abdur Rahman Khan's reign in 1880, a number of early reforms regarding women occurred. A woman did not have to remarry her husband's next of kin should he die; marriage registration was required; a girl given in marriage before puberty had the right to refuse or accept her marriage at full age; and women could sue for alimony or divorce in cases of cruelty and nonsupport. King Habibullah Khan tried to lessen the expense connected with marriage.[4]

Afghanistan immediately modernized when it gained independence in 1919, writes Aziz. King Amanullah and Queen Soraya took a position against the seclusion of women. The government ordered that women no longer had to walk in parks covered by the veil. In 1920, says Moghadam, the King abolished slavery, freeing women from concubinage. In 1921, Queen Soraya established the first women's magazine, *Irshadi Niswan* (*The Guide for Women*). The king established Anjuman-e-Himayat-e-Niswan (Women's Protective Association) to promote emancipation. He appointed his sister, Kubra, head of the association.[5] Amanullah introduced a number of social reforms including monogamy, allowing girls to choose their marriage partners, compulsory education for both genders and the separation of religion from politics and the state. According to Moghadam, Amanullah's most audacious acts were to begin a study abroad program for Afghan students and to open the first schools for girls.[6] One example of the Afghans' regard for their women was manifested in sending the first group of Afghan girls to the West for education in 1928.[7] Moghadam concludes, "Afghan legislation was among the most progressive in the Muslim world.... It is not surprising that the family law of 1921 was a major cause of the uprising instigated by the clergy in 1924."[8]

According to Louis Dupree, the ideals of the Afghan society were expressed in the 1931 constitution, but due to its political structure, the ideals were not always enforceable. Article Nine of the constitution says that all persons having Afghan citizenship are equal. Women are not specifically mentioned, but were presumed to have shared in the rights mentioned in Section III. Among those rights were prohibition of imprisonment without due process, slavery, search of personal property without an order, confiscation of personal property, and forced labor. The constitution also dictates compulsory primary education, the appeal of court decisions, and freedom of the press. Dupree says that despite the provisions of the 1931 Constitution, "all persons were not given equal treatment before the law, and women held a decidedly inferior position in Afghan society."[9]

From the end of the 1920s to 1963, customs brought objections against women unveiling in public and their freedom to move about. Many schools for girls were discontinued. In 1929, King Amanullah's program was defeated and he was forced to abdicate by a tribal rebellion led by Habibullah. In the nine months that Habibullah ruled, schools closed, female students abroad returned, and polygamy once again became law.

In 1929, General Mohammad Nadir overthrew Habibullah and proclaimed himself the new king. He made Islam a state religion, and decreed that women must wear veils. He closed schools for girls, and not until the last two years (1932 to 1934) of his reign could girls attend schools; and then, these schools were for girls alone.[10]

Mohammad Zahir, who took the throne in 1934 and ruled until 1973, established separate schools for girls and employed women in professions considered appropriate, such as teaching and medical personnel.[11] Although women's colleges had existed since 1946, women were first admitted to Kabul University in 1959.[12]

Prime Minister Mohammad Daoud, who served from 1953 to 1963 under King Zahir, led a movement in 1959 to unveil women.[13] Nancy Hatch Dupree writes that unveiling was voluntary, which left it up to "individual families to decide."[14] When Daoud was the president (1973 to 1978), he forbade child marriage, declared the dowry to be the property of the wife, established a family court with a woman judge, and recruited women into the police and armed forces.[15]

Moghadam believes that Afghanistan's religious and tribal forces strongly opposed change.[16] Civil law in 1977 abolished child marriage and set the legal marriage age to 16, but the law did not address the husband's right to unilaterally divorce.[17]

Amin stresses the importance of comparing what happened in Afghanistan with what was happening in the rest of the Middle East.

> Afghanistan joined United Nations in 1946, at the time there were only about 55 countries that joined the United Nations. The independence movements that were advocated by a lot of these powerful middle western countries begot a lot of new nations which were infant nations. But at the time, Afghanistan was already existing, it was a state, and so many of the middle eastern societies, by far the Afghans, had shown or exhibited a crescendo in terms of the women's liberation movement. Women were there in all aspects of life, poets, writers, ministers and members of the parliament, already under the 1964 Constitution.

In 1959, women in Afghanistan were actually learning to drive and do many things, says Amin. Louis Dupree notes that 1957 saw women work on the Radio Afghanistan staff, in the factories, in other workplaces, accompany their husbands to overseas posts, compose a delegation to a conference of Asian women in Ceylon, and in 1958 a woman delegate represented Afghanistan in the United Nations. In 1959, Prime Minister Mohammed Daoud decided that, since the veil and the *purdah*, the isolation from all men except near relatives, could not be justified in Islamic law, wives of high officials could appear in reviewing stands during the *Jeshn* holidays with their faces bared. Daoud's decision was a step toward further emancipation of women in Afghanistan.[18] Amin and Dupree agree that the abolition of *purdah* was social, political and economic reform. The potential labor force increased by 50 percent. By the 1960s and 1970s women served as ministers and heads of organizations. Dupree states that, for the first time, women delegates entered the controversy over the meaning of the term "Afghan" in the line in the 1964 constitution, "No Afghan accused of a crime can be extradited to a foreign state." One woman advocated that women should be specifically mentioned, but withdrew her proposal when the constitutional committee assured her that the word "Afghan" included both genders. Dupree concludes that "the emphasis on the legal equality of women is one of the more important aspects of the 1964 constitution."[19] Although women were permitted to vote by the 1964 constitution and by election law, they usually voted only in the larger urban centers.[20] Goodwin says that Rokia Habib, one of the first four women elected to the Afghan House of Representatives in the 1960s, explained,

> Two women were members of the Counseling Committee in charge of drafting the new Afghan constitution. Four others, myself included, became members of the Grand Assembly, which adopted the constitution that same year. The movement for women's emancipation in Afghanistan began long before the communist takeover.[21]

From 1963 to 1973, two women were in the government: Kobra Norzaye, Minister of Public Health from 1965 to 1969 and Shafiqa Ziayee, political advisor, 1972. Four women were elected to the government as deputies in the parliament from 1965 to 1969: Dr. Anahita Ratebzad, Khadija Ahrari, Roqia Abubakr and Masuma Esmati Wardak. Two women were in the Mishranu Jirgah: Homeira Seljuki and Aziza Gardizi. Most women who participated in government were urban.[22]

Hundreds of women students objected to Parliament when in 1968 conservative members proposed that Afghan women be prohibited from studying abroad. The women said the constitution guaranteed equal rights for both men and women. In the 1970s, some women adopted the Western style of clothes, and conservative factions objected.

The organized women's movement in 1964 consisted of two political groups, Feminists and Socialists. The Feminists advocated equality of men and women regardless of class or ideology. The Socialists wanted to change the material bases of women's oppression, the semi-feudal and capitalist relations of production.[23] Conservative forces saw the women's movement as anti–Islam. During a demonstration, a religious leader threw acid on several women. He was arrested, but he said he would do it again. More than 5,000 women demonstrated saying, "Give him back to us!"

According to Jan Goodwin, conditions for women before the Russian invasion depended on where they lived. In urban areas, girls were educated, and many went to college. Most did not wear the chadari, the large head-to-toe pleated garment designed to cover the woman's body completely. Arranged marriages were the rule rather than the exception, but "love matches were becoming common." In rural areas, only boys benefited from education. Women lived in seclusion unless they worked in the field, and their work was long and hard because they also cared for their children and the home.[24]

The government was based on voluntary introduction of change and family attitudes prevailed, even though women were enfranchised by the 1964 constitution, a penal code in 1976, and civil law in 1977 that addressed rights regarding child marriage, forced marriage, inheritance and abandonment. The leftist group in power in 1978 promised full equality for women, but in reality they did not provide it. The emphasis on Western dress, a standard for urban women before the war, does not account for "the fact that all males outside privileged Party members had been conscripted or fled into exile." Women were more visible in Kabul but had no real decision-making or power-sharing roles.[25]

President Daoud was overthrown in 1978 and Afghanistan became a democratic regime, electing Nur Mohammad Taraki, secretary general of the Khalq faction of the People's Democratic Party of Afghanistan (PDPA) as chairman of the Revolutionary Council and president and prime minister. Taraki believed women belonged in the home and counted none as followers.[26] Babrak Karmal, leader of the Parcham faction of the PDPA, became vice-chairman and deputy prime minister. Shortly into the term, the Parcham faction members were removed from the cabinet.

In 1979 the Khalq and Parcham factions united with Russian influence, writes Emadi. President Taraki was killed in a fight that occurred because Premier Amin would not resign. President Amin, once elected, tried to normalize relations with the United States. The Soviet Union eliminated Amin and put in President Babrak Karmal. More women were employed in industry and social services because men were enlisted to fight. The Khalq Organization of Afghan Women (KOAW) was renamed the Women's Democratic Organization of Afghanistan (WDOA), which was the only women's group that supported the Russian invasion.[27]

Women and men were declared equal "in all social, economic, political, cultural and civil aspects."[28] Dr. Anahita Ratebzad, who had become

Afghanistan's first woman doctor in 1963 and won a seat in parliament in 1965, was appointed minister of social affairs to promote the cause of liberating women. Ratebzad formed the Parcham-founded Women's Democratic Organization of Afghanistan, which became the Khalq Organization of Afghan Women led by appointed President Delara Mahak. The Khalq faction outlawed arranged marriages, limited amounts of the dowry, and campaigned against illiteracy by opening night schools with the intent of politically indoctrinating women.[29]

In 1979, when the Soviets took over, they instituted changes in the status of women. Decree Number 7 forbade forced marriages and required a minimum age to marry, with an imprisonment penalty up to three years for violators.[30] According to the Online Center for Afghan Studies, this decree advocated the liberation of women but its agenda was a "direct and open attack on Afghan culture and honor."[31] Valentine M. Moghadam says that the new marriage regulation coupled with compulsory education for girls, "raised the threat of women refusing to obey and submit to family (male) authority."[32] When villagers sometimes would not attend literacy classes, the communists used physical force. Some who fled to Pakistan cited as their reason the use of force to have women attend literacy classes. Reasons for Afghans' objections were not uncomplicated, explains Moghadam. While some reasons were a product of male chauvinism, others were that educating the women brought dishonor to the women and to the household because they were not in *purdah*, and still others perceived it as "unbearable interference in domestic life." Forbidding the brideprice, payment due from groom to bride either for her widowhood or to her father for loss of her labor, also prevented traditional transactions that ruined the economy of households that needed the brideprice as convertible capital in the future.

Nancy Hatch Dupree explains that the Afghan dissent over the "total disdain" for their values led to bombings of civilians, often including attacks on mud-brick housing occupied only by women and children. Many Afghan women fled without male relatives. However, during exile, there was no evidence of rape and "the innate respect for women characteristic of Afghan culture is not only articulated but practiced."[33]

Goodwin interviewed Ratebzad in 1985 and learned that five years into the Soviet occupation, the organization was still only offering six-month literacy courses and needlework classes. The program was not as successful for its students and it did not reach as many women as the propaganda claimed.[34] Emadi writes that nonetheless Afghan women continued to demonstrate during this period.

In fact, many women, says Aziz, helped to form the mujahideen in

1979, and then later, again played a role to free the country from the Soviets. Aziz profiles a woman, Nooria Jehan, who participated in the Jihad or holy war. Two of her seven children were killed. She fought because she says the Russians "came to play with the dignity of women so we had to protect ourselves and children and other women." To Nooria, dignity meant all things "rooted" in her country, land and property rights, children, education, economy and military resources. When the mujahideen asked her be a part of terrorist activities, she found it difficult to shoot people, so she learned explosive techniques and taught the men. She was captured by the Russians, sentenced to 18 years in prison because she was a leader, but released in two years in an exchange. Aziz explains that other women, primarily urban and educated, were not supportive of the Soviets but were fearful of losing their new-found freedoms should there be a mujahed victory.[35]

In 1980, the Revolutionary Association of the Women of Afghanistan resisted Soviet occupation. Emadi writes, "Women's role in the national liberation struggle was not restricted to rallies, protest demonstrations, noncooperation with the enemy, etc. They participated in organized struggles such as abduction, assassination and bombing of the enemy positions."[36]

One such leading woman fighter, Tajwar Kakar (Sultan), was beaten and tortured in prison. Other freedom fighters include a woman that Emadi refers to as Nadia and Commander Rasia.

Afghans Morwarid (Mora) Hashimi and her brother, Rahman, fled to Pakistan in 1983 to escape Soviet oppression and then came to the United States. Rahman describes life before the invasion:

> A normal life, you know. Everything was O.K. We weren't restricted. We were free. We could speak. We could speak with each other. We had free movement. Everything. The Russians came in, and we were restricted. As with other communist countries, you have heard a lot of stories about [East] Germany, of course. The same thing there, you know.... Everything is under control, you know, no freedom, talking, nothing.[37]

Rahman's words help demonstrate that the Afghan people, men and women, lost a good way of life. Afghanistan, described by the Online Center for Afghan Studies, as a "once peaceful and beautiful nation," lost over two million of its people. As genocide embraced a nation, many Afghans were forced to flee for safety.[38] Mora describes how life was and how it became:

> I came to the U.S. on the 28 of September 1983. The main reason that we fled the country, is that the Soviet Union Communist invasion of

Afghanistan took place. After they jailed my brother, and after he was released from jail, he fled the country. And my mother and I were alone, therefore we also left the country, joined him in Pakistan, from there we came to the United States.

The daily life for women in Afghanistan right now is very difficult. Women are not allowed to go to work. They are not allowed to go to school. They are to be completely covered from head to toe when going out, and also they should be accompanied by a male family member when going out, otherwise they are not allowed to get out of the house.

Life in the U.S. is completely the opposite here. The woman has the same rights as the man in the United States. I am free to work, to study, to go out whenever I want and so on.[39]

Anthropologist Audrey C. Shalinsky tells the story of Nadia, who fled with her family to Pakistan in 1983. The value of Shalinsky's study is that it is longitudinal. She first met nine-year-old Nadia, then named Mahbuba, in Afghanistan in 1976. When Nadia was a teen, the family fled to Karachi where they could get help from relatives rather than registering for one of the camps. From Pakistan Nadia came to the United States where she completed high school, attended community college and married. Nadia said that her life differed from her mother's in that she worked outside the home, she did not have to live with her husband's family, and made many of her own decisions about her life. Shalinsky describes Nadia as a person of "great strength," and concludes that Nadia's freedoms "may indeed be an important renegotiation of gender relations and ideology in the immigrant context."[40]

Jan Goodwin profiles Fatima Gailani, daughter of Pir Sayed Ahmad Gailani, descendant of the Prophet Mohammad, former member of parliament and the spiritual leader of many Sunni Afghans and founder of the National Islamic Front of Afghanistan. Fatima represents an Afghan who was in a safer position to speak out. Fatima says,

Thank God I was born into my family. If I had been the daughter of someone who could be easily jailed, or whose house could be burned down, as has happened in Peshawar, or could be driven into exile like Tajwar Kakar, I couldn't do what I do. I have the protection of my family name, my father's position, and because I come from a privileged background, it is harder to wipe me out, kill me, than it is an ordinary Muslim woman.[41]

Goodwin writes that Fatima realizes her advantaged background requires more of her.

The Labor Law of 1984 provided equal job opportunities. Women served in the army and the police and constituted 50 percent of the labor force, according to Cecil Marie Cancel. By the 1980s and early 1990s, says Amin, women were deans of universities and presidents or heads of major hospitals in Kabul. There were women pilots, women diplomats, and women generals. In other words, Dupree says that women did have predominant roles in society.[42]

Mavis Leno testified to the U.S. Senate that

> before the Taliban gained dominance in Afghanistan, women were a crucial part of the workforce. In Kabul, for example: 70 percent of teachers were women; 40 percent of doctors were women; over half the university students were women; schools at all levels were co-educational; Afghan women held jobs as lawyers, judges, engineers, and nurses; and Afghan women were not required to cover themselves with the burqa.[43]

Scholars and activists see Afghan women in struggle, but they see them also as strong and as women of accomplishment. Catherine Daly says, "As in many countries' cultures, it's women that really pass on the traditions. Afghan women, as most women, are very hard working individuals, and they're very, very committed to their families, their children, their husbands."[44]

Angela E.V. King, special advisor on Gender Issues and Advancement in Women in the United Nations, reported in 1997:

> External observers and interlocutors often mistake symptoms and causes: the *burqa*, for example is not considered a major problem for most Afghan women with whom the Mission spoke, but is treated as such by many assistance workers in the country, agency personnel at headquarters and sometimes, opinion-makers outside the country.[45]

Moghadam's research confirms the findings of others that women are not "passive targets of policies or the victims of distorted development," but that "they are also shapers and makers of social change—especially Middle Eastern women in the late twentieth century."[46]

Afghan women continued to be involved in the political arena, says Nancy Hatch Dupree. In 1996, 150 poor beggar women demonstrated in front of the governor's office in Kandahar, and successfully persuaded the governor to order shopkeepers to accept small bank notes, or they would be closed. Later in 1996 in Kabul, when the Taliban protested against foreign interference, a female judge in General Dostum's administration provided inspiration as women held a five hour rally in Mazar-e Sharif producing slogans such as "Taliban law is not Islamic law." Toward the end of 1996 in Herat, 50 women protested the closing of women's bath houses. Several were beaten and 20 were arrested.[47]

When they gained control of most of Afghanistan, the Taliban issued decrees on a range of social matters for both men and women. Men were to grow beards. Music was prohibited as were other forms of recreation such as kite flying or chess. House-to-house searches culminated in arrests. Many people have been killed. Women who had been allowed to move freely in society for about 40 years could no longer do so unless they covered their bodies with the *burqa*, a long, head-to-toe garment designed to cover the body completely. Major restricted freedoms included the right to be educated, to be employed outside the home and to receive medical care. Lara Paul reminds us of the greatest danger of all to women in Afghanistan: "the new rules are not just restrictive. They are life-threatening. No woman may seek medical treatment from a male physician."[48]

Peter Marsden says that "there are no easy labels with which to define the Taliban." Since the Taliban are mostly Pushtun and rural, they are, in part, influenced by the code of honor in Pushtun law. Thus, they are concerned that girls will be corrupted if they are taught anything other than pure Islam. They seek to return society to the way it was before Daoud's reforms, the PDPA coup and 14 years of the Soviets, and rule by Islamist parties and the presence of Western agencies.[49]

The name "Taliban," "loosely translated, means seekers of wisdom … seeking to establish their version of a true Islamic state, a state where an adulterer can be stoned to death and where a woman is forbidden to work outside the home. And where if she does venture out without being covered from head to toe, she can be hit with a rifle butt."[50] Although the cultural and social barriers were always a factor, the Taliban took the situation further than the barriers. Under the Taliban rule, not only must women remain at home, but the windows of their houses must be painted black. Initially, much attention was given to the Taliban's activity, and not so much attention was given to the complexity of the situation, a problem that author William Maley, other scholars, diplomats and many activists continue to try to rectify.[51]

Many freedoms for men and women alike came to a halt when the Taliban gained dominance, but the freedoms of formal education, work outside the home, moving about in society, and health care ceased primarily for women. The far reaching effects of refugee life pose the especially difficult problems for women of dislocation, developing new notions of home, and handling the balancing act of family and the new outside world. In 1998, the executive director of Physicians for Human Rights, Leonard Rubenstein, said, "We are not aware of any place in the world in recent history where women have so systematically been deprived of every opportunity to survive in the society—from working to getting an education to walking on the street to getting health care."[52]

The Physicians for Human Rights study states that the Taliban restrictions on women have been highly publicized, but very little is known about the experiences and opinions of Afghan women.[53] They contend that their study invalidates the Taliban's assertion that gender segregation is based in Afghan history and culture. The study points to women's long history of participation in Afghan society. Almost all of the 160 women interviewed agreed that women should regain their freedoms.

Unfortunately, the reforms that the male-dominated political government in the 1920s granted Afghan women, such as the right to vote, to travel, and to be educated, were also taken away. The beginnings of women having a voice in Afghanistan were stripped by the following decades of war.

## Afghan Society and the State

### SOCIAL ROLES

Moghadam noted that Afghanistan scholarship "has emphasized geopolitics over gender politics and neglected the place of the woman question in the reform program of the DRA [Democratic Republic of Afghanistan] and the opposition of the Mujahidin."[54] Her research demonstrates that political and cultural projects such as uncovering women, educating girls, legislating hejab (general Arabic term for body covering), requiring burqa and honoring women's family roles are highly gendered, and that government initiatives to modernize have resulted in tribal rebellion.[55]

Moghadam notes that the most evident divisions are between the sexes, but there are role patterns within the country that are less patriarchal and more complementary. These patterns are based in economics. If a husband's first wife, for example, produces all girls, he may marry again. Women have power over their husbands and sons. They also have the brideprice. As a state Afghanistan is weak because of its inability to realize goals or regulate social relations and use resources in determined ways.[56]

Hafizullah Emadi believes that the condition of Afghan women is one of inferiority and that they are discriminated against from birth, since a male child is preferred, inherits the property and carries on the family name. Women are bought and sold. A woman's virginity is a symbol of honor. Not remaining a virgin until marriage is considered scandalous and, in a few instances, the woman is subjected to death by her family.

Sexual affairs may condemn her to death. Women are subject to strict social traditions that forbid them to talk with strangers, and that separate them from the men at such events as funerals and in public transportation.[57]

Aziz writes that women's involvement outside the home does not weaken the tradition that women are the heart of the family, because honor and status of the family lie with the women who are controlled and protected by the men. In other words, whether a woman involves herself beyond the family is in part determined by the ethnic group she belongs to and where she lives. Aziz writes that Hazara and Tajik women have more freedom than Pushtun women.[58] As does Amin, Peter Marsden suggests that social roles be examined in the development of policies pertaining to women's roles since the beginning of the 20th century. The primary role for agrarian women is wife and mother and passing Islam from one generation to another. The protection of women is connected to the protection of the society. In Pushtun society, the honor of society is dependent on the honor of women. Contact with others is defined by rules. Northern and central Afghan women are under similar restrictions. The nomadic women are an exception to the norm.[59]

Nancy Hatch Dupree writes that "Afghan society is consistent in its innate belief in male superiority, giving men the prerogative to determine the dos and don'ts for women. Few challenge this. The Taliban are reinforcing the patriarchal norms wrapped in the mantle of Islam." Yet, the Taliban's interpretation of Islam, she concludes, is viewed as extreme, harsh and unacceptable.[60] Peter Marsden believes that the footsoldiers have taken a simplistic and extreme view of Taliban policy regarding women.

After 20 years of continuous war, one ascribed role of women is widowhood. The increase in widowhood began during the Soviet occupation and continued throughout the efforts of the Mujahideen. In 1996, Pamela Collett of Save the Children, Pakistan, found that up to one-third of female refugees are widows, because women have no right of safe return to Afghanistan. Since all women are to be protected by a male family member, widows no longer have right to employment, benefits or guarantees of security. Yet, they must support their families. Widows also live in fear of being targeted for revenge killings by factions or tribes should they return to Afghanistan.[61] Sue Emmott found that a number of widows had some security through their husbands' families, although others found that the husband's family may not be financially equipped to help. Middle class families, accustomed to some economic protection such as a pension, found the destruction of the social fabric as much a burden as the physical destruction of Kabul.[62]

Emmott found that a relationship existed between stability and land ownership; that is, if a family owned its home rather than rented, the family would feel a greater loss because owning a home often meant also owning the land. Thus, the family might be able to return to its home, provided it was still standing. If the home was destroyed, and family members had no way to earn a living, they felt they probably could not rebuild their home. If the family lost its land to hostile forces, family members felt the loss was permanent. Nomadic Afghans worked for a landowner and earned food and shelter and did not experience loss of the security of food and shelter. Emmott found homelessness worse for men since they often lose their sense of identity from loss of their means of supporting their family. Yet, the men can leave the home to find socialization; women cannot.

The sense of loss over home is coupled with adapting to refugee camps, and some develop a sense of dependency and do not wish to leave. Thus, the camp becomes a settlement. Emmott writes, "The very strength and solidarity fostered through the women's networks means that women may be less anxious to leave the camps and move onwards to a more sustainable way of life."[63] The lesson to be learned for aid workers in an emergency setting with a gender perspective "is very different from implementing the paternalistic 'women's programmes.'"[64] Widowhood is a predominant factor affecting women's economic roles in Afghanistan today under the Taliban regime.

Nancy Hatch Dupree argues that because "access to women under the Taliban is so perplexing," it is useful to view the "totality of Afghan women as a pyramid."[65] The base of the pyramid represents the majority of Afghan women and is sound, she says, consisting of those women who live in rural areas. Progress exists within this base. These women's aspirations almost exclusively center around family.

At the tip of the pyramid are the women who "bear the full brunt of the Taliban ire": assertive, working women who have led the liberation of women that began in 1959, and who advocate equal participation in all levels of decision making. The center of the pyramid is the growing, solid middle class composed of professional teachers, medical practitioners, engineers, judges, administrators, businesswomen, social workers and civil servants. The core of the pyramid must be unleashed, Dupree says, if Afghanistan is "to recover and move forward." These women believe Afghan women can function in society without compromising Islam. This group has been lost through resettlement and those that remain are in need of training; those that have training most likely will not realize their potential.

## ECONOMIC ROLES

Hafizullah Emadi maintained in 1991 that the capitalism imposed on Afghanistan "did not alter the feudal mode of production or its corresponding ideology, politics and cultural practices."[66] Although major cities reflected some change in women's status, capitalism did not give women emancipation. Since the advent of the Taliban in 1994, excluding women from employment has increased. Apart from traditional work of women in agriculture, women are forbidden to leave the home unless accompanied by a male relative. In urban areas, especially Kabul, women were forced to stop working except in health care and only then in restricted circumstances. An estimated 30,000 widows in Kabul, a large number after 20 years of war, are the most affected. They sell all of their possessions and beg to feed their families.[67]

Paul Clarke, U.N., says, one explanation for the high levels of food insecurity in urban areas is that the restrictions on women taking part in economic activities are more strictly enforced in urban environments than in rural ones; thus the households dependent upon female labor find it harder to survive in the city. In addition, when women do work, the lowest incomes, in most cities, are those earned by women and children performing paid work. So, when households are dependent upon the work of women and children for income, they are very poor. For urban women, examples of paid labor include processing agricultural produce; performing domestic tasks; baking; needlework; and tailoring and handicraft manufacture. The recent U.N. World Food Program's Vulnerability Analysis and Mapping surveys in Ghor and Badghis provinces indicate that many women own and work the land, but this varies from area to area.

Paul Clarke reminds us to avoid the assumption that just because a household is food secure all of its members have food security. He says, "It is quite normal in much of Afghanistan for women and children to eat after the men have finished, and in many parts of the country there seem to be taboos as to what sort of food young children should eat."[68] Yet, no conclusive evidence exists that intra-household distribution means higher levels of food insecurity among certain age groups or among women. Clarke believes that the situation calls for research; even so, employment opportunities for women are needed to assure food security in Afghanistan.

## EDUCATION

The Women's Alliance for Peace and Human Rights in Afghanistan reports that before the Taliban occupation, "women in Afghanistan were educated and employed: 50 percent of the students and 60 percent of the teachers at Kabul University were women, and 70 percent of school teachers, 50 percent of civilian government workers, and 40 percent of doctors in Kabul were women."[69]

Emmott describes the vibrancy of prewar Kabul along with women's improved status. Women enjoyed education, work, pensions and wore sleeveless dresses or jeans and T-shirts. "They covered their heads when and if they wanted to, rather than by decree."[70]

Nasrine Abou-Bakre Gross illustrates Afghanistan's modernity in her book *Qassarikh-e Malay: Memories of the First Girls' High School in Afghanistan*, which is written in her native language. Gross showed me the pictures in the book, and as she did she stressed that the Taliban restrictions placed on the Afghan women are

> not a creation of Afghanistan. My book will help you understand the Afghan woman and her context of the 20th century. There are 172 pictures from 1920 to 1998 of Afghan women who went to this high school which was the first high school for girls in Afghanistan. A lot of the pictures are from the girls at that time, but very few of them are of just inside the school. So you see the girls in their everyday life. When you see the girls living, for example, you see in 1947, one of the first graduates, 1963, and 1976, with short skirts, nylons on their legs, nail polish on their nails, lipstick on their lips, short hair with hairdos in Bridget Bardot style, no scarf. It is not a scene from a play in a theater. This requires an entire culture to support the nail polish. It's a whole chain of events that gets you to have nail polish. So it speaks volumes for the Afghan girl in the 20th century.
>
> This is a girl going to a parade on the Day of Independence in the stadium. Look at all the men looking at her and all of the men attending this. It's the same stadium where now they are cutting off hands and feet. Look at this civilization in the picture, and just imagine a civilization that thinks that cutting off hands and feet of human beings is the answer, the two civilizations are worlds apart. It is not Afghanistan that cuts off arms and feet; it is colonization. Look at these girls and their basketball outfits in the 1960s. This is Madame Pompidou, the wife of the President of France, who came to visit in the 1960s. This is a picture in 1947; look at these girls. Do you think they are savages? Look behind them. Look at the lawns. The lawns are manicured and turfed. Look at the walls. Look at the houses. Do you think people live in such houses and then become savages and cut off hands and feet?
>
> This picture is in the 1960s. This is five generations of Afghan women that were connected to the same school. This lady, who was a wife of a prince, first gave up the veil in the 1920s and became the director of the match making factory. After the new dynasty came to power, she became kind of an orderly in the corridors of our school. She kept

discipline with all of us girls. This is her daughter who was educated, her granddaughter, her great granddaughter, and her great great granddaughter, the youngest generation.

These are the cleaning ladies who took care of the corridors. This is a gardener. This is the traditional garb of Afghan women in the fields. They wear the scarf to cover themselves from the wind and the dust. A lot of times when there is no dust, they take it off to till the land.

These are some of the men who worked in the school. This is me. It goes on and on and on. This is 1946. How different are they from you and me today? They are not.[71]

Gross's work preserves the history and cultural context of her country. She wanted to assess the effect of modernization and modern education on the 20th century Afghan society. Her book, she indicates, is more than a collection of stories:

When you have a society where there is no institutional schooling, girls are not socialized. So, at the beginning there were more skill classes. One woman has written that she was tops in ironing. We laugh nowadays, you don't learn ironing in school. Then it was important. Also, there were not enough teachers to fill all classes. They had cooking, they had sewing, they had baking, they had flower making, and they had washing and ironing. They had several other skills in home economics types of courses to fill the curriculum. From the 8th or 9th grade, when they were old enough to be young ladies, they studied in the morning and taught in the afternoon. So, they were being recycled: work and study, work and study. Every year, when new graduates finished, they were not allowed to stay at home. One of the most important phenomena in Afghanistan and one of the most under appreciated is that the girls and women all went back into society to keep building it. Through my research, I am convinced that it was the Afghan woman who was really the cornerstone of the 20th century Afghan society.

Gross notes that she belongs to the second generation of educated Afghan women. She graduated in 1964, and she says "that means another generation of 20 years of war that either has not seen education or has not been educated for the Afghan situation. So, education being so young and now interrupted means the country will have to enter another dark ages and this time, much harsher, unless we interrupt the dark ages itself."

## WOMEN AND HEALTH ROLES

A good example of the Taliban-supported militia's extremism can be observed in medical and development efforts. Although there have always been social and cultural barriers to women being attended by men, development programs of the past, and other approaches, have attempted to improve health care by building a local capability to train nurses.[72] Eventually, women became doctors.

Most Afghans lack any access to adequate medical facilities. In 1999 the Taliban relaxed some of the restrictions they imposed in 1997 when they segregated men and women in hospitals, and reduced women's access to health care. In an effort to centralize women's health care, services were to be provided by a single hospital still partially under construction. Later women could be treated by female medical personnel in particular locations. In June 1998, a woman could receive treatment from a male physician provided she was accompanied by a male relative. In practice, women were excluded from most hospitals. Kabul's widows found treatment impossible to attain. When a woman is treated by a male doctor, she has to be fully clothed during the examination and he cannot touch her. With lack of adequate physical medical care, women's mental health also suffers.[73]

## DRESS

Catherine Daly's research differs with the view of many outsiders that head coverings are a form of female oppression, an ethnic stereotype and a kind of religious orthodoxy. She offers a balance by providing insider views of the practice. She says that women's dress, including the chaadar, the partial veil or head covering, and chaadaree, the complete body veil or body covering, visually communicates the wearer's affinity to hejaab, the Islamic practice of covering the body. The chaadar is the more customary head covering worn by Afghan women. It can indicate generational, gender and socioeconomic status of a woman, her family; in Taliban-controlled areas, the chaadaree in contrast to the chaadar can serve as protection for both the woman and her family. Daly concludes from her research that certain Afghan women wear the clothing out of love and respect for their husband and family. Interviews Daly conducted provide examples of Afghan women's point of view, "We are not oppressed as Americans would believe," and "We just want to be able to practice our religion." Daly's response is, "wearing a *chaadar* signifies this choice."[74]

Megan Reif believes that more responsible action in the use of images is needed because in the long term, emphasis on the burqa harms the Afghan women that we are trying to help. The burqa image reinforces stereotypes. The world's 1.1 billion Muslims are a diverse group and not all are "powerless women under the thumbs of turbaned, gun-toting men."[75] She contends that efforts should be redirected toward providing humanitarian assistance for women and pressuring governments to address the underlying political and economic problems, and that Afghan women will then, again, decide for themselves what to wear. Some *Christian Science Monitor* readers strongly disagreed with Reif and argued that "the burka is a perfect symbol of what is wrong with not only Afghanistan, but other strongholds of fanatics."[76] M. Catherine Daly says that the present-day portrayal of head coverings and related practices by Muslim women by outsiders has tended to "depersonalize, essentialize and even objectify Muslim women as no more than a head covering."[77] Anaga Dalal reached a different conclusion. It is the veil, she says, that "has prevented women from seeing the world and each other."[78]

Nancy Hatch Dupree says that most professional women may not like the inconvenience and image of the chadari, but they are willing to put it on when necessary to deliver humanitarian assistance. Rural women, who do not usually wear it, will also put it on if they travel to the city. In fact, the chadari is a status symbol and worn in different colors and styles and with pride. It is in Kabul that the Taliban have insisted on a "standardization," but even there and in other cities, women have begun to wear it in different colors and styles, a far cry from policy intent.[79]

Some contend too much emphasis is placed on forcing Afghan women to wear the burqa. Although the burqa is not without controversy, it is a symbol of a series of restrictions and problems, because the burqa is part of some Afghan women's total context. The restrictions on women go beyond those of dress. The atrocities committed against the Afghan woman cannot be denied. Even women whose lives are spared and who flee find problems of dislocation, such as shelter and new notions of home.

## The Strength of Afghan Women

If women have made dress codes work to their advantage, as Nancy Hatch Dupree suggests, they will also make or break other policies to Afghanistan's and their own advantage. Catherine Daly says one of the contributions of Afghanistan's women is the strength with which they prevail in their hard lives, as they continue to provide a continuity for their people by passing on cultural traditions.[80] In this way, as Abdul Raheem Yaseer notes, it is most meaningful to look beyond the dress code, to other Afghan cultural perspectives and Western positions to fully understand their strength.[81]

Mavis Leno, who is working to end gender apartheid in Afghanistan, sees beauty and strength in Afghan women. She says that there is not to be found

> a more benign, hard working, honest group of people than Afghan women. They were just holding their country together which had been through so much. And, working and feeding their families.... They were minding their own business and being good decent human beings, and these big bully boys come in and just strip them of everything. And there's no special pleading. If you're a woman, that's it. There's no other circumstance that there could be about you that would redeem your fate.[82]

Suffering is not a sign of weakness, but aside from their suffering how the courageous Afghan women are dealing with their crisis is powerful. Scholars and activists provide insight on their spirit, and help us understand the women's experiences. Their fierce and spirited lives are also reflected in collections of their stories.

The value of profiling Afghan women from secondary sources is that it allows a broader base of study. Researchers have compiled hundreds of interviews. Two members of the Feminist Majority staff did extensive interviews with women under the Taliban who had just crossed the border into Pakistan. Some women were interviewed within days after escaping Afghanistan. These interviews provide a good idea of what has been going on in Afghanistan recently and what the current situation is.[83]

Valentine M. Moghadam explains that the Democratic Republic of Afghanistan began as a secular regime that sought to extend women's rights, but has become a captive of religious fanaticism. "Women have become all but invisible."[84] The outcome is divergent and unintended regarding Afghanistan's tribal patriarchy and underdevelopment. Because rulers practice a branch of patriarchal Islam, the 1990s saw drastic outcomes for Afghan women. Or is Afghanistan's current situation as Amin describes it: "The Taliban have not been able to provide women with any means of sustenance or any means of living, and so what you make out of this is neither Islamic nor Afghan. Any Taliban soldier has become virtual law unto himself."

Angela E.V. King reports her conclusions about the future for women in Afghan society. First, she believes, changing attitudes and behavior will take a long time because the present condition of the Afghan people has existed over an extended time, and this situation is exacerbated, but not created, by policies and behaviors of controlling authorities. Second, external forces often mistake symptoms, such as dress codes, for causes. Third, assistance agencies have not been able to effectively pursue opportunities in areas were there is an absence of customary interlocutors in a central government. Fourth, recent edicts have less effect in the rural areas, but assistance programming has not taken advantage of possible opportunities that less restrictive atmospheres present. Fifth, women are viewed as passive beneficiaries of assistance and their participation in decision making is very limited. More understanding is needed at the policy-making level of the "crucial relationship between mainstreaming and the need for transitional women-specific programming." Sixth, edicts restricting women's work have adversely affected their access to health care and have hindered the delivery of health services. Even where the edicts have been reversed, the interruption has affected training and reduced the number of female health care personnel. Rehabilitating the health care infrastructure is critical in order to provide emergency care. Seventh, reproductive health care needs constitute 30 to 40 percent of women's needs and are generally ignored in assistance programs. The traditional preference for survival of sons reduces the value of life for women and girls and increases the incidents of disease among women. Eighth, educational opportunities are limited, traditional low enrollments due to favoring of sons and bans on girls' education has been instituted, and thus the disparity between female and male literacy rates is growing. Restrictions on female employment have affected the educational system. Adaptability of assistance is limited. Ninth, limiting women's work and movement violates their human rights, threatens their economic well-being and contributes to the decline in national human capital resources.[85]

## Conclusion

In 1993, scholar Valentine Moghadam wrote that the analysis of societies and regions is "incomplete without attention to gender and its interaction with class, state and the world system." The Middle East is undergoing profound change in its roles and relationships of men and women, and the change has been "met with the politicization of gender and family law, the preoccupation of Islamist movements with women's appearance and behavior, shifting state politics, and cultural debates about authenticity and Westernization.... Women are at the center of change and discourse about change in the Middle East." Moghadam believes that an "unintended outcome" of women's activism is women's increased participation, political savvy, and demands of men within their own movements. Moghadam says that we have seen such a movement of women in Iran. Iranian female activists undermined patriarchy and thus accelerated the transition into modernity.[86]

As Afghan women continue to reclaim their country, they emerge with a new strength. Because the war has claimed so many of the men, by necessity the women will realize more political participation. They will not only reclaim the rights they once had; they will be their country's "center of change."

# Women's Roles in Islam

*Islam ... is a religion of peace, compassion and justice.*
Zieba Shorish-Shamley, WAPHA[1]

The conservative and moderate Islamic sects in Afghanistan claim their religion is the one accurately grounded in the Koran and Islamic law. All claim to have the true interpretation of the Koran and the law about women's religious and societal roles. The conservative beliefs of the Mujahidin and the extreme beliefs of the Taliban clash sharply with the beliefs of the moderate Sunni Muslim sects about women's roles. A study of the Koran and Islamic law reveals which beliefs about women are the most accurate.

## Women and Islam

Early Islam, says Louis Dupree, did not consider women inferior and they played active political, social and economic roles. Yet, for centuries, the custom of purdah, the isolation of women from all men except relatives, was justified as a religious sanction. Before 1959, women in urban centers were required to wear the chadari or burqa outside the family compound. Dupree maintains that a careful examination of the Koran, the Hadith and the Hanafi Shari'a of Sunni Islam, "reveals no definite, unqualified requirement for purdah and the veil." He notes that the dress code was not practiced by rural women who worked in the fields.[2]

Emmanuel Todd writes that Islam is formulated in "vague, general and moralizing language." The Muslim woman is protected in theory and in practice in the sense that the Koran, as a doctrine, seeks to improve a woman's position and her marriage, psychologically, within a specific tribe or similar social unit, but "protection is not equality." The tribal system is basically "embodied in a separation of the sexes." Todd believes the cultural price paid for the social elimination of women is the retardation of education and long-term social stagnation.[3]

Zieba Shorish-Shamley says that Islam, in theory, gives men and women equal rights in every aspect of life: marriage, creation, spiritual status, education, work, owning property, having wealth, being able to inherit, and the right to live. Islamic law forbids forced marriages. In addition, the Koran grants a woman the right to own her own mahr, which is the payment that the husband makes to the wife as part of the marriage contract in relation to divorce. She also has equal rights to divorce. The Koran contains a number of controversial verses concerning men and women. According to Sura 2, Verse 228, "...women shall have rights similar to rights against them, according to what is equitable. But men have a degree (of advantage) over them. And Allah is Exalted in Power, Wise." Some see the degree as a degree of intelligence; others, superiority; and others, relevant to maintenance of the family in that degree is based in economics. Sura 4, Verse 3 addresses the marriage of a man to two to four women in order to deal justly with orphans and war widows. In verse 129, the Koran states that a man is not capable of treating all wives equally and justly in every aspect of life. Shorish-Shamley says, "Thus, in truth, Islam encourages marriage with only one woman." And Sura 4, Verse 11 states, "Allah (thus) directs you as regards your children's (inheritance): to the male, a portion equal to that of two females..." Some argue this verse does not benefit females economically while others say it is fair because a man is legally obligated to "maintain" his wife, children, parents and other relatives in need, and a woman is under no obligation to maintain her family.

Shorish-Shamley says, as does Haron Amin, that Taliban edicts are neither Islam or Afghan. She clarifies that, in Islam, God grants human rights that cannot be changed, and are applicable to all the human beings (Koran Sura 5, Verse 44). Further, she says, Islam is very specific in its goodness:

> Islam has granted rights for security of life and property and protects the honor and dignity of human beings (Sura 49, Verse 11–12). Islam protects the human rights to security and privacy (Sura 49, Verse 12 and Sura 24, Verse 27). Under Islamic principles, no one can be imprisoned unless his/her guilt has been proven in an open court. To arrest and imprison individuals on the basis of suspicion without due process is not permissible in Islam. Islam has given human beings the right to protest against government's tyranny (Sura 4, Verse 148). Islam protects individuals from being arrested or imprisoned for the crimes of others

(Sura 35, Verse 18). Islam grants humans the rights for freedom of thought, of expression, of associations and of formation of organizations, on the condition that these rights be used for the propagation of truth, virtue and justice and not for evil purposes. Islam also protects the human's freedom of conscience, of convictions and of religious sentiments (Qur'an Sura 2, Verse 256). Islam ensures that the human's religious sentiments are respected and nothing will be done that may encroach upon these rights. Islam recognizes the rights of humans to the basic necessities of life (Sura 51, Verse 19). Islam grants humans equality before law and does not hold the rulers above the law. Islam also grants humans the right to participate in the affairs of their State (Sura 42, Verse 38). Islam has granted all human males and females the right to education and work (Sura 35, Verse 28 and Sura 4, Verse 32). Islam has laid down some universal fundamental rights for humanity as a whole that are to be respected and observed by all human beings (Sura 5, Verse 8).[4]

Abdul Raheem Yaseer speaks from experience about how the Afghan woman is looked upon:

Women are very much esteemed. They are important members of the family, and religiously they are put in a very high position. Our books and beliefs have taught us that paradise is at the foot of the mother and if anybody other than God deserves to be worshiped, it is the mother; and it is the mother that forms the life of her family and she is the center and the focal point of attention and respect. Her freedom varies. Freedom for a woman in Afghanistan is something different than freedom for a woman in the United States. Women are equal in the eyes of God according to Islam, but men and women are complementing each other not equal to each other due to such factors as physical conditions, physical restraint, responsibilities, such as bearing children and raising children. The man is responsible for providing. Also Islamically, a woman has all the rights on what her husband owns, and the husband has no rights on anything that the women earns or receives in heritage.[5]

Professor Yasser's philosophy is not unlike that of some American women who believe that women can be equal without being identical.

Islam expanded rapidly, not allowing new converts time to become educated. Thus acculturation and Islamic education of converts were unsynchronized. Growing wealth and new mores produced a fear for the chastity of its women, and the result was a deterioration of the Muslim women's position, status and role. Shorish-Shamley concludes, "It is not the Islamic ideologies that determine the position of women in the Islamic societies, it is rather the pre–Islamic patriarchal ideologies existing in a particular society, combined with the lack of education and ignorance, that construct the Muslim women's position."[6]

William Maley says the Koran has a "powerful warning against missionary utopianism" in that it commands there "shall be no compulsion in religion."[7] Haron Amin says,

> The Taliban don't believe in diversity even though the Koran specifically says that we have created you into tribes and groups so that you will get to know each other (Koran Chapter 49, Verse 3). The Taliban have interpreted it so that you can actually get to kill each other. That's the distinction that they make. The Koran whenever it talks about the state of man and woman, men and women, female and male, says females and males, we created you mankind, we've created you from a single blood clot. I don't know any part of it that says that women are supposed to be doing it and men are not supposed to be doing it. It is very balanced.[8]

Hassan Hathout, director of outreach at the Islamic Center of Southern California, writes that more distressing than the shocking Taliban implementation of their interpretation of Islam, is that they announced their practices as a fulfillment of the teachings of Islam. He believes that the Taliban know that the Prophet says, "The pursuit of knowledge is obligatory over every Muslim, male or female." Hathout explains that Muslim women became teachers, had the right to manage their wealth, generate income, and to have individual, independent ownership. The whole medical corps of the Prophet's army was an all-woman corps, and, interestingly enough before their Western sisters were legally allowed to serve as soldiers, in some battles Muslim "women took sword and shield and joined active combat, to be later praised by the Prophet." Further, women engaged in public affairs. Um-Salamah, the wife of the Prophet, diffused the crisis among the Muslims at the Hudaybiah treaty. Caliph Omar, the second successor to the Prophet as head of state, appointed a woman judge, Al-Shaffa, over commercial affairs. When Omar gave directives regarding the marriage dowry, a woman in the mosque corrected him by citing the Koran. Omar responded, "The woman is right and I am wrong."[9] Hathout concludes, "Men and women are equal, and obligations (and prohibitions) of Islam apply to them equally."[10]

The Muslim Women's League adds its voice to these philosophies: "Taliban's stand on the seclusion of women is not derived from Islam, but, rather, from a cultural bias found in suppressive movements throughout the region." The Taliban claim that their laws are temporary, but the league believes that history has demonstrated that other Muslim countries have been subject to the same atrocities and women continue to be oppressed.[11]

The organization Women Living Under Muslim Laws (WLUML) works inside Afghanistan and Pakistan. Its members believe that historically the Afghan society continues to follow primitive codes of conduct set since prehistoric times, such as patriarchy, and that dictatorial governments and misinterpretation of religion have limited women's rights. WLUML shares excerpts from a brief received from an organization requesting anonymity: "Most steps taken to protect women against violence tend to address women rather than men. These steps don't enforce laws or take action against men." The anonymous organization adds, "Legal aid is non-existent for Afghan women."[12] The group writes that violence always existed in Afghanistan, but it escalates in times of conflict and crisis, and the family exerts more control over women and the state represses women more, increasing their burdens. Women may have gained security from some atrocities, but at a price. The anonymous group believes that women have not come a long way from a time when they were treated worse than livestock:

> There have been times when women were imprisoned and used as sexual slaves and later their body parts were removed one by one as the women still lived, and finally the remains of the body was disposed of in the streets. War and anarchy produced trafficking of women across the country.[13]

Catherine Daly says that the factions in Afghanistan represent the conflation of culture and religion; the interface of tribal codes of conduct of the Pushtun majority and Islamic codes presumably derived from the Koran and Shari'a Law. Both Pushtun culture and the religion of Islam have politicized women's issues. Although Afghanistan is a very patriarchal society, patrilineal where in marriage women go to live with the husband's family, etc., there is also internal or tribal conflict among various groups, a vying for power. In addition, historically, there is the overlay of the superpowers, whether starting with the Timurid dynasty in 1370–1506 or with Alexander the Great in 329 to 327 B.C. The more recent approaches of the English, the Soviets and the United States continue the struggle for control of human and natural resources. Daly, whose area of expertise is Muslim ethnic identity expressed in dress, reminds us that

> Muslims and non–Muslims perceive dress differently based on their own cultural and religious bias. Non-Muslims tend to critique all patterns of dress of Muslims as Islamic in nature rather than influenced by culture. For example—it's not real clear to me if dress is truly an Islamic prescription or if it is cultural. Certainly, there's a consistency in Muslim dress as which means loose clothing that covers the arms, legs and upper body of both men and women. Dress for both genders should be loose fitting and certainly nothing that was transparent. The Taliban have placed further restrictions on women to minimize body dominant

characteristics, i.e., no perfume, cosmetics, nail polish, certain kinds of foot coverings, ankle bracelets.[14]

Religion and state are one in the fundamentalist Islamic world. Sometimes leading theologians have as much or more power than political leaders.

## Taliban Style of Islam

Ahmed Rashid's *Taliban: Militant Islam, Oil and Fundamentalism in Central Asia,* tells of the young, orphaned, Taliban who grew up in Pakistani refugee camps with the vision of an idealized Islamic society as defined by the Prophet 14 centuries ago. They know nothing of their own country's history or clan structures and have no vision for the future. They were locked into male brotherhood without knowing the company of women, acquired their skills from Mujahedin along with a warped version of Islam. Reviewing Rashid's work, Michael Church concludes that, in issues related to women, the Taliban are "quite unbothered that their erasure of women from public life has also erased the bulk of teaching and nursing forces and driven aid agencies staffed by women out of the country."[15]

Abdul Raheem Yaseer describes the Taliban policy enforcement as stemming from two things:

> There are Muslim fanatics and extremists from Pakistan, Saudi Arabia and other Arab countries who have been teaching the Taliban in madrassas in Pakistan where they trained them. They taught them their very restricted form of Islam to make them very brutal fighters. Secondly, since these Taliban are immature and they haven't had any background in Afghan history, Afghan culture and Afghan tradition, and Afghan values, training has been very one sided, not taking into consideration the cultural sensitivies, historical background, traditions, and habits of the people. The Taliban deal with the situation in a very ignorant manner, insensitive, and the plans are according to strict lines they have been given, for example, women should not be seen in public, women should cover themselves, and they go to the very extreme.
>
> They misinterpret instructions, like if they say to all people, women should not expose themselves, then they say while they are inside their house, they should paint their windows so they should not be seen from outside. When Islam says all women should be modest and moderate and modestly dressed, then they go as far as to say they should cover their face and hands and feet too, which is not culturally acceptable and religiously

correct. And then they say women should not go to school. They should study at home. They should not learn the worldly things but they should concentrate on the religious subjects. These are all against the main-stream Islam which says that men and women are all obliged to acquire knowledge from the cradle to the grave and they should seek knowledge even at the furthest spot from their place of residence.

And, these are all the sayings of the Prophet Mohammed in the instructions from Koran, but Taliban interpret it in a very restricted way and take it too far. And, it is mainly because of their political views, their ignorance, and the push of their supporters and patrons and mentors and those outsiders. This whole thing has been imposed from outside on the people, all these rules and regulations under the name of Islam and the politics and people keep suffering.[16]

The Taliban have decreed that men shall pray five times a day. Women are not allowed in the mosques and must pray at home. Shia and other minority places of worship were "cleaned" and taken over by the Taliban, who converted them to Sunni mosques. Religion was a factor in the very bloody takeover of Mazar-i-Sharif in 1998 that included shooting of peo-ple in the streets, systematic searches and killing and arrests of men sus-pected of having a weapon, using the captured as hostages or transporting them to another city, summary judgments with public executions, often by throat slitting, that are sometimes extended to the families, and abduct-ing and raping women and girls whose whereabouts are still unknown. Although the conflict between the Hazaras who are predominantly Shi'a Muslim and the Taliban is political, military and religious, the mass killings, in particular, of the "Shi'a Hazaras by the Taliban in newly occu-pied territories in the north reflected a decline in religious tolerance."[17]

Many restrictions were placed on women in the name of Islam con-cerning dress, movement, work, education and medical care.[18] A Physi-cians for Human Rights 1998 survey found that 22 percent of the women surveyed were detained and abused by the Taliban; of these incidents, 72 percent were related to alleged infractions of the dress code. Most inci-dents resulted in detentions of one hour or less, but 84 percent also resulted in public beatings and two percent resulted in torture.[19]

Religious freedom in Afghanistan is determined by "unofficial, unwritten, and evolving policies of the warring factions."[20] In the mid–1990s, Taliban leader Muhammad Omar was successful in "melding reli-gious fervor with the tribal patriotism" of the Pushtun.[21] The Pakistani Inter-Services Intelligence agency, the Pakistani extremist religious party Jamiat-ul-Ulema-e-Islam and radical Arab Muslims including the terror-ist network of Osama bin Ladin supported Omar and Southern mullahs, religious leaders, who were also part of the Taliban. Peter Tomsen says, "Together these forces unleashed a powerful coalition," that ultimately gained control of 90 percent of Afghanistan.

Many argue that the Taliban style of Islam is not the true interpretation of Islam. The Taliban's extremism and brutal enforcement of that philosophy make one prone to agree with Haron Amin that the Taliban's restructured Islam is a "religious mask that Pakistan put on the Taliban."[22] Christiane Amanpour reported that there are many Muslims who argue that what the Taliban are preaching has nothing to do with Islam.[23] The view that the Taliban are enforcing their interpretation of Islam and the perspective that the Taliban-supported militia may, themselves, be operating behind a veil, is provocative food for thought.

Ahmed Rashid provides us the name of "the most feared man in Kabul," Maulvi Qalamuddin, head of the Department for the Promotion of Virtue and Prevention of Vice. Qalamuddin says, "We lost 2 million people in the war against the Soviets because we had no shari'a. We fought for shari'a and now this is the organization that will implement it."[24] The shari'a is not only the constitution, but the only true interpretation of Islam, says the Taliban leadership. Some Muslim leaders say the Taliban interpretation is giving Islam a bad name.

The Taliban regulations make it difficult for women to receive humanitarian assistance in that they are not allowed to work for international aid agencies. The young men who patrol the streets sometimes enforce regulations with a stick. Extreme regulations have elicited strong criticism from fundamentalist Iran and "gentle persuasion" from Saudi Arabia, says Rashid.[25] Women must not entice men who cannot behave appropriately with women. Thus, the Taliban issued edicts for separate transportation, and bans on women wearing makeup and high heels and making noise when they walk.

Amanpour believes that, although women have borne the brunt of their harsh brand of Islam, other acts were extreme, such as "not just closing down movie theaters, but torching the film, cutting music cassettes, smashing statues, crushing the demon liquor and forcing all men into the mosques to pray, ordering them to grow beards, threatening the most brutal punishments."[26]

Strangely, women's bath houses were closed in several instances, for example, in Herat in 1996. The significance of the women's bath houses is that one has to be clean in order to pray.[27] The bath or ablution (wodou) entails "cleaning by water of mouth, nares, face, ears, forearms to the elbows, wiping head and ears and washing the feet." Women are exempted from prayers during menstruation, but "at its cessation a bath is necessary

(Tuhr)." Otherwise, one bath may be sufficient for several prayers, "but has to be repeated if the person passes urine, stools, flatus or falls asleep. Sex necessitates a full bath."[28]

Nancy Hatch Dupree says Afghan women have heretofore been on the periphery, but now "Afghan women stand centre stage in the full glare of world opinion." The Taliban and the international community, she says, hold the position of guaranteeing women a dignified role, but, in actuality, they are far apart. "The divide lies in the complex realms of defining roles and determining appropriate means by which these roles may be realised." The Taliban's position is to install a pure Islamic state, the unfinished agenda of the Jihad, the holy war. She says that their stated purpose is to produce a secure environment to preserve the chastity and dignity of women.[29]

Many people contend the acts of the Taliban have nothing to do with Islam. Scholars are offended that the Taliban say their interpretation is the fulfillment of the teachings of Islam. Some believe the situation to be an interface between tribal loyalty and religion. Most believe that Islam teaches that in the eyes of God men and women are equal, and that men and women do not have to be identical to be equal. The Afghan culture should not be evaluated by Western standards, but the atrocities of the Taliban-supported militia are unacceptable whether committed in the name of religion or tribal customs. Hillary Clinton, speaking at a human rights conference in Tunis, Tunisia, condemned the acts of those people in both Algeria and Afghanistan who brutalize women in the name of religion: "Those who perpetrate these hateful deeds pervert the great religion in whose name they claim to act."[30] Haron Amin believes that the Taliban have an interpretation of Islam, but it is an interpretation that is very narrow and not the true view. Taliban Islam is much more intolerant and chauvinistic. Amin asks, "Didn't the Prophet allow women outside of their houses? Couldn't they go to the mosques? Why have women been banned from going to the mosques? According to the Taliban, women are impure. The clicking of shoe heels tempts men. So, this is the cursed view of women being temptresses to men."

Amin suggests examining other historical periods and events, including the witch hunting that happened in Salem in the United States, the Medieval period to the 30 Years War in Europe, and even the *Scarlet Letter* by Nathaniel Hawthorne, who in 1844 wrote the following entry in his notebook: "The life of a woman, who by the old colony law, was condemned always to wear the letter A, sewn on her garment, in token of her having committed adultery."[31] The Taliban's actions lead Amin to conclude,

> The whole thing is witch hunting. It's a social crisis emerging in a
> different part of the world. The problem is there, it's backwardness and
> this is exactly what we are facing. The Taliban are doing more than inter-
> preting Islam, they are restructuring Islam. It is not necessarily that this
> [Taliban interpretation] is truly Islam, but it is mankind failing to real-
> ize he is utilizing religion for the purpose of his own realization of what-
> ever fantasies he might have in his mind.[32]

The Taliban, Amin says, have misrepresented and misstated the
Afghan woman, and created feminization of poverty and gender apartheid
in Afghanistan. Thus, while some say the Taliban tout fundamentalism,
Pamela Collett says that many believe the Taliban are fascist, because their
interpretation of Islam is not a true interpretation of the Koran and their
representation of Afghan society is not that of the traditional patriarchal
culture.[33]

Fatima Gailani, daughter of Pir Sayed Ahmad Gailani, former member of Parliament and spiritual leader for many Sunni Afghans, reflects a
belief held by some Afghan women. She says that no matter how oppres-
sive a forbiddance may seem to the Western world, "I will accept it because
I believe in God, believe in the Prophet and believe in our Holy Book. The
divine mind knows what is best for us.... I think the duty of man and
woman is different in Islam."[34] However, if Fatima does not believe a certain practice is not required in Islam, such as veiling, she will not accept
it. Fatima believes the majority of women are moderate Islams who must
acquire a thorough knowledge of their religion in order to take a stand
against the hardliners.

While the Taliban are particularly violent toward women, The
Human Rights Watch Report illustrates that Afghan males and religious
minorities are also subject to abuse:

> To ensure that religious practices were strictly enforced, Taliban police
> continued to arrest men for having beards that were too short, for not
> attending prayers, and for having shops open during scheduled prayer
> times. As in previous years, the Taliban enforced its laws according to
> its interpretation of Islamic Shari'a, with weekly public executions, flog-
> gings, and amputations in Kabul's stadium and other cities under its
> control. Several men accused of sodomy were punished by having walls
> pushed on them by a tank. In one case, a man who survived the ordeal
> after being left under the rubble for two hours was reportedly allowed
> to go free. In September, the Taliban issued new decrees aimed at non–
> Muslims that forbade them from building places of worship but allowed
> them to worship at existing holy sites, banned non–Muslims from crit-
> icizing Muslims, ordered non–Muslims to identify their houses by plac-
> ing a yellow cloth on their rooftops, forbade non–Muslims from living

in the same residence as Muslims, and required that non–Muslim women wear a yellow dress with a special mark so that Muslims could keep their distance.[35]

The alarm that has greeted the Taliban's edicts against women and men in Afghanistan is justified. Historically, Islam has honored women and included them in all aspects of life. Clearly the Taliban are at odds with Islam.

# Afghan Women, Contemporary Wars and Geopolitical Forces

*But, these lackeys of aliens*
*Keep selling you to master after master*

*These three battle cries shall we never forsake:*
*With Democracy shall we turn your night into dawn*
*With Justice shall we dress the people's wounds*
*Your Freedom shall we attain once more*

*These three banners shall we hoist over our land*
*Forward we march, no danger do we fear!*

"Grieving Mother," Patriotic Songs of RAWA.[1]

In April of 1978, the communist regime was established in Afghanistan with Soviet aid. To save the regime in December of 1979, the Soviet Union invaded Afghanistan. The invasion caused deterioration of normal relations between the Chinese and the Soviets as well as between the United States and the Soviet Union.

The fundamentalist power base was created soon after the Soviet invasion, says Jan Goodwin. The United States supplied the Afghan Mujahideen with arms and nearly $3 billion in aid that was "the largest covert military-support operation run by the CIA since Vietnam." Goodwin explains:

> But because the Afghan Resistance was based in Pakistan, President Zia demanded that the money be funneled to the Afghan parties through his military officers. And as part of his Islamization program, he heavily favored the fundamentalist parties over the moderates. Over a twelve-year period, 75 percent of American funding was channeled to rabidly

anti–American Afghan Islamists by Pakistan, a move the U.S. State Department now acknowledges was an error.[2]

In addition, Saudi Arabia's financing of the archconservatives of the resistance was openly equal to that of the United States. Libya was also involved in support of Gulbuddin Hekmatyar, a brutal leader. It was at this time, says Goodwin, that the term "Great Game," coined for the political and military schemes played out in this very region in the 19th century between Russia and the British Empire, took on a new meaning, making Afghanistan a modern day example of how "moderate Islam was subsumed through the hegemony and petro-dollars of Islamic theocratic states."

The war was not easy on women. Many were killed, others lost family members, others became refugees. In her book, *Searching for Saleem*, Farooka Gauhari describes her desperate, unsuccessful search for her husband Saleem after the April 1978 coup. She writes about her family who lived in Afghanistan, but fled, about the people left in Afghanistan with whom she can no longer communicate and about her children. Her book is also a cry against wars and executions and a plea for peace and justice. Her story is one of strength as she tells of her efforts not to arouse the suspicion of government officials in search of Saleem.[3]

In May 1995, Amnesty International (AI) wrote that Meena Keshwar Kamal, health worker and founding member of RAWA, was assassinated with two members of her family, reportedly by members of the Hizb-i Islami (Hekmatyar) in 1987 in Quetta. She had reported threats proceeding the murders.[4] AI describes RAWA as a left-of-center group that campaigns for women's rights and provides education and health facilities for women and children. Like many organizations supportive of Afghanistan's situation, RAWA's journal, *The Burst of the "Islamic Government,"* is filled with profiles of Afghan women whose voices were silenced.

## The Role of Pakistan

"The Pakistani government, at the time under General Zia, had its own goals for the future, and for the geopolitical necessities of Pakistan in the region," observes Haron Amin. He adds,

> General Zia was a man with vision who had convinced the Pakistanis as well as Pakistani allies that any sort of thrust by the Soviets would actually cause major realignment of the countries in the region and therefore, called for an all out resistance against the invasion of the former

Soviet Union in Afghanistan. At the same time, Zia had outlined what was very, very pivotal in significance for Pakistan which for the longest period has been a state with security dilemma. At the time, it had one or two organizations which further created more organizations and so, in its entirety, seven major political resistance organizations were established in Pakistan; some more pro–Pakistan; some less pro–Pakistan.[5]

Amin explains that the situation grew more complex. Pakistani and Saudi interests then were reciprocated with other countries' interests in the region.

"Subsequently," Amin says, "with the pullout of the former Soviet Union from Afghanistan, 1989, of course being subsequent to the Geneva talks, and the negative symmetry between Soviet Foreign Minister Eduard Shevardnadze and also George Shultz, the U.S. Secretary of State, the withdrawal of Soviet troops from Afghanistan went very well and was completed by February 15th of 1989." The war in Afghanistan seemed to have ended, and there was a reduction of the international or superpower-involved status of the Afghan conflict down to a regional level.

Shabana, a RAWA activist, notes that the Jehadis or Mujahedin (Freedom Fighters) and Opposition Forces have committed atrocities against women and men. RAWA participants remember these acts and do not solely focus on the extreme violations of the Taliban.[6]

Amin provides further background:

> The Communist Regime was still intact under Dr. Najibullah. A shift in the military makeup of Afghanistan caused rifts in the military, and in April of 1992, led to the split in the Communist Regime, and the Communist Regime wanted to surrender to the Resistance. What happened afterwards was that six major organizations in Pakistan, excluding Gulbuddin Hekmatyar, agreed on the formation of a government in Afghanistan. Hekmatyar had requested a unilateral takeover of Kabul. Hekmatyar's ambition would not stop him from destroying Kabul which he subsequently did, and from April of 1992 all the way to 1995, almost half of Kabul was destroyed and many of its citizens were killed. At one point, as many as 600 rockets in one day were sent into the city, while Hekmatyar was at the same time reinstated by the Pakistani as well as Saudi Arabia to be the Prime Minister. Pakistan's goal with Hekmatyar did not end, but there was a shift in the Pakistani policy in Afghanistan. Hekmatyar was not able to deliver Kabul to the Pakistanis. So Pakistan resorted to creating the Taliban.

The Taliban is not an indigenous movement that started from southern Afghanistan, Amin contends. He says as do others that the Taliban did not just come out of some sort of a spontaneous combustion theory,[7] but that the Taliban were created in Pakistan, that these religious students had been educated in the Pakistani religious schools and that is where they learned the idea of Sunni Deoband, a form of Islam that originated in the Indian subcontinent. He says that this was the religious mask that covered the Taliban phenomena. In addition, there is also the geopolitical, geostrategical aspect of the Taliban. He describes Pakistan as having felt since 1947, the year of its creation, that compared to India it is a vulnerable state. When Pakistan split from India, the country was separated by India. There were Pakistan and East Pakistan. In 1971, East Pakistan became an independent nation, Bangladesh, under Sheikh Mujibur Rahman. Says Amin:

> So, Pakistan, when it comes to nuclear power, when it comes to manpower, when it comes to population, when it comes to economic power, when it comes to the military power, considers itself to be vulnerable. Kashmir was never really resolved, that still remains the case and India and Pakistan have fought at least two wars over that. The recent imbroglio in Kashmir also is a manifest to that claim. Pakistan has looked for what is called a strategic depth or some background room or some backyard in case of a war with India.

Barnett Rubin states that "Pakistan is a fundamentally and existentially an insecure state that feels the need to achieve military parity with its neighbour India, with seven times its population and economy."[8] Pakistani Finance Minister Shamshad Ahmad referred to Afghanistan as Pakistan's fifth economic province.[9] Amin reasons to the conclusion:

> We understand from the Pakistani recognition of the Taliban immediately that Pakistan is behind what is happening in Afghanistan, that Pakistan needs a subservient state in Afghanistan. Pakistan needs Afghanistan for whatever Pakistani's interest asks. General Zia's doctrine of strategic depth or as it was called at the time, Pan Islamism, is the idea to promote Islamic belts around the whole region and to swallow up countries of central Asia. As its geopolitical, geostrategic need, Pakistan, in order to survive its current economic crisis and, of course, with it being a democratically failed state with the latest coup by General Pervez Musharraf, there is the need to export things to central Asia given that they have the essential industries over in central Asia, they need to export things over there and also get a cheap supply of oil and natural gas to Pakistan. So, that's the political situation in Afghanistan.

According to Peter Tomsen,

> It's a very complex situation. The Afghans naturally have divisions. Their neighbors are competing in supporting various ethnic groups inside

Afghanistan, like Pakistan supports the Pushtuns and Iran is supporting the non–Pushtuns, and the Russians go back and forth, although they
are now supporting the non–Pushtuns like the Northern Alliance. And
the Saudi government too, although it does not state this publically, in
effect, it's permitting Saudi citizens to send considerable amounts of
money and support to the more extremist Pushtun factions which are
represented by the Taliban. So it's a very difficult situation. It's not exactly
a civil war. It has the character of proxy wars by outsiders using Afghan
groups inside of Pakistan.[10]

Amin says that what we have seen unfold in Afghanistan is not
Afghan culture. The Afghan culture is a very, very moderate culture that
has been uprooted. It is not the fanatic culture that the Taliban represents:

The Taliban social engineering edicts and daily issuance of everything
else has inflicted a tremendous amount of suffering on the people of
Afghanistan. Not only the women, of course, they really suffer the brunt
of everything, but also the men of Afghanistan. In fact, this is a Pakistani style religion, Deoband, plus traditional customs of Pakistan
exported and somehow mixed with southern customs of Afghanistan,
a very, very dangerous concoction, you see in Afghanistan.[11]

Abdul Raheem Yaseer says that each of the many factions in Afghanistan is supported by one or more external parties, mainly the close neighbors, such as Pakistan, Iran, India, China and all the newly independent
former Soviet Republics like Turkmenistan, Uzbekistan or Tajikistan, each
of which had a group inside Afghanistan whom they want to use for their
own purpose. Therefore, they extend their monetary, military and moral
support to those groups. Because of the external interferences of unpre-
dictable duration, the future is very bleak: Nobody can tell when things
will improve. Yaseer goes further to say, "I think the main factor that might
stop and bring peace in Afghanistan is if a few people of power, like the
government of the U.S., the United Nations and some other countries, give
serious attention to the situation and try to discourage the foreign interference and let the Afghans decide their own fate. And then, you know,
things will turn normal. Other than that, it will keep going the way it has
been going on for almost 22 years now."[12]

"It is dangerous to treat the Taliban as if they are a monolithic force,"
William Maley writes, even though the Taliban have "distinctive fea-
tures."[13] That the Taliban are religious students is accepted by many, but
not all, as part of their definition. Some aspects of the Taliban identity
remain ambiguous and unsettling. Peter Marsden writes that one interpretation is that they began in early 1994 as a small spontaneous group

of religious (Islamic) students in Kandahar, who were outraged with the Mujahidin leaders' corrupt behavior. Their mission was "to create a society that accorded with Islam." The unclear aspects of the Taliban include how they moved from a small group to a major force; how they benefited from the willingness of young people to serve the ideological premises of the movement; how they receive their training; and the roles of Pakistan, religion, and tribal influence. Their "absolute leader" is Pushtun Mullah Muhammad Omar, whose supreme religious title is Amir Al-Mu'minin, Leader of the Faithful. Omar was a member of one of the traditionalist Mujahidin parties.[14] In addition, the Taliban movement's governmental functions are performed through its key governing body, "the Inner Shura (Council) based in Kandahar, and by ministries based in Kabul."[15] Rubin testified that the Taliban originally succeeded largely because of the military aid they received from Pakistan.[16]

Assistant Secretary of State Karl F. Inderfurth testified before Congress in July 2000 that although the Taliban control 85 percent of Afghanistan, "their popularity and legitimacy now appear to be in decline."[17] Tomsen says that the Afghan nation has resisted subjugation. Its moderate Islam rejects the radical Deobandi, Wahabbi and Ikhwani influences from Pakistan, the Persian Gulf and the Middle East. Other reasons for hope exist. The Taliban will probably be driven from Kabul by the end of the year. No ethnic group within has "separatist aspirations." The U.N. Security Council also seeks a legitimate regime in Kabul as accepted and chosen by Afghans.[18]

The United States and the United Nations do not recognize the Taliban, or the Islamic Emirate of Afghanistan. The United Front for Afghanistan, known as the Northern Alliance, is also present in Afghanistan and is headed by nominal President Burhanuddin Rabbani, who holds power with de facto Defense Minister Ahmed Shah Masoud (assassinated Sept. 23, 2001), Rabbani's primary military backer. Rabbani retains the U.N. seat. The U.S. State Department explains the Northern Alliance this way: "Rabanni received nominal support from General Dostum, and a faction of the Shi'a Hazara Hezb-i-Wahdat. Another faction of the Hezb-i-Wahdat nominally allied with the Taliban early in the year [1999]. Rabbani and Masoud control the northeastern, largely Tajik, portion of the country, including the strategic Panjshir valley north of Kabul."[19]

The United States does not support the Taliban, in part, because Afghanistan's rulers welcomed and protected terrorist leader Osama bin Laden, who has been living in Afghanistan since 1996. Bin Laden's Afghan quarters were attacked by America's missiles in August 1998.[20] In addition, the Taliban have breached international standards and law, and human rights. Their methods are harsh, brutal and violent. Pakistan and Saudi Arabia support for the Taliban adds a complexity that reminds us that no country is an island. Karl F. Inderfurth reports that another element of consideration is the destabilizing effect of the Taliban on Central Asia and Kashmir. Afghanistan's Central Asian neighbors, along with Iran, fear the spillover effects of what is taking place in Afghanistan today, including drugs, terrorism, religious extremism and persecution of ethnic minorities leading to destabilizing refugee flows.[21]

United States support in the late 1980s was meant, in part, to contain Russian imperialism, but the backing was costly, and the United States disengaged.

Today the fundamentalist Taliban control most of Afghanistan and harbor anti–U.S. terrorists.[22] The reasons the United States now does not recognize the Taliban include their behavior. In 1998 Barnett R. Rubin stated:

> They continue to shelter Osama bin Laden and his colleagues, thereby contravening requests from both the U.S. and Saudi Arabia; they violated firmly established norms of international and, if I may say so, Islamic law by executing Iranian diplomats. Their troops appear to have massacred large numbers of non-combatant Shia Muslims from the Hazara ethnic group after the capture of Mazar-i Sharif; and they continue to insist on unacceptable conditions on the delivery of humanitarian assistance, especially to women.[23]

Rubin believed that U.S. policy should be aimed at weakening the Taliban because of their strategic location in the region.

In May 1999, Peter Tomsen wrote:

> Peace and a political settlement, however, will not be realized in Afghanistan unless Pakistan terminates its covert support to Islamist radicals like the Taliban today and the ruthless Gulbuddin Hekmatyar before the Taliban's ascendancy. Since the Soviet pullout in 1989, the single largest obstacle to a successful settlement process has been the Pakistani military intelligence agency, the ISI (Interservices Intelligence Agency). The United States, through the CIA, funneled more than $1 billion of weapons, equipment and cold cash to the ISI following the Soviet invasion, including during three years after the Soviet pullout. The ISI unilaterally conveyed the great bulk of this aid to the Afghan Muslim extremists, who concurrently were receiving large sums from radical Islamist sources in the Persian Gulf region.[24]

Tomsen says that the U.S. vital interests lie in the regions around Afghanistan, and that American positions will have considerable weight among the Afghan and external parties involved, including Pakistan. He believes that Afghanistan will have peace and stability only when the Afghan people are able to "choose their leadership in a process seen by them as credible and not imposed from the outside."

Ahmed Rashid believes that "the dangerous behavior of Afghanistan's new leaders is no longer a local affair," and that "thousands of foreign radicals now fighting alongside the Taliban in Afghanistan are determined to someday overthrow their own regimes and carry out Taliban-style Islamist revolutions in their homelands." He urges the United States to put "serious pressure" on neighboring countries not to supply arms inside of Afghanistan, thus "drying-up" the warlords' supply, and, one hopes, presenting opportunities to negotiate peace.[25]

The U.S. Department of State reiterated in 2000 that the Taliban imposed their extreme interpretation of Islam in all the areas they controlled, but that enforcement was stricter in cities, especially Kabul. The Ministry for the Promotion of Virtue and Suppression of Vice acts as the enforcing body and regularly checks passersby to see that Taliban requirements of dress and appearance are met.

Nuclear weapons remain a major concern. Rubin says that Pakistan faces the prospect of institutional disintegration and violent civil conflict. U.S. interests would best be served by stability created by an inclusive, decentralized government in Afghanistan that respected the rights of all groups of Afghanistan's population and recognized the legitimate interests of all that country's neighbors. The greatest threats to such an outcome right now are the Taliban and their Pakistani and Saudi supporters (though Saudi Arabia may be moderating its support). Earlier allies are now the greatest threats to U.S. interests, and U.S. policy should aim to weaken the Taliban both from within and from without Afghanistan. Within Afghanistan, weakening the Taliban might enable factional division to ultimately force them to become more moderate and inclusive. Rubin did not advocate military assistance to any of the anti–Taliban forces because he believed that Afghanistan could not withstand more war and violence. To weaken the Taliban from without, Rubin contends, means to weaken or break their tie with Pakistan and requires denouncing Pakistan's aid to the Taliban. In the long term, Rubin believes that the U.S. goal must be to foster a new regional settlement over pipeline and trade routes, protection of cross-border minorities, and non-interference in Afghanistan.[26]

Nasrine Abou-Bakre Gross says that she has a political philosophy of life, and believes that "the current situation around the women's human rights issue in Afghanistan is purely political."[27]

The Afghan woman is being used as a political tool of colonization. It is actually wrong for another country to want Afghanistan. Afghanistan has had a major link with the United States. In the 1980s, Afghanistan was the most decisive factor that made the United States the sole superpower that it is today. In fact, Afghanistan gave the CIA its biggest victory; its biggest success story, and we must not forget that. We must do everything we can to use Afghanistan as a friend. Our best interests lie in an independent Afghanistan and that we must do everything we can to stop the use of Afghan women as a political tool of colonization for other powers. If our policy is involved in that colonization, we must really rethink. There are other ways we can have our best interests insured in Afghanistan than to annihilate and destroy an entire culture, an entire people; an entire country. This is worse than Nazi concentration camps.[28]

Gross becomes very worried when people talk about Afghan women in the contexts of their families, their culture, their religion and their history, and then conclude that the Taliban constitute a natural phenomenon. The Taliban serve as an army of occupation for colonization. Says Gross:

If we write about Afghan women without understanding the political situation, we are going to hurt them even more. It's a disservice. We must understand, because she is being used as a political tool of colonization, her woes come from the political needs of colonization. Her woes today do not come from Afghan men. Her woes today do not come out of Afghan society. Her woes come from a political force which through militias took power, and overnight revoked the rights of Afghan women. This has got nothing to do with Afghan woman's family, society, religion, or culture. As soon as we bring these other things up, we are diluting the colonizing dimension. I assure you, that if the Taliban are gotten rid of today, tomorrow, the streets of Kabul and every city will have women without chadari. And not a single Afghan man will go demonstrating, "No, we want our wives and daughters to wear chadari." I also assure you that the very next day, all Afghan men will shave their beards. And none of them will say, "We are less religious, less Muslim because we don't have a beard." So you need to understand that the beard and the chadari serve the same political purpose for colonizing power. They are equal. It is a way to control.

Gross says that what is happening in the country is not a creation of Afghanistan. Afghanistan is a very traditional society that loves family values, but it has never been a fanatical society. Gross provides provocative insight on how the colonizing power controls men as well as women:

Through controlling women, the colonizing power is controlling the Afghan men. Traditionally, wearing a chadari, working outside the home, and education, were the purview of the men in the family; never the government. When the Taliban came, they took that authority away from the men for themselves. So, what did they do to the men? In essence, they castrated the men. They disempowered the men. And when you are disempowered, you cannot fight back. Afghan women are being restricted more and more and more every day, not to punish the women, but to insure that the men stay castrated. The women of Afghanistan are the honor of the men, and when you dishonor the men, you disempower them. The creation of the Taliban and the way they use these techniques and the way they abuse the traditions of Afghanistan is a master creation, albeit, totally evil.

In *Steps of Peace and Our Responsibility as Afghans*, Gross concludes that the first round of colonization was with the Soviet Union. The men of Afghanistan were the guerrilla fighters. The men ate away at the power of the Soviet Union with the help of the United States, and they were finally victorious.[29] She believes the Taliban are the second round of colonization and that "in the second round of colonization the women can develop a mission of eating away at the power of the Taliban in the same guerrilla way that the first round did; maybe not with stinger missiles, but with other means."

After 21 years of genocide and a proxy war between the United States and the Soviet Union, says Sima Wali, and after "2 million killed, 1 million the victims of land mines, 12 million dispossessed of their homes and livelihood, and atrocities committed against women, Afghans continue to remain the largest refugee and internally displaced population in the world. Yet little or no coordinated relief is in sight."[30] Wali is among those who believe that it is not the *burqa*, but the politics behind Afghanistan's problems that have kept its women isolated and dehumanized.[31]

The Human Rights Watch report of 2000 states, "Governments in Pakistan and Afghanistan failed spectacularly to uphold women's rights, and violence against women was a pervasive problem in the region. There was no improvement in the status of women in the parts of the country controlled by the Taliban."[32] Both the United Front and the Taliban were responsible for violence resulting in civilian casualties by rockets, bombing, burning people's houses, killing suspected supporters of the opposing side, deporting men, or separating families by arresting or shooting men and taking women and children to Kabul or Pakistan. The Taliban are, however, particularly violent toward women, and beat them when they perceive any of them to have violated a rule.

The U.S. State Department's report concluded that "the human rights situation for women was extremely poor" in 1999.[33] Violence remains a problem. Rape, kidnapping and forced marriage occur especially in areas beyond Taliban control. In Taliban-controlled areas, treatment of women and girls has improved slightly. Nonetheless, the Department of State describes Taliban restrictions as widespread, institutionally sanctioned and systematic. The stability the Taliban brought was offset by their continued threats and actual beatings of women to enforce their dress code. There were unconfirmed reports of Taliban soldiers and foreign volunteers who fought with the Taliban raping and abducting women.

Barnett R. Rubin perhaps best describes Afghans as citizens: "In general, the concept of Afghan people as citizens of Afghanistan has been lost. This is the case de jure for women under Taliban rule, but it is true for anyone who is not commanding an armed group."[34]

## The Refugee Woman

In 1996, Sue Emmott, the Oxfam United Kingdom/Ireland country representative for Afghanistan, wrote that conversations in 1994 with women in a camp for the displaced in Jalalabad revealed what it meant for women to lose their homes, particularly during ongoing instability and conflict. One-third of the Afghan population fled to Pakistan and Iran during the Soviet occupation. When the Mujahidin captured Kabul in 1992, the people in Kabul who stayed did so because they could not afford to leave. In 1992, 20,000 needed assistance leaving Kabul for Mazar i Sharif, and in 1994, 100,000 left Kabul for Jalalabad. When the Taliban seized Kabul in 1996, approximately three million Afghans fled, and about a million and a half of these are displaced.[35]

Once displaced, however, Emmott discovered that the women found it hard to talk about the notion of "home." They understood what home was "not," but not what home "is." Home was not the tent or where they slept. Nor was home the "space" they occupied with little privacy or that which their children wandered purposelessly with no school. The environment was more unfamiliar to middle classes who were used to modern facilities, but surroundings were also unfamiliar to the poor. Further, even though women were sharing the same experience, class still affected relations.[36]

"But for all," the UNHCR said in June 2000, "that drought affecting Afghanistan, Iran and Pakistan has resulted in the suspension of UNHCR's assisted returns of Afghan refugees from Iran and Pakistan to four drought-stricken southern Afghan provinces."[37]

According to the U.S. State Department, the Taliban said in 1999 that they were putting together a new constitution to guarantee the rights of all based on Shari'a, the Islamic law, which includes the Koran, the Sunni and Hanafi jurisprudence. The two names given to Afghanistan by each organization within the country indicate that both factions believe in promoting Islam as a state religion. The Taliban's official name for the country is the Islamic Emirate of Afghanistan, and the anti–Taliban organization, the Northern Alliance, calls it the Islamic State of Afghanistan.

In October 1998, after two years under Taliban rule, Kabul reflected the efforts of the Taliban to isolate its citizens from the outside world. Brent Sadler, CNN correspondent, says, "Laws are so strict that Afghans live in fear of breaking them."[38] The Taliban captured the city of Herat, the country's cultural center, and banished all books on the Koran. "They had their own brand of the Koran and the Kalashnikov."[39]

When the Taliban entered Kabul, they publicly hanged Najibullah, the figurehead Soviet president, and introduced their own harsh version of Islam. Glyn Davies, U.S. Department of State spokesman, said in 1998 that there was nothing objectionable to imposing Islamic law on the areas the Taliban controlled. The Taliban reportedly received large sums of money from Saudi Arabia and some of the Gulf States. United States officials appeared to welcome the Taliban taking of Kabul in spite of the manner in which they did so, because they believed the Taliban would help them with two big problems: controlling international terrorism and the heroin industry. Afghanistan is considered the biggest center of terrorist activities, and the world's second largest producer of heroin.[40]

Ambassador Peter Tomsen believes that in some areas, particularly rural, the Taliban are more a social movement than a regime: "The Taliban don't really have an infrastructure. It's more of a movement than a regime: They don't have a government per se with offices that are very significant with personnel out in the provinces and districts."[41] Barnett R. Rubin, director of the Center for Preventive Action and senior fellow council on Foreign Relations, testified to the U.S. Senate that the Taliban are a trans-border movement, led by Afghans, funded and aided by Pakistan and Saudi Arabia, and linked to social networks in both Afghanistan and Pakistan.[42]

Marsden concludes that the Taliban movement is a product of the 1978 socialist coup and 1979 Soviet invasion; the Afghan weariness of resistance leaders who failed to form a stable government; the Great Game; the fear of the Soviet Union that if the United States gained control in Afghanistan, its southern provinces would be vulnerable to attack; and the failure of political movements to form a government. The Taliban, then, appeared to represent potential stability to countries with interests in Afghanistan, like Pakistan and the United States. These countries provided support for the Taliban.[43]

Nancy Hatch Dupree wrote in 1998 that it was "a valid but little heeded point"[44] that the Taliban movement was still coming to grips with establishing a government. The very young militia is the power base to the central government that is not functioning effectively. Very conservative Islamic seminaries or madrassas train the Taliban, for example, in the beliefs that unveiled women appearing in public are immoral and the duty of the Taliban is to rid a city of the sinful ways Kabuli women represent. The Physicians for Human Rights (PHR) add to the definition of the Taliban as a movement and as a military and a political force. The organization claims that Taliban means "students of Muslim religious studies," and that the students are poorly educated rural Pushtun youths recruited from refugee camps and religious schools in Pakistan.[45] PHR rejects the perception that while the Taliban are repressive, at least they have stopped the war and ended violent crime in the capital after the Soviet occupation.

## Who the Taliban Say They Are

The Islamic Emirate of Afghanistan has its own responses to the question: Who are the Taliban? Although the answers are not unidimensional, the Emirate begins with the claim that "Taliban are the blessing of Allah Ta`ala which He in His graciousness has bestowed upon the people of Afghanistan in lieu of the innumerable sacrifices they have made. They are a source of honour and liberation to all the oppressed Muslims of the world."[46]

They say that the Taliban are well-known people who are trained and study "pure Islam" and earn the "Degree of Trust" at Deeni Madaris, or Madaris-e-Islamiyyah. They are the true leaders, sincere devotees, and fearless fighters. Their movement began to help the widows and the weak. Shari'a law is the governing force. They argue that weapons of war were seized from the enemy and food is taken with thanks to Afghan families. When addressing the human rights of women, the Emirate states that what rights a woman has is a matter of definition. The Taliban adhere to the definition determined by Allah Ta`ala, not by the Western world. Further, whoever would give women their rights as defined by the West would be denying women their rights, which is against the principles of the West, so, giving women their rights by Western definition is not intelligent and is coercion. As for women who are demanding freedom from Purdah in order to be employed, these women are not Afghan, but are from neighboring countries. When the war comes to an end, women will be educated

TABLE 3.1
POLITICAL PARTIES AND LEADERS IN AFGHANISTAN

Harakat-i-Islami (Islamic Movement)
*Mohammed Asif Mohseni*

Harakat-Inqilab-i-Islami (Islamic Revolutionary Movement)
*Mohammad Nabi Mohammadi*

Hizbi Islami-Gulbuddin (Islamic Party)
*Gulbuddin Hikmatyar faction*

Hizbi Islami-Khalis (Islamic Party)
*Yunis Khalis faction*

Hizbi Wahdat-Khalili faction (Islamic Unity Party)
*Abdul Karim Khalili*

Hizbi Wahdat-Akbari faction (Islamic Unity Party)
*Mohammad Akbar Akbari*

Ittihad-i-Islami Barai Azadi Afghanistan
(Islamic Union for the Liberation of Afghanistan)
*Abdul Rasul Sayaf*

Jabha-i-Najat-i-Milli Afghanistan
(Afghanistan National Liberation Front)
*Sibghatullah Mojadedi*

Jamiat-i-Islami (Islamic Society)
*Burhanuddin Rabbani*

Jumbesh-i-Milli Islami (National Islamic Movement)
*Abdul Rashid Dostum*

Mahaz-i-Milli-Islami (National Islamic Front)
*Sayed Ahamad Gailani*

Taliban (Religious Students Movement)
*Mullah Mohammad Omar*

*Source:* Afghanistan Online, "Political Parties and Leaders in Afghanistan." Available: http://www.afghan-web.com/politics/parties.html, Jul. 13, 2000.

in an Islamic madrassas. Notably, the Taliban movement is "purely religious" and "spiritual." Prejudice and discrimination are "contrary to the spirit of Islam."

In response to the alleged terrorism of Osama bin Laden, the Emirate says that even Rabbani, the leader of the opposition faction, had said that bin Laden is a guest in the country, and therefore, Afghanistan's responsibility is to protect him. The Emirate says that Osama bin Laden does not deny or apologize for the three charges that America has made against bin Laden, that he was behind the killing of American soldiers in

Somalia, the bomb-blast in Riyadh, and the decree to kill Americans anywhere in the world. Bin Laden has sacrificed most of his life and given of his wealth for Jihaad, the Emirate says.[47]

## Taliban in 2001

Despite statements made in 2000 "by some Taliban officials that the ban on women's right to education, employment and freedom of movement would be lifted, these restrictions remained in force."[48] The Taliban militia persisted in 2001 with repressive edicts on its people that continued to concern deeply human rights groups and governments. In the name of its perceived interpretation of Islam, the Taliban destroyed two ancient statues of Buddha in Bamiyan and other religious statues. They decreed that all non–Muslims must wear identification tags. The Taliban said wearing the tags was to protect Afghanistan's Hindu population.[49]

Since the Taliban's emergence in 1994, it has been shown to have provided terrorists with "logistical support, travel documentation, and training facilities."[50] Although radical terroristic groups, including Osama bin Laden's Al Qaeda, were in Afghanistan prior to the Taliban, "the spread of Taliban control has seen Afghan-based terrorism evolve into a relatively coordinated, widespread activity focused on sustaining and developing terrorist capabilities."[51] The combining of Pakistani movements with the Taliban and their Arab-Afghan allies has seen ties between these groups strengthen. The religious extremists are willing to strike outside of their immediate country. This willingness is shown in the 1993 bombing of the World Trade Center and the September 11, 2001, attacks on the World Trade Center and Pentagon. These events raise the question: does the Taliban militia host bin Laden or does bin Laden host the Taliban?

The sinister and pervasive nature of the Taliban became most apparent as the U.S. and the world investigated the attacks on the World Trade Center in New York City and the Pentagon in Washington, D.C., and the jetliner that crashed in Pennsylvania on September 11, 2001. When the Taliban refused to turn over bin Laden and the Al Qaeda network to the United States, on October 7, 2001, the United States and its allies attacked the Taliban in Afghanistan.

## Conclusions

The subject of Afghanistan continues to evolve. Bleak as it is, there may be hope. Peter Tomsen argues that there is opportunity to bring stability to Afghanistan. The Taliban's days appear to be numbered and he says, "I hope that we can help the Afghans reclaim their country and for the first time since the Soviet invasion get a chance to establish a truly legitimate Afghan government and not one that's imposed from the outside."[52]

Although the young "religious" males who form the Taliban militia were originally welcomed by the Afghan people and by the United States, there is no doubt that the Taliban-supported militia have imposed cruel, inhumane and deadly discipline on the Afghan people. The countries in the region around Afghanistan are not without their own agendas. Nuclear weapons and terrorism loom on the horizon. Into this quagmire, the United States had, in the eyes of many Afghans, deserted Afghanistan both by disengaging from the quest for a peaceful solution in the post–Soviet period and by supporting the countries that support the Taliban.

Although some believe that the Taliban do not have a legitimate interpretation of Islam, Afghanistan's religion is part of its total context. More importantly, it is the cloak of a far more sinister agenda. Some believe that it is not Islam that the Taliban practice, but a form of extremism of the moment.

# Afghan Women Under the Rule of the Taliban

*The Taliban have not been able to provide women with any means of*
*sustenance or any means of living, and so what you make out of this*
*[situation] is neither Islamic nor Afghan.*

Haron Amin[1]

When the Taliban gained dominance, they moved swiftly to impose restrictions on women. The Revolutionary Association of the Women of Afghanistan (RAWA) compiled an "abbreviated" list of 29 restrictions placed on women and 11 restrictions applicable to all Afghans. The list ends with the words, "and so on..." (Appendix C). RAWA says that even if the number of rapes and killings fall, "Taliban restriction—comparable to those from the middle ages—will continue to kill the spirit of our people while depriving them of a humane existence."[2]

Media Action International posts 16 decrees to the people, translated verbatim from the office of Amr Bel Maruf wa Nai as Munkar, Ministry for the Promotion of Virtue and the Prevention of Vice, the religious police. (See Appendix C.) About 15 additional decrees apply to international and national agencies. Adding to the harsh rigidity of existing edicts, the impact of still other decrees is not clear until they reach the headline of a newspaper or appear on TV. Although these bizarre rules affected men as much as women, some that affected women appear in the following items gathered by Media Action International:

> "Women now risk beatings in the streets for wearing white socks." (*International Herald Tribune*, Sep. 25, 1997)
>
> Nur Mohammad, Governor of Herat: "Women just aren't as smart as men. They don't have the intelligence. We categorically refuse to let women vote or participate in politics." (*Sunday Times*, London, Mar. 24, 1996)

"Women in Kandahar were outraged at being banned from using the city's ancient public baths." (*The Times*, London, Oct. 8, 1996)[3]

Media Action International concludes with a section on examples of Taliban justice:

> Beating with whips and imprisonment for minor offences, amputation of hands for theft, execution for murder, and death by stoning for adultery or "multiple intercourse" (sleeping with two men in one month) if witnessed by at least four people.

In 1996, the *Women's Health Journal* referred to violence against women and girls as a "daily reality throughout the world," and that the Taliban movement "drastically" curtailed the rights of women.[4] To denounce violations representatives from Afghanistan and other countries met in Latin America in November 1996 at the World Meeting of Women Victims of Violence.

The restrictions on women include but go beyond those of dress and consist of constraint of movement in society, denial of education, work and health care. The atrocities committed against the Afghan woman cannot be denied. And finally, even those women whose lives are spared and who may flee, find new problems in dislocation and refugeeism. All of these effects are not limited to the lives of women, but reach to the lives women touch, especially those of their children.

## *Effects on Children*

Mavis Leno says

> We can never remind people enough that whatever happens to the women in a culture, happens to their children. If you don't have a soft heart for adults, then think about the children living in this situation. For many of them their mother was the only wage earner and is the only adult family member. There are far more women than men in Afghanistan because so many men have died in the wars. So, if their mom starves, they starve.

Leno cites the Physicians for Human Rights study that found

> both women and many children in profound clinical depression, a huge upsurge in suicide among women including very painful suicides because their means of killing themselves are limited under these circumstances they find themselves in. There are women drinking household bleach

and things like that to kill themselves—so very painful deaths—rather than live in these circumstances. In the day-to-day living and conducting of their lives, they have virtually no access to medical care, and they are not allowed to work.[5]

Leno's warning about the effects on children is illustrated by the August 1998 Mazar-i-Sharif massacre, in which "men, women and children were shot, while baby girls were kicked or beaten to death."[6]

The consequences of "erasing" women are predictable, says Michael Church. The July 1999 UNICEF survey in Kabul verifies the effects on the children. "Two in three children did not trust adults, had seen people blown to bits and did not themselves expect to survive."[7] In Afghanistan, children at risk ranked behind only Angola and Sierra Leone in factors related to environmental conditions, mortality rates, nutrition, primary education, security, and health.[8] The Human Rights Watch Report of 2000 notes that 30 percent of the daily landmine victims in Afghanistan are children.

## Health Care and Children

The issue of the needs of children ties directly to the lack of health care provided women, particularly their reproductive health care needs, which constitute 30 to 40 percent of women's health care problems. In 1995 the *British Medical Journal* said that only Afghanistan and Haiti were among the 21 countries not in Africa that were considered in the very high reproductive risk category. The journal stated that the low status of women in many societies perpetuates early and frequent childbearing. In addition to giving women access to reproductive health services, educating girls and providing economic opportunity for women, and educating men about women's health needs were important.[9] According to a U.N. report, reproductive health care needs "are largely ignored in assistance programs," and "similarly, traditional preferences for the survival of sons has reduced the value of life for women and girls and increased the disease burden of women."[10]

## Constraint of Movement

All restrictions on women affect their movement about in society. Women can not go anywhere without wearing the burqa, and they must be accompanied by a male relative. Some cannot afford a burqa. Many no longer have a male relative. Thus, they are to remain at home behind windows that must be painted. The PHR reports that in other instances, a woman may have the appropriate attire, but her ankle might show, and she will be beaten.[11] For the most part, education and employment are forbidden. Women must be treated by women medical personnel, but women medical personnel are severely scarce. Haron Amin of the United Nations reminds us that these things that happen to the women of his country are not easy to talk about. He says,

> There are women who have contemplated many, many times suicide. That was not a phenomenon in Afghanistan, even the women who take refuge in Pakistan. A lot of these women they have been forcibly pushed to have sex with men and to be sold as prostitutes and things like that. These phenomena were not known in Afghanistan. Afghanistan was a very closed society with a very, very high degree of dignity and honor. The effects of the crisis in Afghanistan will not be known for at least some time, because the trauma and everything else will hit hard in the next 5 to 10 years. Usually, when you have mass movement of people in a society, the actual effect can only be seen afterwards. From the mass mobilization, from the mass movement of the people, people generally have social crisis. And the social crisis from Afghanistan, the impact on these women becomes traumatic on their children. The impact is great on these women who will bear the guilt as is the impact of psychological torture on a woman who has a child by a man who raped her.

He adds,

> Women are locked in their houses. The Taliban have told them to actually paint the windows black. So they are confined to their houses, cannot go out. What are they doing? I really don't know. They have become selfless physical nonbeings that have to live. They have become nonbeings, yet they exist. They exist. They breathe, but it's a life full of torture. It's like stripping somebody of their entire identity, and it is cursing God for having created woman as well. One of the ministers of the Taliban said that there are two places for a woman: one is the husband's bed and the other is the graveyard. He has said that; this is an official quote that is the woman's place in the world.

Amin says that people need to "actually open a window and take a glimpse of what the world might be like for that woman. It's hard to see how much she is trying to avoid in speaking out, and what she really internally feels."

Equally disturbing is that the restrictions for women affect children and men. Since women represented most of the employed teachers, restriction of women's right to be educated and to work affects boys and girls who now have no teachers.

## Education

One of the Taliban's first rulings prohibited girls and women from attending school. A young female graduate of Kabul University bemoans the lack of educational opportunities: "[...]Afghan women have no rights today. They are all walking deads."[12] Humanitarian groups established projects to restore this right. Schools were established in private homes where the girls were taught to sew and weave. On June 16, 1998, the Taliban ordered the closing of more than 100 privately funded schools. The Taliban issued new rules for nongovernmental organizations providing the schooling: education must be limited to girls up to the age of eight, and restricted to the Koran.[13] Damning education had effects on both boys and girls. Books were removed from Herat. Since the majority of teachers were female, boys experienced a shortage of teachers.[14] In January 2000, UNICEF reported that 90 percent of the girls in Afghanistan and 75 percent of the boys were not attending school in Taliban-controlled areas, a drop from previous statistics.[15]

Nancy Hatch Dupree believes that, of all the restrictive rules and regulations applied to women, the international community is most concerned with the restrictions on education and employment. Providing education for women is complicated by the challenge of how to give international aid without compromising national cultural perspectives.[16] A 1996 U.N. survey further demonstrates how the restrictions placed on women affect boys. The survey reported Kabul had 158 public schools, 148,233 male students and 103,256 female students; of 11,208 teachers, 7,793 were women.[17] UNICEF found that the 10 percent of girls who attend school do so in a non-governmental organization (NGO) school, mosque school or home school. In 1999, about 300,000 to 350,000 children attended schools run or funded by various assistance agencies and NGOs. The Swedish Committee for Afghanistan (SCA) reported serving 175,000 students in 567 schools, of which 39 were home schools. In a few areas, over 50 percent of students were girls. The SCA said 20 percent of the students in its formal schools are girls, but these schools are located in rural areas. Boys are also educated in home schools because Taliban-run schools have administrative problems. Girls represent a high proportion of the students in the Northern Alliance–controlled territory. In newly Taliban captured cities such as Hazarajat, schools have been reopened. In Herat, captured in 1995, girls' schools are closed, but 20 percent of girls are enrolled. In Kandahar, girls represent 5 percent of the students. Refugees and returnees have demanded education, and some have sent their girls abroad to get an education.[18]

Illiteracy is growing as a result of the ban on education. The United Nations Educational, Scientific and Cultural Organization's literacy rate indicators show only two countries, Burkina Faso and Niger, with a lower estimated adult illiteracy rate than Afghanistan in the year 2000. In Asia, it is the highest.[19] A whole generation of Afghans are growing up without any education.[20]

In April 2000, *BBC Worldnews* reported that Afghanistan had one of the worst records on education in the world. Although only one school survived near Kabul through development agency aid and local community support, more girls are getting educated. Their schools are unofficial and without support. Religious law is still emphasized over other subjects, but the Mujahedin with the help of an unnamed American university, introduced the standard alphabet textbook. In the villages, the situation is better. Children, both boys and girls, learn reading, writing and math as well as Islam.[21]

At least some children in Kabul are learning, according to *Time*. In a tiny school a few young, dedicated Afghan women are teaching girls. The women obtained permission from the government in January 2000 after lobbying nine months to open the Naswan Shashdarak school to girls in grades one to six. The school's headmistress, 25-year-old Nilab Zareen, is taking a risk, but the school's doors are kept shut to avoid informers.

Female literacy was never high. Only one percent of Afghan women graduated from high school before the Soviet invasion. The United Nations estimates that in Kabul "only a few thousand girls—out of a total population of 2 million—are receiving some form of schooling."[22] The Taliban have also allowed a small group of women to finish medical training at Kabul's military hospital.

In March 2000, the Co-operation Centre for Afghanistan (CCA)conducted a survey inside Afghanistan on the status of girls' education. Although they say their results are preliminary, one comparison alone tells a stark story. In 1921, Mustorat, the first girls' school, had 34 students. Also in 1921, another girls' school, Esmat, was established bringing the total number of students to about 200. One glance at their zero projections for 2000, both in number of schools and estimated students, tells us that the trend of women's education is no longer a trend.[23]

The Taliban turned the Mariam Girls' High school into a market, and

TABLE 4.1
ILLITERACY RATE INDICATORS, SELECTED COUNTRIES*
(Listed in descending order by illiteracy rates of women)

| Country | Estimated adult (15+) illiteracy rate (%), 2000 | |
|---|---|---|
| | F | M |
| Niger | 91.7 | 76.5 |
| Burkina Faso | 86.9 | 66.8 |
| Afghanistan | 79.2 | 49.0 |
| Guinea-Bissau | 78.6 | 47.0 |
| Sierra Leone | 77.4 | 49.3 |
| Benin | 76.4 | 47.8 |
| Nepal | 76.2 | 40.9 |
| Yemen | 75.0 | 32.6 |
| Guinea | 73.0 | 44.9 |
| Senegal | 72.4 | 52.8 |
| Pakistan | 72.2 | 42.4 |
| Mozambique | 71.6 | 40.1 |
| Mauritania | 70.5 | 49.4 |
| Bangladesh | 70.5 | 48.3 |
| Gambia | 70.4 | 56.2 |
| Bhutan | 66.4 | 38.9 |
| India | 57.9 | 31.4 |
| Iran (Islamic Rep. of) | 30.0 | 16.3 |
| China | 22.6 | 7.7 |

*Source:* United Nations Educational, Scientific and Cultural Organization, 2000. Online. Internet. Available: http://www.un.org/Depts/unsd/social/literacy.htm, Jun. 2, 2000.

*The United Nations Educational, Scientific and Cultural Organization defines an illiterate person as someone who cannot, with understanding, both read and write a short, simple statement on his or her everyday life.*

in 1998 they attacked the United Nations' special schools in the Macrorayan area that were allocated for girls' education.[24]

Christiane Amanpour reported that in 1997 one aid agency held classes for a very few of the very young, "but if a Taliban with a gun decides he doesn't like it…" the school is closed. In 1998, Amanpour reported that girls were forbidden to attend high school because authorities say the purpose is to keep the sexes apart. When Taliban are confronted with the fact that schools were already segregated, their response is that they are

## TABLE 4.2
### TREND OF WOMEN'S EDUCATION IN AFGHANISTAN

| Type of Education Institutions | Number | | | | Estimated Students | | | |
|---|---|---|---|---|---|---|---|---|
| | 1980 * | 1991 ** | 1996 | 2000 | 1980 | 1991 | 1996 | 2000 |
| Women Literacy School | 576 | 700 | 400 | 0 | 10431 | 12663 | 0 | 0 |
| Primary Schools | 443 | 600 | 600 | 0 | 155000 | 189000 | 218000 | 0 |
| Secondary Schools | 63 | 73 | 73 | 0 | 28200 | 34500 | 38000 | 0 |
| Women Medical School | 7 | 7 | 7 | 0 | 2530 | 3087 | 3395 | 0 |
| Total | 1089 | 1380 | 1080 | 0 | 196162 | 239250 | 259395 | 0 |

Source: Co-operation Centre for Afghanistan (CCA) "Education Rights." "Status of Girls' Education at the Beginning of 21st Century in Afghanistan" [Peshawar Pakistan] CCA Newsletter (Apr. 2000) VII:2 1. Reprinted with permission from Dr. Amir S. Hassanyar, Director, Co-operation Centre for Afghanistan.

Legend:    *CSO (Central Statistic Organization) 1982 Publ. (20).
           **Interview and projection

Note: Many primary schools as well as higher educational institutions were co-educational. The total estimated number of girls in all educational institutions was estimated to be over 3,000,000.

trying to bring peace to the country so that girls can be educated. Amanpour says, "a five-minute drive from the girls' school is the boys' school and it's full of students."[25] In spite of official oppression, efforts to educate girls persist. In 2000, the New York Times reports that by word of mouth, women in Kabul opened a school. Schooling for girls is still prohibited, but a few exceptions are being made. A few mullahs have been able to use their mosques as classrooms for girls, though the instruction is primarily religious. Some schools have opened in homes, some secretly, others discreetly. The United Nations estimates that 10,000 young girls are going to classes in Kabul. The number is increasing. Fatima, a teacher, says, "Most girls have lost four years of education. Children with illiterate parents have suffered the most."[26]

## Employment

Physicians for Human Rights reports that in 1998 one of its researchers "saw a city of beggars—women who had once been teachers and nurses now moving in the streets like ghosts under their enveloping *burqas*, selling every possession and begging so as to feed their children."[27] The PHR concludes such restrictions on work, schooling, mobility and health care "are life threatening to women and their children."

The prohibition on work makes it very difficult for widowed women with children who are forced to beg on the streets. The PHR reports, one widowed mother said, "...there are beatings for showing up in public without a male chaperone or showing your face. Worst of all is not being allowed to work. How can a widow survive like this?" The pressure is so great, some women flee. This woman's story is truly painful:

> He [my husband] was sitting in his office when a bullet passed through the window and hit him in his heart. After his death our home was destroyed by a rocket, and we moved to a different part of the city. I suffered a lot from the loss of my husband. My children were young when their father was killed. The pressure was too much on me: I had to be a father and a mother for them. I was working two jobs, and we had an okay living until 1996 when another disaster happened. The Taliban took me out of work and my daughters out of school. This was unbearable and sickening for me and my entire family. I almost lost my sanity, and I did not have anyone to support me financially.... Without a source of income and with the dramatic rise in prices, I didn't have a way to support my family. If I hadn't left, I would have gone crazy.[28]

## Prostitution

The Co-operation Centre for Afghanistan reports cases of prostitution narrated by the people. In some cases, women in prostitution are not professionals but rather are forced into the work by economic need. Some of Kabul's prostitutes live in brothels and must share their income with a madam and the resident pimp. The business survives because of frequent relocation, bribing of judicial authorities, and by entertaining the Taliban free of charge. The Taliban claim that "communists and lechers" have infiltrated the Taliban ranks.[29]

Prostitution and trafficking of women has alarmingly increased among refugees. Some international aid workers say the increase is due to the Taliban's restrictions on women working and going to school, thus increasing the poverty, thus forcing women to flee to Pakistan. Many of these women have lost their male relatives. Accelerating poverty and increasing despair perpetuate the trafficking and prostitution of widows and young girls.[30]

## TABLE 4.3
## TALIBAN POLICY EFFECT ON WOMEN

| Effect | Response (%) |
| --- | --- |
| Employed before Taliban takeover | 62 |
| Employed, last year in Kabul | 20 |
| Decline in physical health status | 71 |
| Decline in mental health status | 81 |
| Decline in access to health care, last two years in Kabul | 62 |
| Symptoms of posttraumatic stress disorder | 42 |
| Symptoms of anxiety | 86 |
| One or more family members killed | 84 |
| They or family member detained and abused | 68 |
| Extremely restricted social activities | 68 |
| Support for women's human rights | 96 |

*Source:* Zohra Rasekh, Heidei M. Bauer, Michele M. Manos, Vincent Iacopino, "Women's Health and Human Rights in Afghanistan," *JAMA*, 280:5, Aug. 5, 1998, 449–455. Available: http://www.ama-assn.org/special/womh/library/readroom/vol_280/jsc80298.htm, May 7, 2000.

The PHR survey concluded that the results suggest "the combined effects of war-related trauma and human rights abuses by Taliban officials have had a profound effect on Afghan women's health," and "that Taliban policies regarding women are incommensurate with the interests, needs, and health of Afghan women."[31]

Frayba Wakili, a refugee from Afghanistan, told the Feminist Expo 2000 international conference of the Feminist Majority in Baltimore, "The Taliban abused and used our religion to oppress women. I cannot hold a job or go to school, and so would be forced to beg for food like thousands of others."[32]

In 1998, Western journalist Marion Lloyd reported extensively on Afghanistan's difficulties. Women in Kabul, unlike their rural components, were used to Western-style freedoms and about half held jobs. Career women can no longer work or are afraid to go to work. The mental hospital is filled with women who suffer from depression or see the hospital as an escape from boredom. Lloyd spoke with a 25-year-old former physics teacher, Fazona, described as sitting "slumped on a cot in the cheerless, freezing, women's ward, her eyes desperate and fearful." Afraid that the Taliban would make a surprise visit, Fazona kept her voice very low, fading into a whisper, as she said, "I am angry; I am upset; I stay every day in a room. I am a teacher; I am too educated to wear a burqa…. The Taliban are everywhere." Lloyd concludes, "It's a grim echo of the Muslim mantra, 'God is everywhere.'"[33]

## Health

The 1998 Physicians for Human Rights survey of 160 Afghan women found high levels of poor health, multiple specific symptoms and a significant decline (71 percent) in their physical condition since the beginning of the Taliban takeover. Seventy-seven percent reported poor access to services in Kabul, 20 percent reported no access. Access (62 percent) and quality (58 percent) were worse than the previous year. Fifty-three percent had occasions in which they were seriously ill and unable to seek medical care and 28 percent reported inadequate control over their reproduction.[34]

The PHR found that women's fear of being publicly beaten or arrested by the Taliban deters them from seeking health care. In some cases women had no money to pay for a burqa so that they could not go out on the street to seek health care. Women begged the PHR researcher to send them some burqas from the United States so that they could go out on the streets. Yet, says the PHR, the burqa may contribute to health problems. One woman reported that walking in the burqa is difficult. Seeing is difficult. The burqa is unhealthy for women with asthma or hypertension. PHR concludes that the burqa may cause eye problems, poor vision and hearing, skin rash, headaches, increased cardiac problems and asthma, itching of the scalp, hair loss, and depression. In addition, many women do not receive humanitarian assistance, since a Taliban decree in 1997 stated that women could not pick up food or aid. A male relative had to pick up and deliver the aid to the women. In the case of widows, this restriction was doubly harsh.[35]

In 1997 *Lancet* reported that, although the Taliban had banned women from most occupations, some female doctors and nurses were allowed to continue their professions because Taliban rules of work state that women should only be attended by female physicians. The negative side to the Taliban's allowance is that many female doctors and nurses are beaten or forced to watch beatings of their female colleagues. Women are often beaten because they seek medical attention. If they are fortunate enough to get to a hospital, they still might not receive treatment. In one hospital 80 female patients were ordered home because their modesty couldn't be preserved in a crowded ward. Male doctors are not allowed to treat women or girls unless they are relatives. The need for health care is exacerbated by landmine incidents, Taliban or warring faction–inflicted gunshot wounds, by the decay of public utilities breeding infectious disease, and by Taliban-inflicted wounds of torture such as broken bones, bruises, fractured skulls and serious burns. The Taliban view health care professionals with hostility and some health care workers have fled to other countries.[36]

Physicians for Human Rights "mobilizes the health professions and enlists support from the general public to protect and promote the human rights of all people."[37] The PHR contends that the restrictions on women are highly profiled in the media, but very little is known about the experiences and opinions of Afghan women. Stories of refusal of treatment and dire consequences abound.

A 20-year-old mother in Kabul told how her two-and-one-half-year-old daughter died from diarrhea. The first hospital refused treatment and the second refused intravenous fluids and antibiotics. The mother says,

> Her body was handed to me and her father in the middle of the night. With her body in my arms, we left the hospital. It was curfew time and we had a long way to get home. We had to spend the night inside a destroyed house among the rubble. In the morning we took my dead baby home but we had no money for her funeral.[38]

A Kabul health worker says that even though she has permission from the Ministry of Health, working outside the home is still a big risk: "One day the religious police may stop me on the street and ask where I am going. At that point, the fact that I have 'permission' may mean nothing to him; he can beat me or harass me or arrest me at his whim. Every day I leave my house and I pray that I might get back home safely at the end of the day."[39]

A 35-year-old professional woman described the decline in quality of health care from 1996 to 1998: "There are no qualified doctors, no medication, and no medical equipment in the hospitals. The patients are not treated properly...."[40]

A most sad physician revealed,

> Under current policies, this situation will only get worse. Already there are a limited number of female obstetricians that women are supposed to see exclusively. And now the training of more women health professionals has been halted completely; so there is no way there will be women doctors for future generations.[41]

And the somber result is explained by an Afghan pharmacist: "A lot of pregnant women die at home and in hospitals and clinics."[42]

Christiane Amanpour, in a CNN report on Sept. 30, 1997, said it best: "The latest crisis, say aid agencies, is in health care, women now get practically none." The Taliban "had just banned women from the main hospitals and dumped them in a crumbling building with no window panes, no running water, no proper operating theater or the electricity to power equipment as basic as a sterilizer." At that time Amanpour reported that when efforts were made to try to visit the hospital, all, including the aid agencies and the accompanying press, were arrested at gunpoint and detained for several hours. Amanpour concluded that the Taliban's rage caused by the presence of the press illustrates not only their reign of terror over Afghans, but also the difficulties they make for any kind of meaningful international intervention.

## Displacement

The loss of a family member to war and displacement are common to Afghan women. Mental stress from trauma is common. All but one of the 160 women in the PHR survey had been displaced at least once. Eighty-four percent reported one or more family members killed in war. The most mentioned hardships were poverty (69 percent); disease (68 percent); emotional difficulties (63 percent); lack of health care (54 percent); lack of education (51 percent); and inadequate sanitation (50 percent).[43]

Amnesty International testified before the U.S. Congress that "Afghan civilians have been the main victims of a human rights catastrophe." To illustrate their conclusions, they reported, "during a rare lull in the bombardment of Kabul in 1994, a woman left her home to find food. Two Mujahedin guards grabbed her and took her to a house, where 22 men raped her for three days. When she was allowed to go home, she found her three children had died of hypothermia."[44]

Men also suffer atrocities. On May 9, 1999, when the Taliban recaptured Yakaolang, they systematically killed hundreds of men who remained in the town. The Taliban also recaptured Bamiyan on May 9, and carried out summary executions of hundreds of men upon entering the city.[45] All Afghan civilians suffered atrocities whether torture or murder upon being detained, or ethnic mass killings, kidnapping, murder and other means of excessive force such as firing upon student demonstrators.

Men, like women, suffer restrictions. All the men must grow beards,

Christiane Amanpour of CNN reported in 1997. "They're beaten if they're not bushy, not Islamically correct enough. Men can play sports but not in skimpy sports gear."[46] Men must also wear Islamic clothes and a cap.[47] According to the Physicians for Human Rights, men not only also must bear restrictions, but also suffer severe consequences if they do not obey.

> The Taliban's abuses are by no means limited to women. Thousands of men have been taken prisoner, arbitrarily detained, tortured, and many killed and disappeared. Men are beaten and jailed for wearing beards of insufficient length (that of a clenched fist beneath the chin), are subjected to cruel and degrading conditions in jail, and suffer such punishments as amputation and stoning. Men are also vulnerable to extortion, arrest, gang rape, and abuse in detention because of their ethnicity or presumed political views. The Taliban's Shari'a courts lack even a semblance of due process, with no provisions for legal counsel and frequent use of torture to extract confessions.[48]

Despite the Taliban's freeing of 46 prisoners in 2000, the International Red Cross estimates as many as 4,000 men are held prisoner.[49]

A RAWA activist described the Pol-e-Charkhi Prison in Kabul. The prison has 18 blocks, each block has 116 rooms, and each room has 40 to 50 prisoners. The more than 2,000 prisoners in the first block are mostly small shop owners and the poor working class people. Some have been prisoners for three years. Once a day, each prisoner gets a dried-up 180-gram loaf of bread. Every 24 hours every six prisoners get 450 mg of boiled rice. Although the Red Cross sends aid to the prisons, the prisoners do not receive all of it. Twice a day, from 8 to 10 in the morning and again from 4 to 6 in the afternoon, prisoners may use the restrooms. In between those hours, prisoners use a bucket given to them by the Red Cross for water to take care of their bodily functions. Torture, sodomy, and robbery are other atrocities that happen to the prisoners.[50]

The suffering of parents and their children is exemplified in Amnesty International's story of a 15-year-old girl who in March 1994 was repeatedly raped in her house in Kabul's Chel Sotton district after armed guards entered the house and killed her father, supposedly for allowing her to go to school. Girls have often been sold into prostitution when they were no longer wanted by the commanders. To avoid this fate, some women have committed suicide. Some family members have kept silent in fear for their own lives.[51] Some women have been killed by family members to prevent their suffering.

Children, whether or not they are kept with their families, do not

fare well. Alla Auddin Orphanage is the only refuge in Kabul, but sometimes children left there are not without at least one living parent. Robin
Wright gives this picture of the orphanage and one of its orphans, Uddin:

> ...Uddin shares a bed and filthy blanket with a larger boy in a small
> room with 38 other orphans. A putrid stench in the hallways comes from
> bathrooms without running water, because the vintage generator that
> powers lights and water pumps recently broke down. Medicine is too
> expensive, so waves of maladies sweep through the concrete-floor wards;
> one child recently died of measles. Meals consist of bread and tea for
> breakfast, rice for both lunch and dinner; dried milk once provided by
> a foreign charity is long gone. When asked what the kids do to play,
> Uddin replied with his own question, "What's a toy?"[52]

Children kept by their families are also unfortunate, says Wright. In
the heat of the day children as young as five spend their days throwing
dirt in rocky chasms along the rough road to Kabul. Children hope drivers will throw them a little money, but not many do. Other children try
to sell the travelers old Pepsi cans filled with water from the muddy Kabul
River. "In Kabul, nearly 30,000 kids are estimated to survive by brazenly
begging or scavenging through garbage and war ruins."

The Co-operation Centre for Afghanistan reported that there are
several prisons with hundreds of women. In Kandahar at Karez Bazaar
from 400 to 500 women are kept as prisoners. The prison in Welayat-e-
Kabul has about 60 women prisoners. Women prisoners receive two loaves
of bread a day and are not allowed access to their relatives.[53]

## Refugees

According to Amnesty International, over six million people fled
Afghanistan during the Soviet occupation. Many refugees returned after
the Soviets withdrew, but "there are still over two million Afghan refugees
in Iran and Pakistan, making Afghans the largest single refugee group in
the world."[54] The destruction of their country has left Afghans displaced
and dispossessed. Nor is it safe for them to return. But while they wait,
says Amnesty International, "the end of flight does not necessarily mean
the end of danger, and this has been the unfortunate reality for a number of Afghan refugees." They suffer abuses within the countries to which
they have fled, including poverty, discrimination and dislocation. In addition, many are murdered by armed Afghan border groups who exert control over the camps. It is a testament to the Afghans' strength that in spite

of the unrest, many make the decision each year to return either on their own or through repatriation programs such as those sponsored by the United Nations High Commissioner for Refugees (UNHCR). According to Amnesty International, in 1998, UNHCR assisted the return of about 107,000 refugees. In July and August 1999, UNHCR helped 2,564 families or 14,024 persons return from Baluchistan and the North-West Frontier Province of Pakistan. Deportations from Iran occurred at about 1,000 per week.[55]

London journalist Robert Fisk asks, "But why do you need a programme if all is well in Afghanistan?" He answers, "It's not, of course, as the U.N. well knows. If the Taliban have provided security, they have created a state without a government, a theocracy without a nation."[56] Fisk calls the refugee camp outside Marden a desolate "half society," "a land of eternal age" where "lines and hanging flesh mark the faces of the young." The refugees live in fear of theft, kidnapping, and overnight shooting. There remains anarchy in the camp.

The United States Committee for Refugees reported at the end of 1999 that Afghan refugees numbered more than 2.6 million, and in 2000, about 3.6 million. In 1999 the largest numbers were in Iran and Pakistan, 1.4 million and 1.2 million respectively. Smaller numbers are in India and Central Asian Republics of the former Soviet Union. The committee reports that the United States has admitted 81,072 refugees from 1986 to 1999. In 1998, the United States admitted 88 refugees, and in 1999, 364. Although the number of refugees has remained relatively constant for Iran and Pakistan, the number of Afghans who were counted the previous year as having fled may be offset by Afghans who repatriated. The committee's figures are estimates. Some factors that affect trying to assess the number of voluntary repatriates include forced repatriation, for example, from Iran, internal displacement within Afghanistan, and legal or policy definitions of refugee status. The 1998 report (for 1997) stated, "Women, probably more than half of the refugees, and non–Pashtun minorities are understandably more reluctant to return to Afghanistan under current circumstances, and should not be pressured to repatriate."[57]

According to a study in *JAMA*, women and children constitute three quarters of the refugee population.[58] Fisk shares insights of women and girls in the Marden camp: an 18-year-old mother with an eighth grade education can not complete her schooling because her future in-laws will not allow it; 15-year-old girl twins can not advance their education beyond grade six because the bus transports men and boys only; Rahmina, a 30-year-old woman with seven children who looks 50, believes life is better in the camp because she has two rooms instead of the one she had in

TABLE 4.4
ESTIMATED NUMBER REFUGEES IN THOUSANDS

| Country | Year | | | |
|---|---|---|---|---|
| | 1996 | 1997 | 1998 | 1999 |
| Iran | 1,400,000 | 1,400,000 | 1,400,000 | 1,400,000 |
| Pakistan | 1,200,000 | 1,200,000 | 1,200,000 | 1,200,000 |
| India | | | 16,000 | 14,500 |
| Central Asian Republics | | | 8,000 | 17,000 |
| *Internally Displaced* | | | | |
| Total | 1,200,000 | 1,000,000 to 1,500,000 | 540,000 to 1,000,000 | 500,000 to 750,000 |
| Tajiks | 18,860 | | | |
| *Voluntary Repatriation* | | | | |
| Iran | | 8,367 | 2,233 | 14,000 | 62,000 |
| Pakistan | | 120,770 | See note | 93,000 | 92,600 |
| India | | | | | |
| Central Asian Republics | | 30 | | | |
| Tajiks | | 1,435 | | | 63 |

*Source:* U.S. Committee for Refugees, "Worldwide Refugee Information: Country Report for Afghanistan," 2000. Available: http://www.refugees.org/world/countryindex/afghanistan.htm, Jun. 10, 2000.

*Note:* Not given since offset by new refugee arrivals.

Afghanistan. She has no education, and her husband will not permit her to go to school. Although the Taliban closed down the women's university in Peshawar, some school teachers continue to study and teach. Malika's husband takes care of their three children and his four from a previous marriage while she attends the Pakistani university in the morning and teaches in the afternoon.

Amnesty International reminds us that many who were forced to flee from their homes fled to another place within Afghanistan, such as one of the camps near Jalalabad and Herat, or to another remote area or another city. Approximately one million Afghans have been internally displaced since 1992. Although it is clearly against international standards to inflict harm on civilians, the Taliban justify the destruction as a military necessity.

Barry Bazarak says that in spite of the "human wreckage" the Taliban left behind in October 1999, Afghans who had only their houses burned or crops destroyed often apologized because their story was not bad enough. These Afghans are among the refugees who fled to a safer place within Afghanistan. Refugees who escaped to the Panjshir Valley in the Himalayan Mountains numbered 65,000. There is a continuity in the stories of the refugees, with accounts of people shot in their homes, fires everywhere, and beatings. Bazarak reports the reactions of a 45-year-old woman with six children: "The Taliban took my husband out of the house and cut him down. They were killing everyone who looked young, thinking they must be soldiers. I screamed then, and I cry now. We have nothing left. We returned once to see our house. The ceiling is now on the ground."[59]

Under the Taliban, some Afghan refugees believe they cannot return for practical reasons. Grim economic conditions make it necessary that girls be educated and women be allowed to work.[60]

## Danger and Death: Some Women's Stories

Preserving the words spoken by Afghan women that describe their experiences is important to a full understanding of the catastrophic events which the Afghan people continue to live through. Some women have chosen to be politically active for the cause of women even though danger and death linger close.

I submitted a set of written questions to the Revolutionary Association of the Women of Afghanistan to be answered by an activist of their choosing. The following is that interview.[61]

AU: I was told there would be several possibilities as to who would respond to my interview questions. Whom am I interviewing?

SHABANA: My name is Shabana.

AU: What is your position within RAWA?

SHABANA: I am a member of the cultural committee of RAWA.

AU: Tell me about you.

SHABANA: I am 28 years old. I got the membership of RAWA eight years back. The main reason that led me to this decision was my deep hatred of fundamentalism and therefore I found RAWA as the sole organization combatting the fundamentalists in Afghanistan.

AU: How many belong to RAWA? Are they all women or are they men and women?

SHABANA: RAWA has hundreds of members. According to our organization's rules, only women can get membership of RAWA, but we have got some male supporters as well.

AU: Does RAWA do most of its work inside Afghanistan or outside?

SHABANA: Our base is inside the country but we are also active in Pakistan.

AU: Is there a project or activity that RAWA considers its most important?

SHABANA: We are firmly of the opinion that knowledge is a great power that raises the awareness of women and the new generation of their rights and place in society and enables them to understand social and political problems of the country, therefore we focus our activities mainly in the field of education.

AU: Do you believe that the Taliban is losing power in governing Afghanistan?

SHABANA: Everyone knows that the survival of these mediaeval-minded hypocrites is associated with the generous support of the regional and world power and once this support ceases the Taliban would in time disappear.

AU: Do you believe that the Taliban will be overthrown by a democratic government? If so, when do you think that will happen?

SHABANA: Unfortunately the democratic groups in Afghanistan don't enjoy any support from any source and are being constantly attacked by the fundamentalists, therefore they are not in a position to be counted as an organized alternative.

AU: Are the conditions in the refugee camps in Pakistan getting worse, about the same or better?

SHABANA: We can say that the situation is getting worse in the camps.

AU: Of all the atrocities committed against Afghan women, which does RAWA find most objectionable?

SHABANA: The atrocities that are committed by Taliban and their Jihadi brothers are all inhuman and barbaric.

AU: What progress and successes has RAWA had in its efforts to help the Afghan women and restore democracy?

SHABANA: Since its inception, RAWA has struggled hard for democracy and women's rights and has had a lot of achievements in this regard: Our demonstrations and functions are getting crowds of large numbers of women from different provinces year by year. Among them are some women who actively attend our demonstrations without making their husbands aware of it.

We have been nominated and received several human rights awards, which are proof of our striving for human rights and democracy. Just a month ago the French National Advisory Commission granted an award of human rights to RAWA.

RAWA has now been recognized internationally as the only democratic Afghan organization combatting uncompromisingly the fundamentalists, and many world democratic organizations have established close ties and shown solidarity and cooperation with RAWA's struggle.

We have been invited by many feminists and democratic organizations around the world to attend their respective conferences, but due to our grave financial condition we could accept invitations only from those that paid the whole travel expenses.

The expanding number of letters received, e-mails and articles concerning the miserable condition of Afghan women from around the world indicate our progress in our activities.

Our site is being visited by hundreds of people daily who use it as a base reference that provides sufficient information about women, reports, photos, movie clips, etc., from fundamentalist-blighted Afghanistan. And it was nominated and received several prizes for its valuable contents.

It has been a unique event in the history of Afghanistan that women themselves sell their publications in market and RAWA did break this tradition and its members had the audacity to accept any risk and sell their publications.

AU: What do you want me to know about RAWA that I have not already asked you in the questions?

SHABANA: For knowing more about RAWA I have the useful following items for you:

RAWA is the sole women's organization in Afghanistan which has been fighting for peace, democracy and women's rights since 1977. RAWA is the *only* organization which highlights the crimes and human rights violations of the fundamentalist gangs to the world through its website, demonstrations, publications, press conferences, as well as by informing Amnesty International and other human rights organizations about the brutalities of the Afghan fundamentalist warlords.

It is still the only feminist organization which is fighting firmly against the fundamentalist Taliban and other fundamentalist gangs and exposing their anti-democracy and anti-women nature. RAWA was the first Afghan women's organization to launch many humanitarian projects in education, healthcare and income generation fields in and outside Afghanistan during the [Soviet-backed] puppet regime and after the fundamentalists' takeover.

It was the first Afghan organization to stage anti-fundamentalist demonstrations, and its rallies have been attacked by the fundamentalists of all brands and its activities are receiving death threats for their opposition against the Taliban and Jehadi (Rabbani-Masoud & Co.) RAWA is the only feminist organization whose founding leader went to Europe to air the voice of the deprived Afghan women and when she returned, she was assassinated along with her two aides at the hands of the fundamentalists and the KhAD (Khadamati Itlil-dat'i Daulate) henchmen in Pakistan.

It is the only women's organization which holds both the Taliban and the so-called Jehadi forces equally responsible for their treacherous anti-democracy, anti-women, anti-human right acts since the fall of the puppet regime in 28th April, 1992, and is one of the few Afghan organizations which marks 28 April (taboo for others) as the Black Day in the history of Afghanistan.

RAWA is the only organization which still runs home-based schools and literacy courses for women and young girls inside Afghanistan. It is the only organization that observes some days of the year including 10 December, International Human Rights Day, 27 December, the Afghan Soviet invasion, 8 March, International Women's Day and 28 April by organizing demonstrations and functions. RAWA is the only feminist organization which has clearly declared its adherence to secularism as the cardinal pillar of democracy.

It is worth mentioning that we have experienced imprisonment in Pakistan and have been persecuted and pressured by certain of its agencies not to make propaganda against the Jehadis and Taliban. Amnesty International is aware of it and has taken urgent actions in connection with the kidnapping and cruel investigation of one of our technical aides. Our telephones and post box are tapped and controlled.

In May 2000, Katha Pollitt of the *New York Times Magazine* interviewed two RAWA activists, Sajeda Hayat and Sehar Saba.[62] They use these pseudonyms in travel, because of the danger in which their work places them. Saba explains that RAWA has schools for girls and mobile health-care teams. All courses and all home-based classes are completely underground. They support income-generating projects for women, for example, carpet weaving. "In Afghanistan, that's revolutionary," says Saba. Both Hayat and

Saba are in their 20s, have been in demonstrations where they have been attacked twice and, as Hayat says, "...hit with sticks, arrested, put in prison. Our male supporters beat them back. We women fought, too. I was also beaten by the Pakistani police. We've been arrested for selling our magazine." Regarding the harm that could befall them, Hayat says,

> ...We make jokes, we pretend to make up our wills. Older, more experienced members say we should have all preparations. But we don't talk much about it. When you think about what's going on in Afghanistan, you stop caring so much about your own safety. And we have ways of staying cheerful. We read books by women who've been brave—Iranian, Vietnamese, even Joan of Arc. If I get depressed and lose hope, then what will other women and girls my age have to look to?

Saba concludes,

> If the Taliban caught me inside Afghanistan they would definitely torture and kill me, stone me as a quote-unquote prostitute. So the punishment has already been decreed. But I can do it. I'm ready for everything. Someday we will die but maybe it will be a prouder death than from some natural cause.

Unfortunately, some women have died as a result of their experiences with the Taliban-supported government, and cannot tell their stories. They still contributed mightily. This author's 99-year-old father, Warren V. Keller, often said, "Sometimes we do not live to see the benefit of our efforts." Such is the case of the many Afghan women who have been killed in the era of war and repression.

Other accounts found in newspapers, magazines and learned journals help provide the context to what is occurring today in Afghanistan and the impact on its women. The profiles in this section begin with Belquis Ahmadi, who told her story at the White House.

### BELQUIS AHMADI[63]

On December 6, 1999, an Afghan refugee now living in St. Louis, Belquis Ahmadi, told President Clinton of a woman who died "at the gates of a hospital" after medical services were suspended to Afghan women. "I felt that I had no hope at all. I hated to be a woman. I asked myself if the world cared about women in Afghanistan." Ahmadi, a law student in Afghanistan and founder of the Afghan Women's Network, came to the United States with her two sisters and a brother as part of a refugee resettlement program. She says that the treatment of women in her country has gotten worse and that she saw people crying. The *St. Louis Post-Dispatch* also reported Ahmadi's assertion that "The Taliban ordered that women had to cover themselves from head to toe and could only go outside accompanied by a close male relative or they would be beaten." One year earlier she had informed the United Nations Commission on Human Rights that "Afghan women have lost lives, family members, basic human rights, human dignity and the right to be respected."

## Humera Rahi

Humera Rahi, poet, teacher and mother, is a professor of Persian literature at Bamiyan University and a member of the Women's Committee of the main Hazara party, the Hizbe Wahadat. She has seen the fighting during Afghanistan's 20 years of war. Rahi began writing poetry 30 years ago and is published in literary journals in Iran, Pakistan and Afghanistan. Her poetry is an inspiration to soldiers. Since she writes in the tradition of Central Asian epics, her poems could take hours or days to recite. Thus, her poetry was learned by heart and passed down through time.

In 1997, Rahi helped found Bamiyan University, which is coeducational with 300 students and 16 teachers. She says, "So many women have fled Kabul because of the Taliban's attitude to women, and they wanted to continue their higher education so we started a university." And she did so not without great personal sacrifice, leaving in Mazar her husband, also a teacher. "I have not seen him since then," she says, "but it's a small sacrifice when the entire nation is suffering." It is also hard raising children alone. She says she will "continue writing poems about the war until there is peace and then I will write about our beautiful country."[64]

And no doubt the Hazaras will prevail, because from 1996 to 1998 they led an alliance of ethnic minorities against the Taliban. That heritage is reflected in the lines of a poem that *The Canberra Times* used as part of the headline of an article about Humera Rahi, "best known woman poet of the Hazaras."

> O victorious army of Hazarajat, may your foes' chests be the target of your rifle barrels. You are the winner, the victorious, god is with you. By midnight prayers and my cries at dawn, and the children saying "O lord, O lord!" and the tears and sighs of the oppressed are with you.[65]

## Sidiqa Sidiq

When the Taliban first arrived, Sidiqa Sidiq, an archaeology professor, courageously appealed to them to let women go to work and school. She also appealed to the Afghan women.

Based on the orders of the holy Koran, I am requesting all the concerned brothers and individuals to release us from this detention and these chains and let us continue our education and our jobs. Under the Islamic law that is the prime need for the development of our ruined homeland.... Oh sisters, we have to be determined and must not be like our grandfathers expecting assistance from our compatriots abroad and from foreign organisations and countries, because they are shouting only for political propaganda.[66]

## ZOHRA RASEKH

Penney Kome writes that Afghan refugee Zohra Rasekh, researcher for Physicians for Human Rights (PHR), "was one of the lucky ones." After Rasekh's first visit to Afghanistan since the Taliban-supported government's rule, she said, "I thought I was in hell."[67] In 1998, Rasekh interviewed about 200 women and the results were published in *JAMA*.[68] Rasekh told Kome of her visit to her country, "I had a 50 percent chance of getting arrested and killed." She had a visa, but the Taliban are not accountable for beatings or killings. Her compelling motivation: "I saw it as a public health issue. A driving force for me was knowing that women were not allowed to seek medical care." Rasekh says although women are forbidden to work, men have difficulty in finding work. People are forced to beg in the street and sell their belongings. "The whole city looks like a yard sale. In all the time I was there, no one smiled."

Kome writes that Rasekh traveled with U.N. humanitarian aid officers in a truck. The father of a family of four ran in front of the truck and dropped his three year old child. Rasekh yelled to the father, "What are you doing, are you trying to get your baby killed?" The father answered her, "Yes, kill him, it is better than living here."

Understandably, some Afghans under the Taliban-supported militia believe that living is a fate worse than death. And, yes, Rasekh was one of the lucky ones. She escaped with her life. Many women were not so "lucky," their lives were not spared. Their stories lend continuity to the accounts of suffering related by those who escaped with their lives.

## The Voices Silenced

Conquering injustices from within is part of Afghan women's legacy. Research demonstrates that individual women "did defy patriarchal traditions and revolted against social oppression."[69] Rabia Balkhi was a 10th century poet who refused to marry a man whom her brother chose for her. While imprisoned, she wrote a poem on the prison wall with her own blood. She condemned society for not permitting her to marry the man of her choice. She died in prison. Other women wrote folk songs depicting their desire for freedom. In the 1960s and 1970s minstrel women were permitted to sing in public expressing desire for freedom, as long as they performed for a special occasion and in the women's quarters. The Islamic resurgence that began just before the Soviet occupation restricted women's social activity.

## Khadija d/o M. Auob and Zhara Ahmad

It is difficult enough for women in the best of situations to cope with a brutal regime, but women in a far worse situation are totally without support. RAWA writes of an effect of forced marriages when the husband is "a drunk and adulterer." Unable to find assistance under the Taliban-supported government, the woman, Khadija d/o M. Auob, "burnt herself to death by spraying kerosene on her body." In a similar circumstance, a teenaged woman, Zhara Ahmad, forced into marriage, returned home only to be beaten by her father in an effort to force her return to her husband. She poured a gallon of gasoline on herself and set herself on fire.[70]

## Conclusions

Christine Aziz reminds us that Afghan women have born the brunt of a long war. In Kabul alone, 30,000 widows must provide for their families. Amnesty International reports that thousands of unarmed civilians have been killed by surprise attack on their homes, mostly in Kabul. Other women have been killed for a variety of reasons, such as resisting whatever the Mujahed groups wanted. Among the atrocities women have experienced are abduction, rape, being sold into prostitution, taken as wives and being stoned. Some have simply disappeared. Women face an uncertain fate merely by stepping into the street. The Mujahideen are gone, the Taliban are present, and the women remain alone, exhausted, poor, and homeless. According to Aziz, the "quiet defiance of women in the face of tyranny" gives Afghanistan hope. That the women continue to study, often secretly and in makeshift schools, is but one example of their defiance.

# Profiles of Afghan Women

*... [The] perspective on the Afghan conflict that has remained hidden to the West— the perspective of the Afghan women and men whose voices have been silenced ... should be heard.*

Sima Wali[1]

### The Voices Heard

Interviews with Afghan refugee women reveal vividly how they are affected. The women's stories bear a common thread of death, violence, threats of violence, denial of education, denial of work, and the breaking up of families, but also demonstrate their ongoing, unmitigated and unique courage. These women have lived through two bloody regimes, the Soviet occupation and now, that of the Taliban.

The interviews in this chapter were conducted by and translated by the Revolutionary Association of the Women of Afghanistan (RAWA). RAWA provided for this book 30 interviews with Afghan women who either recently had fled, or who had fled after the Soviet occupation.[2] The interviews were received during March, May and July 2000. The interviewees were asked five broad, open-ended questions:

1. What experiences have you had since the Taliban took power?
2. How is your life changed as a result of the Taliban?
3. What was your life like before the Taliban came to power?
4. Do you think your life would be better or worse if the Taliban were no longer in power? Explain.
5. What else would you like to say about your experiences in Afghanistan?

The numbered responses in the interviews correspond to the above numbered questions.

## SALEEMA

1. When the Taliban came, they beat up my husband very seriously and said that he had weapons, but my husband was a farmer and did not have weapons. For some days they detained him and during the investigation they beat him. By paying a small amount as a bribe, we got him released from prison.

2. The change which came to my life was that that the Taliban set to fire our home and the wheat we had in our home. They forced us to go to Pakistan with lots of difficulties, and I was injured during the rocketing of the Taliban.

3. Before the Taliban, our life was harsh and bad. During the past 20 years our life went from bad to worse with the passing of every day, and we had a dog's life.

4. Our life will become stable and good under a government which the people will select and where there is no oppression and brutality.

## ASTHMA

1. The Taliban's first work after capturing power was the closure of girls' schools, and then they started their oppression against women and men.

2. The men cannot trim and shave their beard. Above all, the women have not the right to education and to work in offices. If they go somewhere, they have to cover their body from head to toe with a veil, so that nobody can see them. If the Taliban sees a woman without veil, they beat her very seriously.

   During the Taliban, our life became harsh and unbearable because we could not go to our work. The Taliban closed the only source of our income, i.e., schools and offices. After that, our economic condition became so much worse that we could not buy even a scrap of bread. Then we decided to leave the country and took refuge in Pakistan.

3. Before the Taliban our life also wasn't good. The Jehadis were more brutal than the Taliban. During the Jehadis, every day we were in fear of hunger, rape and other uncountable problems. Many young girls committed suicide just to save their chastity from the filthy hands of the Jehadis. Hundreds of families sold their children very cheaply because they hadn't anything to feed them.

4. Under whatever organization or government that is in favor of democracy, education and rights of women, our life will become better. If they

are against these wishes our life will become worse than the Taliban regime.

## SHAMSIA

1. The Taliban don't allow the women to go outside home. They closed girls' schools and forced the women to wear a veil. They don't allow women to work and even in the beginning, they deprived women of going to the doctor.
2. With the coming of the Taliban, we were forced to stay at home and nothing changed for the better.
3. The Jehadis and the Taliban are chips off the same block. Our life under the Jehadis was also miserable. They both are the arch-enemy of the Afghan people.
4. I don't know that what will happen after the Taliban, and what sort of government will come to the power. If those who are in favor of democracy and women's rights come to power, our lives will become better. But if the Jehadi parties once again take power that would be another catastrophe.
5. The Jehadis were not better than the Taliban. They raped and looted our people. During the Khaliqi-Parchami regime our villages were under heavy bombardments. Finally, after the killing of a number of our villagers and relatives, we were forced to come to Pakistan.

## PALWASHA

1. As the Taliban come to power, they curbed freedom of the women and men. During the Khalq-Parcham regime my brother was in Iran. When he came back, the Taliban detained him and beat him pretending that he had weapon. When we gained his freedom by paying a lot of money as a bribe, we fled from the country leaving behind our property and home.
2. The change that came to my life was that I again became a refugee in one of the refugee camps in Pakistan, running my life with uncountable difficulties.
3. In general, since the Khalq-Parcham era, all my life has been in wandering and hopelessness. If that situation continues, we will never enjoy happiness and prosperity.
4. If a good government based on democratic value and respectful of women's rights comes to the power, and prepares the way for our

children's education and well-being and opens the door of work for women, our life will change for the better. If it is like the previous regimes, there will be no change in our life. And we will die in hope of that day.

5. All in my life, I have had shocking and heartbreaking experiences. I was 14 when I emigrated to Iran. During the reign of Khalq and Parcham, I got married to one of my brother's friends. I had three children when my husband was killed in an ambush by the Russians as he was on his way from Iran to Afghanistan. I, along with my three children, was living in one of the Afghan refugee camps in Iran with my brother, but the difficulties forced us to go to Afghanistan.

## NOORIA

1. Destitution, oppression, crime, poverty and the closure of school and putting the women behind the walls of home are things that I have got from the Taliban.

2. Emigration from my home-province to Kabul city and from here to refugee camps in Pakistan is the result of the Taliban takeover. All we know is hunger and wandering from here to there in search of food and shelter in the refugee camps in Pakistan.

3. The Taliban and the Jehadis are both from the same origin. There is no fundamental difference between them.

4. If a government that sincerely works for the people comes to power, our lives will change for the better.

5. Forty days passed from my birth to when my father passed on. Now I am 18 years old and live with hunger and poverty in one of the refugee camps.

## FLORAN

1. The experience I have got since the Taliban came, is that that whatever government is based on religion and fundamentalism is the most dangerous one in the world. In the guise of religion, what atrocities are in the world that the Taliban do not commit against our people? I have come to the conclusion that politics should be separated from religion. In our country, the fundamentalists committed uncountable crimes in the name of religion and their first and easy victims are women. I saw hundreds of times how the Taliban whip the women in the streets. Once I went shopping with my sister. The weather was

warm and I couldn't take a breath under my veil. I said to my sister that I wanted to raise my veil for a minute. She had forbidden me to do that. So when we reached an alley, we both raised our veils assuming that the Taliban were not there. A few minutes later we heard a terrible voice that echoed to our ear that "aren't you ashamed showing your faces to strangers?" We both stopped and begin to shiver. In that moment, we thought about those women who are beaten by the Taliban. The Talib who shouted at us wasn't the member of the infamous ministry of "do what are prescribed and don't what are forbidden." Whenever I remember his abuses, I think that we are the most unlucky and ill-fated women of the world. If in some countries the women have been struggling for their rights, we in Afghanistan don't even have the right about what we have to wear on our own body. Our clothing is according to the Taliban.

2. The change which came to my personal life since the Taliban, is that, as I am student, I cannot go to school. We women don't have permission to go to the market. If we do, we must wear a veil. We are always in fear. If the Taliban see us in the street without hejab, they beat us very seriously. It is the whip of the Taliban which mostly makes me prefer to stay at home rather than to go outside and face their cruelty.

3. The television station was closed and the radio programs are full of religious propaganda. There is no music program and the news is a pack of lies. Nobody can hang pictures on the walls of their home or in their shops. Photography is forbidden according to their self-interpretation of the shari'a.

   All the women workers and officials have been prevented from working. We are paid a salary after three or four months which is insufficient. With that salary, we cannot even run our life for a week. Although the security is better than the past, unfortunately nowadays the Taliban themselves intentionally create security problems by robbery and thievery. The Taliban failed to uproot the poverty which is deepening every day.

4. In the past, although there was no security, schools and colleges were open for girls and boys.

   From one side the Jehadi groups fought with each other which resulted to the destruction of Kabul city and from the other side, these groups raped women and young girls. A lot of families didn't allow their girls to go outside. In short, the atrocities of the Jehadis know no boundary.

5. About the Jehadis, I expressed my view in the above passage, but about the Khalq and Parcham I don't have any idea in my mind now because

during that time I was a little child. But people say they are the real cause of the current situation. I myself know that they forced our people to emigrate to neighboring countries.

### Marzia

1. When the Taliban emerged in our land, they behaved with us very inhumanely. They beat my husband and brother and told them to hand over their weapons or face lashing and punishment. As they didn't have any weapon and were against Khalq and Parcham and the Jehadis and the Taliban alike, they were forced to flee to Pakistan. Then the Taliban come to our home and compelled us to give them money equivalent to two weapons.

2. We are far from our homeland. Our life is not good. The destiny of our children is not clear. They are not educated and cannot go to school. Our children are working in a carpet-weaving factory. With their insufficient salary we are running our life. I have got six children. My husband works in a brick kiln. But money is the real problem.

3. Before the Taliban, we were in our home-province. We had a small land. But now we are refugees and are wandering in a strange land.

4. I think our life will become worse and the problem will deepen, because every group is just working for its own sake. They are not working for the country's prosperity and bright future.

5. In the past, the Jehadis and the Khalqi and Parchami oppressed our people and uncountable young girls have been raped by the Jehadi forces. The puppet regime of Russia destroyed our villages, detained our people and tortured intellectuals. At the end, I strongly appeal to the U.N. and other democracy-loving personalities and forces to help the people of Afghanistan to put an end to that unfortunate situation.

### Shakeba

1. The Afghan people dreamt of a future full of prosperity and happiness. They awaited that, after the withdrawal of the Russians, the situation would get better. But unfortunately, everything's turned upside down. When the Taliban captured power, they did every inhumane thing in the name of Islam and shari'a. Their interpretation of Islam is contrary to the order of the day. They didn't even get a lesson from the past 20 years. The puppet regimes of the Russian commit innumerable crimes and then began the turn of the Jehadis, and now the Taliban

white-washed their faces with the passing of every day. Women cannot go to work and are forced to wear a veil.

2. I myself am in Pakistan. Whatever the Taliban put into practice in Afghanistan in the name of shari'a I am fully aware of. In the given situation, I don't hope to go to Afghanistan. Under the Islam which the Taliban forcibly imposed on our people, the women cannot work or have the right of education and studying. In short, this situation really vexes us.

3. I have never seen better days in the past two decades. All the previous regimes oppressed our people and the Jehadis too misused Islam and shari'a. They killed our people in the name of Jehad and Islam. Our economic situation is very bad. We have been living hand to mouth all our life. If our children get sick, we don't have money to go to the doctor and buy medicine. We cannot work because the Taliban don't allow us to work. We cannot solve our day-to-day problems. Our economy goes to the dogs.

4. If our people have got the proper lesson from the past 20 years, I think they will, shoulder-to-shoulder, select their real and just representatives and establish a just and democratic government. We hope that in the near future our land will be liberated and in a free and independent future Afghanistan, the real responsible parties of the current situation will be punished accordingly. Anyway, tomorrow never dies.

5. Since the 27th April coup, I have so many bad and disturbing experiences that it would take sheets of paper to be written down. But in short, every force and government which has come to the power 'til now, did the same thing , i.e., brutality, torture, killing, rape and destruction.

## FREBA

1. I, with my one son and a daughter, was living in Kabul before the coming of the Jehadis. I lost my husband during the reign of the puppet regime of the Russians. I was working in one of the schools as a handmaid to make ends meet. I, with the salary got, just could save myself and my children from dying. Though I had never better days, life was good then compared to now under the Taliban. The Jehadis didn't pay us on time so I was obliged to go to my brothers and other relatives to borrow money. The moment the Taliban entered Kabul city, they announced that women cannot work. The school where I was teaching was for girls and so it was closed down. The teachers, students and all the maids were sacked from their jobs. My life went from bad to

worse. My son wasn't of age, and couldn't find any job. My economic condition was bad, so I had my 16-year-old daughter married in hope that her husband will help us and could find a "legitimate" relative. But prosperity and happiness left us forever. My bridegroom was poorer than we. He could earn only enough money to feed his own family.

2. Before the Taliban I was also a refugee, now and then I moved from one place to the other. I was in fear that someday or the other, the Jehadis would rape me or my teenage daughter. I was in fear of my children's death because of hunger and cold winters. Every day the martyrdoms of my relatives shocked me. So I was forced to emigrate to Pakistan. Now I live in one of the refugee camps in Pakistan while facing lots of economic problems. There is nobody who can save the Afghan people.

3. If a government which works according to the people's wishes comes to power, our lives will change for the better. But I never have the least hope for my future. I've suffered so much that all my hope has died.

4. During the Khalq and Parcham regime, I lost my husband and 'til now I am in deplorable condition.

5. First the henchmen of the puppet regime didn't tell me that they had killed my husband. I searched for my husband from one prison to the other. I had faced ill treatment and bad handling and got no answer. Finally, I have learned that my husband has been killed. I was the only bread-winner and protector of my two little children.

## HAMIDA

1. The Taliban gave people painful experiences since their eruption. Their first move was against women. They shut down the door of girls' schools and banned women from any public appearance, ordered men to sport beards and women to be clad in burqa and if find anyone deviating from these restrictions, they would give her severe punishment. I myself was the witness of an incident when a teenager Talib was lashing an old man because his beard didn't touch the limit the Taliban had prescribed. Seeing that really shocked me and aroused my aversion to the Taliban. When you visit the Taliban offices in Kabul and other cities, they have hung large banners written on white cloths and almost all of them are anti-women slogans. It would be interesting to see if most of these anti-women slogans are based on sayings of Prophet Mohammad. A banner I remember was from a saying of the Prophet, that "I have finished all the enemies of the mankind and there

are no harmful people but women who are the worst enemies for Muslim people, be careful about them." The Taliban never quote some noble sayings of Prophet in favor of women like "education is necessary for both men and women."

2. With the coming of the Taliban the lives of most people have been changed completely though the previous rulers have left nothing to them. The 20 years of war brought our unfortunate country to the brink of elimination but the Taliban dragged our country more and more in the vortex of economical, political and cultural collaboration. Beggary and prostitution have prevailed in each corner of our country and poverty has reached to the maximum.

   As it was done in other places, I was sacked from my job. I had to feed my family, the little amount that my sons earned from the workshop was too small and therefore I decided to do something at home with my two daughters who are both under 15. I borrowed money from my brother-in-law and bought a carpet weaving means. We work from dawn to sunset and can finish a carpet in a month. From each carpet we can earn about 8 lacks Afghani which is equivalent to 1,000 rupees, but now I can't do work any more because I have a back problem and can't sit for too long. I really see my future as bleak because my children are all illiterate.

3. I was a teacher in a primary school, my husband was killed in the war with the Russians and my salary could hardly feed my five children. My two sons who were six and nine years old at that time were working together in a workshop and earned just enough to buy their schoolbooks and stationery. We lived in a house that had a small garden at its back and could supply us some fruits in the summer. Our life under the Taliban is really disgusting. Sometimes I come to the conclusion that there is no way but to commit suicide, but then I feel what will happen to my children and then I scold myself.

4. Naturally, if the elements that have committed thousands of atrocities and introduced the most backward laws were overthrown and not replaced by a successor worse than them, life would be much better. The Taliban since their emergence has brought up our misery-stricken country to the brink of total economic bankruptcy.

5. The only experience that I have got since the giving of the destination of our people into the hands of the fundamentalists is that fundamentalists of all shades and color will never bring welfare and justice to the people because they are anti-people and anti-democracy in nature and therefore if I was given a chance to comment on the issue of

Afghanistan I would have said that democracy and welfare would come only if these fundamentalists are swept away.

## ZAKIRA

1. The three years of Jehadis domination crushed our people both physically and mentally and when they were overthrown by their rival brothers, our mournful people were in the hope that the Taliban will end up their miseries but the Taliban proved them to be worse than the Jehadis. The Taliban claim that they have established peace and stability but what is happening in our country show the opposite. Apart from continuous fighting, the Taliban have imposed restrictions on our people and particularly women. They have kept women locked in the closed walls of their houses and stopped girls from going to school. I haven't seen such miserable life in my lifetime. I know many women who are suffering from depression, a girl in our neighborhood yells a few times a day and asks her parents to hide her because the Taliban are coming to rape her.

2. The Islamic Emirate of Taliban gave people a lot of miseries. Closing girls' schools and banning women from work brought thousands of women into the home. My three daughters were in school in Pakistan. When the Jehadis snatched the power from the puppet regime, we went back to our homeland with the hope that they would get education there in their own country, and we thought that this will be an end to our long and sad story and the hardships of living in very bad conditions in Pakistan. I admitted them in a school but the studies over there were totally rubbish and the Taliban then struck the last blows to their education.

3. We had a relatively good life. My husband was a shopkeeper and my elder son worked in a mechanic shop.

4. What I have experienced in the last three years under the domination of the Taliban, I can say it certainly that life would be much better no matter who would take their place and I don't think there would exist an element more brutal, backward and anti-women than the Taliban.

5. The 20 years of war and especially the last eight years of Jehadis and Taliban rule gave me a lot of experiences and I reached to some solid conclusions that unless there is foreign meddling in internal affairs and unless there is fundamentalist peace, freedom, democracy and social justice would remain at the level of dreams and imaginations.

PARVIN

1. I have a lot of experiences of the tyrannic rule of the Taliban. The Taliban are against our people and especially the helpless women. They are not Muslim. What they are doing with our poor people is totally against the Islamic law. Where else and who else has seen the way people are beaten in the street for not obeying the ridiculous restrictions the Taliban have imposed? Where else are women given punishment because their shoes make noise while walking? The Taliban are committing thousands of atrocities in the name of Islam. They have shut the doors of girls' schools and at the same time don't allow women to be treated by male doctors. It has stuck in my mind and I still remember the whole story of a girl who was beaten by a Talib near our house. Brutal!

2. My husband had a cosmetic shop at the Shahri Now market in Herat city. The backward Taliban, without giving any warning, smashed all the items because, according to them, cosmetics are un–Islamic. My husband requested from the Taliban to give him a few days so that he could take his properties to Iran but the Taliban didn't listen and crushed everything to pieces. This was our only source of income but after that blow our condition started shrinking. My husband is handicapped and the only work he could do with was as a shopkeeper. We had neither saved money nor any property to start another business. My two sons who are 14 and 16 left school and began to work in a workshop which give them each 250,000 Afghanis (U.S. $7), and with that salary we can only buy the flour we need, therefore we had no other option but to leave our house and rent it out and move to the village where we had an old house. It took three months to make some repairs to that old house with the help of my two sons and their two other cousins. I had a sewing machine and began to do some business with it at home, which can bring me around 300,000 Afghan ($8) per month. My husband is now searching for a light job in the village but no one is ready to give him a job.

3. We had a very comfortable life before the emergence of the Taliban. My two sons were attending their school regularly. My husband had a cosmetic shop which could provide us with a handsome income.

4. Life would certainly be better if these enemies of our people are kicked out. These elements have brought nothing to our people but misery, destruction, homelessness, increasing poverty, prevailing prostitution and beggary and collapsing the economy of our war-torn country. I do believe, and this is because of my experiences of seven years of

domination by the Jehadis and Taliban, that these creatures would not get in power if they are being openly controlled and backed by the foreign countries, and it is quite right that a foreign country see only its own interest and has no concern for what is coming out of its interference. United States of America and Saudi Arabia through Pakistan from the east, Iran from the west and Russia through central Asian countries from the north squeezed our countries in their claws and each of them snatched a part of it for their benefit. The 20 years of war was nothing but just a war between these aggressive neighboring countries. Through history, it has been proved and this was confirmed that why our country has remained undeveloped and backward lies in this fact, that through the ages these aggressive countries have destroyed our homeland and drained our resources and I must say that we are very proud of ourselves that we always stood firm against these invaders.

5. I got that experience from the tyrannical rule of the Taliban and Jihadis that one should not trust what the rulers says. Taliban and Jihadi have always misused Islam for their personal whims and political interests. They killed thousands of people and made thousands of others homeless in the name of Islam. All of them had Koran in one hand and gun in other. I realized that the real Muslims are those who don't just induce people to pray or obey the Islamic law but they themselves act in accordance to the tradition of Islam.

## GULALAI

1. Before the entrance of the Taliban into Herat city, I had heard about them that they were very pious and good people and they carry the banner of Islam and would sweep away all the Jehadi gangs who had committed lots of crimes. When they entered in Herat I prayed to Allah and thanked him for His blessing that finally peace had come and our sorrow has flown away, but this joy was very short lived. The Taliban, at the very first day, took off their mask and showed their real selves. They proved themselves to be worse than the brutal Jehadis, especially their attitude toward women is very cruel. I realized that when we had a wedding ceremony in our village. According to our traditions, we had brought a music band to the occasion, the ceremony was still going on when a group of Taliban came in and disturbed the ceremony. Like wild animals they rushed to the band and kicked the musical instruments, among these instruments was an expensive electronic keyboard, which was crushed to pieces as an angry Talib hit it

with the gun. The owner was weeping and crying for his keyboard. The wedding ceremony turned to grieving ceremony and ended in the middle. Seeing that ominous act, we all at the ceremony got angry. After that I changed my mind and realized that the Taliban are not the ones who carry the banner of the Islam but are the most corrupted and the most backward minded elements. The Islamic regime of Iran which is famed for being the most fanatic Islamic regime in the world, is much more progressive than these medieval-minded people. In the three years of their domination in Herat, they exposed themselves as the agent of misery, poverty, homelessness and thousands of other sufferings.

2. One of the "reforms" that the Islamic government of Taliban has introduced was banning music and watching television, this resulted in the collapse of the electronic workshop of my husband. My husband stayed in the middle, he didn't know what to do. He had invested a big amount on this shop, now he couldn't sell the devices and he could not open another shop. After three months waiting, thanks to Allah, he was employed as a guardsman in the custom which give him 600,000 Afghanis ($12) per month, but this amount could not meet our basic necessities therefore my husband decided to send my elder son who was about to finish his secondary school to Iran to work there. Crossing Iran's border was very difficult, it needed a permission slip (Nama) from the Iranian government. It was a lengthy process as well as expensive and to some extents impossible. My husband met many people and one of our relatives made a fabricated Nama. Thank God that my son reached Iran without any major difficulty. It has been exactly two years that I haven't seen my son, during that time he has sent once 500,000 Tomans ($60) and 400,000 Tomans ($50) eight months later. But I am always afraid if the Iranian regime capture my son they will send him to a special prison designed for Afghan refugees in Zahedan called "Tal-e-Sea" where they treat the prisoners worse than what the Taliban do with people.

3. Our life was much better than what we have now. My husband had a large electronic workshop. The money we earned was more than enough to meet all our needs plus some extra money, which my husband gave to his widow sister. My three sons and my younger daughter were going regularly to school.

4. I think not only our lives but also the lives of all people would be much better. If you ask any person, he would have certainly some problem with restrictions and some laws that the Taliban have imposed on many

things. The Taliban has closed the girls' schools, which had two bad effects, it deprived thousands of girls of education and cost the jobs of hundreds of women teachers. The Taliban have cost the jobs of thousands of women. The Taliban banned music, television and many other entertainments. The Taliban don't allow people to hold Nowruz (Persian New Year) which is a special tradition of our people rooted deep in the history. What I do believe is that if a force came and opposed these restrictions, life naturally will be better, but if the Taliban are replaced by the element similar to them then the wounds of people will never be healed.

5. Russian invasion and then the civil war between the Jehadi rival and now the tyranny rule of the Taliban destroyed our country and made the life of our people miserable. Though thousands of our innocent people have been killed in the resistance war against the Russians, but it was a war against a foreign aggressor and our people unanimously participated and devoted their whole property. But the seven years of civil war really crushed our people mentally and physically. With my little knowledge of Afghanistan history, I can say that Afghanistan has not seen in its 5,000 years, cruel, uncivilized and anti-women elements like Jehadis and Taliban. Abdur Rahman Khan and Allauddin Ghuri were famous for their cruelty, but the Taliban in many ways have whitewashed them. Some of our people now say the communist regime was better than these dirty criminals. Dr. Najibullah was called "cow" by people, but when the seven so-called fundamentalist leaders, Hekmatyar, Rabbani, Massoud, Sayyaf, Khalili, Mazari, Mojadadi, took power and committed many crimes now there is a joke among our people which goes like "Oh God, please smash these donkeys and return our cow!" This shows the depth of hatred our people have against them.

## Nooren

1. After the coming of the Taliban and fleeing of Jehadis, Kabul's picture has been completely changed. The presence of men with beards and women with burqa is a scene that attracts the attention of everyone. Some people say that the shine our city had before has disappeared and the city looks like a cartoon, men with long beards and a cap in head and women in burqas. Poverty has struck so much that by a glancing through the faces of people one can easily predict their miserable conditions.

   Every day, thousands of men, women and children make rows in front of bakeries waiting for long hours and get breads by the cards that have been distributed to them by the U.N.'s committees. Economic problems are great blows which have struck our devastated people, and for the survival of their children, they have gone to Iran and Pakistan. The majority of the residents of Kabul have sold their property so that they could buy at least a sack of flour. Prices are so much high that most of the people spend their day with only bread. Most of the people say that they have survived the Jehadis's rocket shelling but these bad economic conditions are another way of making our people miserable.

2. I am a student of the 11th class. I was very fond of my studies and my only hope was to become a doctor. Though there was not any proper school neither in Dr. Najibullah era nor during the Jehadi domination, but uncivilized Taliban even took this from our people and in this way doomed our hopes.

3. When I was born my country was burning in the flame of wars but I remember that those time people had a relatively better life. We had a comfortable life, my mother was a teacher and my father was a government officer. I could go to school without feeling any fear and worry.

4. In my opinion if a government is established by an election and grant people democracy and freedom then the lives of most people will get better, but this government must be saved from any foreign meddling and clean from the reactionary and anti-democracy elements. I think women also must have the rights to vote for the future government of Afghanistan.

5. The 20 years have given me a bitter experience that if people are given their own right to decide their fate and no external power meddle in it, certainly peace, security and democracy will come in our country.

## Zohra Samad

1. Khalq and Parcham, the puppets of Russia, have destroyed our country and killed thousands of our innocent people but the religious militia, the Taliban, tortured our people in another way. The Taliban in their very first days disclosed their hostility with women, science and culture. They deprived women of their basic rights. Thousands of women are being lashed savagely in the streets because they don't have a burqa or wear white socks.

   They have allowed only doctors to do a job but in my opinion it is not enough, the next generation would be scarce of doctors if they don't get education. The Taliban must keep the schools open for both sexes otherwise there would be no doctor. I also see it as really ridiculous that the Taliban have banned women to be treated by a male doctor.

Most of the patients that I have treated had different psychological problems because they were mostly widows and it is quite natural. There are many instances that these widows have sold their darlings or left them in the streets because they had nothing to feed them.

Most of the intellectuals living in Afghanistan have a tough life. Intellectuals are very sensitive to the political events and this resulted in their departure from Afghanistan.

2. I am doctor. I have four children. My husband is also doctor. Though no peace and stability was there when Jehadis had the power, the people had a relatively good life than that they have now. There was not any prevention when I was going to my job and the conditions were fine for both my husband and me. When the Taliban came they introduced a lot of restriction on female doctors in hospitals. Once I was in my office treating a patient, when a wild teenager Talib came in and with cursing ordered me to wear burqa. It was really hard for me to bear that rudeness but I convinced myself that the Taliban are not the people who should know how to deal with people. I have decided to help my people any time and in any condition but the conditions over here compelled me to leave the country.

3. Our life was in a relative good condition but it was not as good as it is expected. The Jihadi gangs were not far behind in crimes and atrocities compared to the Taliban. In their four years rule the Taliban have left nothing for our misery-stricken people who have been already crushed and tortured by the Russians and their puppets, the Khalq and Parcham. The different Jehadi parties in Kabul put our innocent mass in their claws and each of them tortured them in different ways. These religious murderers sow the seed of differences between different communities. Pushtun fell in hostility with Hazara and Uzbek with Tajik. The first targets of the Jihadis were women. Apart from depriving women of major jobs and giving no attention to women's education, they have committed lots of crime. They have kidnapped girls and forced them into marriage. Raping was happening every day in Kabul and prostitution has been prevalent over most part of the country. When the Taliban snatched the power from their rival brother, our country was in complete destruction, but the religious militia even didn't have any mercy on the war-stricken country.

4. Naturally, life will be better if these religious militia whose crimes and atrocities have no example neither in the 5,000 years old history of

Afghanistan nor in any other history. But one thing is more obvious, that the roots of all miseries lie in the foreign intervention and therefore I do believe that attention should be paid to this part otherwise talking about the Taliban would be useless. When the Jihadis were in power, everyone was of that opinion that peace and justice would come if the Jihadis were removed from power, but the opposite happened and the reason is clear, the instruments of the machine were changed but its engine remained untouched. And it is also noteworthy to say the world communities, and especially the U.S., are really just spectators.

5. Of what I have read in history during my school time and what I have experienced in 46 years of my life, one thing has been confirmed to be right, that if there is foreign handling of our affairs, our people will never see a progressing Afghanistan. And I must say that our people throughout history have proved their opposition to the foreigner and never have accepted any kind of slavery. I have a piece of advice for U.S., Pakistan, Iran and Saudi Arabia that before taking any decision on Afghanistan, spend a few minutes and flick through the pages of Afghanistan's history, I am sure they would find some useful materials. The 20 years of wars have struck our innocent nation severe blows that they are incapable to speak out against the external and internal aggressors, but a time will come when our people will stand on their feet and sweep out the enemies of Afghanistan.

## SAFIA

1. I have a very bitter experience when the Taliban grasp the control of Istalif. They entered like wild animals, arrested hundreds of people because they suspected that these people might have some kind of linkage with the Massoud's forces. They have burnt our cultivated lands and destroyed our houses.

2. The Taliban changed our whole life. My husband was killed in the recent fighting between Massoud's forces and the Taliban in Shomali. Last year, the fighting struck the first blow to our life when a rocket hit directly in the middle of the garden and burned almost all the trees. It was really hard for my husband to repair his beloved garden. He was working steadily in the garden in his leisure time and completed nearly half the garden. The recent fighting struck the most backbreaking blow, this time it was not the garden but its gardener that became the victim of the fighting. My husband was in his shop when suddenly the

shelling of rockets started, he did hurry to get his shop closed but he was too late. A rocket blew up just in front of the shop and killed him on the spot.

Staying any longer in Istalif was naturally unbearable for us as we and other people were being threatened and insulted constantly by the Taliban, and therefore I found no other option but to leave there. We and five other families covered the whole distance by foot from Istalif to Kabul, and I had my six-month-old baby in my arms throughout the journey. In Kabul, I wondered about where to spend the night. My brother-in-law had a house in Kabul but they had already migrated to Peshawar. We stayed two weeks in Kabul and during that time I arranged for two buckets of water for my two sons and the younger daughter to sell water at a bus stop and I myself began begging in front of a mosque. Our life in Kabul was getting worse every day as we had no place to stay for the night over there. We spent the night under a bridge and I was feeling constant fear from the Taliban that one day they might do something wrong with my 15-years-old daughter. I decided to go somewhere that no Talib should be over there and I found Peshawar the most suitable. Thank God and thanks to the driver that took us here.

When we reached Peshawar, I wondered what to do? Where to go? We spent three nights in a bus station and then a driver told us that most probably we could find a house in Nasir Bagh camp. I found a tent in Nasir Bagh camp which I had to pay 200 rupees per month. This is relatively a safe place to live. My elder daughter stays there and I with my other children come to the city early in morning. I followed the same work as I did in Kabul. My children are selling water at a bus stop in Board and I myself am begging. Sometime when I am recalling the past and remember my husband and our life in Istalif I am shocked. I am very anxious about the future of my children. Believe me that when I am looking at them holding two glasses of water and shouting for one rupee, tears roll down my cheek. My elder daughter, like a prisoner, is stuck in the tent throughout the day.

3. We had a good life in Istalif. My husband was a teacher in a primary school in Istalif and my three children had their classes regularly in that school. Attached to our house was a small garden in which my husband had planted different species of trees. Apart from providing us with fruits and fresh vegetables, it could also bring us some money.

4. If the Taliban are replaced by forces which bring peace and stability and do something to improve the economic conditions of our people,

naturally the life would get better, but if they are replaced by elements that nourish by a foreign country then no change will come. When Jihadis was in power everyone was of the belief that if the Jihadics are eliminated then people will be freed from every misery but what the Taliban show to the people, it has proved that they are worse than Jihadis.

5. I have got that experience from 20 years of war that if a party or group is backed and supported by a foreign country then that party will not have any care for the people and what I see as the causes of the present condition all lie in the foreign interference.

## Torpekai

1. The emergence of Taliban in Kandahar and their spreading over most parts of the country was a great danger to Hazara people as on their first day they exposed their hatred to Hazara. When they dominated over Kabul and made their way to Kabul, hundreds of our people left Bamiyan for Pakistan. They captured Bamiyan after long fighting with Hizibi Wahdat and within that period the land and house that we had repaired after coming back from Pakistan once again were laid into ruin. Their brutal and cruel attitude toward our innocent people resembled the attitude of Abur Rahmam Khan in the 19th century.

2. The presence of Taliban in Bamiyan was unendurable as we were in constant fear and danger. They treated us like animals and were taking money from people by force, therefore we along with 10 other families came here to Quetta (Pakistan). In Quetta, the house rent is too high. Now we are living with three other families in a house and pay 5,000 rupees for the rent. It is too much for us. My husband has a small fruit shop and can earn hardly 3,000 rupees per month. My two young sons are going to school but my two elder sons are 15 and 17 years and are working with their father.

3. We had a relatively good life in Bamiyan. In 1993 we returned to our homeland and we almost repaired our damaged house and lands. Our cultivated lands had been repaired and made ready for cultivation. My husband and my brothers-in-law also had made a new garden in which they had planted 500 different species of trees and also a big grape yard.

4. The factor of all the tragic conditions was the Taliban and I think life would go back to its previous track if the Taliban are put aside.

5. I also have many bitter experiences from the Hizb-e-Wahdat. They were the agent of Iran's regime and, during the four years of domination over Bamiyan, committed lots of crime. They looted the property of poor people and took many girls from their parents by force. I have many examples that the Hizb-e-Wahdat forces married many girls by force and if a father resisted in refusing to give his daughter he would be then threatened with death.

## NELAB

1. The Taliban killed our poor people, destroyed our houses and looted our property. When the Jihadis parties took power we all went back to our country. We had a hope that Hizb-e-Wahdat would improve our conditions but they did not have any care for the people. They were taking money from our people by force and didn't pay attention to the education of our children. When the Taliban seized the control of Kabul, our miseries increased much more than before. Our cultivated lands were burnt and destroyed, many bridges were torn down and large number of houses were destroyed. The fighting and shelling of rockets reminded us the Russian invasion. When the Taliban snatched control of the city from the Hizb-e-Wahdat, at their first day the showed their hostility to our Hazara people. They are so cruel and rude to our people and particularly people that I can't tell you all of their atrocities. They behaved with the people like a man treats his donkey. They even don't consider us as human beings. The restrictions and laws that they have imposed on us I don't think exist in any other country. The Taliban are mostly Pushtun and throughout the history of Afghanistan different rulers had cruel and hostile attitudes toward us.

2. The Taliban made our life difficult to live in Bamiyan because they destroyed everything and therefore we were forced to migrate once again to Pakistan. We left everything behind, our whole property. I had more than 100 hens, two cows and over 200 sheep and goats, my husband had butchery shop.

3. We had a very comfortable life in Bamiyan. My two sons were looking after the livestock and I myself along with my two daughters and two sons who were with me at home looked after the animals. I could collect more than 50 eggs per month, and this brought me enough money.

4. The Taliban are the worst rulers I have ever seen. They have special hostility to Hazara people and I think our life would certainly be improved if the Taliban are removed from power.

5. I have noticed that all the rulers who ruled in Afghanistan were against our Hazara people and the reason is quiet clear: first, because we belong to a different sect of religion and second, because all those rulers were Pushtun who considered Pushtun the most pure people and treated other people like strangers. Since we were not Pushtun we have always received very bad treatment from the different rulers. From all these facts I have reached the conclusion that unless and until these communal and sectarian differences are eliminated, civil war and misery will go on for decades and even centuries.

### QASIMA SHAMSI

1. The coming of the Taliban brought nothing but misery. On their very first day, they axed all the women from public work and shut the door of school for girls. I am not expert in religious studies but I am quite sure what they are doing with the people conflicts with the Islamic law. I remember that once our teacher taught us that in Islam both men and women have equal rights to get education and they share common rights. I wonder who has taught the Taliban and from where they have grasped these harsh regulations and laws. Right now more than 30 Islamic countries exist on the map of the world but none of them apply these laws. Even in Saudi Arabia that stands for a high degree of Islamic value and is the place where the Holy Makkah is situated, no such laws are imposed on the people. These all make us suspicious that there might be something hidden behind this movement and secondly there might be someone directing the Taliban because they are completely unaware of administrative rules and politics.

2. The seizing of power by the Taliban brought about adverse effects on our life. The money I earned from the NGO [non-governmental organization] and the income of my husband from his small shop was enough to meet our demands to some extent. But after I was sacked from my job our life started shrinking. The prices are too high and my husband's income could hardly feed us. With his income we can buy only a sack of flour. I have sold many of my possessions such as furniture and two carpets but this is not the way to get rid of this misery. Our financial capacity doesn't allow us to go to Pakistan but we have this plan to borrow some money and leave Afghanistan. Many women were forced to go into the streets and beg, but I can't do this, I prefer to die and will never accept begging.

3. We led a relatively normal life before the Taliban. My one daughter attended school regularly. She was in 6th grade. Since they have been

expelled from the school and got locked into the boundary of house, the girls have been affected psychologically. They are like prisoners that stay in the house for weeks and months. They can't go outside, can't do shopping, can't venture out for entertainments, etc. As the time goes on, their depression increases.

4. Certainly if the Taliban are removed from power, life would return to normal. But it is obvious that if the Taliban are replaced by elements that have links with foreign countries then the case would be the same. We have that experience from the previous regime. When the Jihadi were in power, we prayed to Allah that these criminals must be overthrown and a new party come that would establish peace and security in the country, but the Jihadis were replaced by elements that proved themselves worse than they. Therefore, I feel life would be better only if an independent party takes power that has no relation to any foreign country.

5. War, distraction and killing give everyone bitter experiences. Twenty years of unprecedented war left our country with its land destroyed and its residents dead. Millions of innocent people lost their lives and large cities laid into ruins.

## ZARMINA

1. The Taliban are very harsh to our people and especially to our women. They beat old men in the street for not having long beards or boys for having long hair. They do everything in the name of Islam. They want to impose the ways of Pushtun on other ethnics.

2. The Taliban made our already ruined life a misery. The fighting between the Taliban and the forces loyal to Massoud blocked the road for a year. This had a bad impact on the business of my husband. We had a large grapeyard which sold more than a ton of grapes every season, and this was our main source of income, but due to the road being blocked the grapes have remained in the yard and we couldn't sell them. Therefore we spent the whole year on borrowing money and wheat from other people. My husband was very anxious about that. He searched for a job in that area but no one would employ him because he is too weak and old. Our loans have increased so much that we found no other way but to sell our grapeyard and go either to Kabul or to Mazar Sharif. Thereby after selling the grapeyard we made our way to Kabul, but the life in Kabul was even worse than that of our village and therefore we came to Pakistan. Now my husband is working as a servant in

a general store in Peshawar. He earned 1,500 rupees ($22) per month. We pay 200 rupees for a very ruined house in Kacha Gali (it is a camp in Peshawar which is occupied by Afghans and houses over there all have no gas supply) and it costs 200 rupees for the electricity. It is really hard to live. My two sons, who were in school in Afghanistan, now work in a workshop that gives both of them 500 rupees ($10) monthly.

3. We had a good life in Ghorband. We had very pretty grapeyard behind our house and my husband worked in this grapeyard throughout the year. The money we got off this grapeyard was more than enough to meet all our demand. I myself kept more than 100 hens which provide us with at least 30 eggs a day. We could hardly eat eight of them daily. My children attended their school regularly. We lived in the village very peacefully.

4. The exclusion of Taliban from power certainly would have positive result on our life, but I think it would take a long time to return to our normal life. We have lost everything.

5. I would like to tell one thing to my people and to the whole world that the root cause of all these fighting and miseries is the interference of foreign countries. Russia destroyed our country and went back and now Pakistan and Iran are meddling for their own political interests and aims.

SHAH GUL

1. The Taliban are the puppets of Pakistan and Saudi Arabia. They are a bunch of Mullah (people who live in mosque and call the people for prayer or give Azan) who don't know the administrative rules nor have any knowledge about politics and economy. They are given money and arms just to fight. Their ignorance and hostility to women is not found in any other country and resemble the era of 1,000 years ago. The Taliban don't consider women as human beings. They treat women like animals.

   My son had a tea business. He bought tea from Takhar and sold it in Kabul. One day when he was going to Kabul, the Taliban got him out of the car and accused him of having relation with Ahmed Shah Massoud. He told the Taliban that he had been doing the tea business for the last of three years and never had links with Massoud, but the Taliban confiscated his tea and put him in prison in Kabul. After a week we found out that Jamshid has been arrested by the Taliban and put in Pulcharkhi prison. My husband went to Kabul to release my son. After giving 300,000,000 Afghani ($600) to the judge, who was a Taliban, my son was released and came back home. After that he stopped his business. The conditions in Takhar was not suited us because my husband had a shop there and the Ahmed Shah Massoud force took money from the shopkeepers by force. Therefore we came to Pakistan.

2. Before the appearance of Jihadi and then Taliban, my husband was a businessman and took imported goods from Tajikistan to Kabul. When the Taliban took the control of Kabul, the Salang Highway was blocked by the Taliban and it became difficult to bring goods from Takhar, and thus my husband's business was stopped. Last year we came to Pakistan. Now my husband drives a taxi and my son has a small shop at Hayatabad Super Market in Peshawar. Though my husband earns a considerable amount of money, renting a house here in Hayatabad is extremely high. We live in a house which has three bedrooms and pay 5,000 rupees ($1,000) plus the high cost of electricity and gas which some month exceeds 8,000 rupee per month.

   Apart from these economic problems, we are separated from our relatives and people. It has been one year that I have had any news of my mother and father. We feel really alone. There is no one to come and participate in our ceremonies. In Eid, only two families who were our neighbors have visited our house. I am alone in my house and don't know what is happening outside. It is really difficult to be away from your people and live in a foreign country.

3. Before the Jihadi came to power we had a very good life. My children attended school regularly. My elder son finished school in Takhar and got degree in business in Russia. But with the coming of Jihadi, my husband's business began to shrink. The continuous fighting between warring factions blocked the road all the time. With the coming of Taliban, his business was collapsed completely.

4. It is the wish of the whole nation of Afghanistan that both the Jihadi and Taliban be thrown from power and have a democratic force replace them. Both the Jihadi and Taliban proved themselves as anti-people and especially anti-women.

5. One thing I want to tell to the U.N. and other countries that if the river does not dry up at its end it has to dry up from its source. If they want to get rid of the Taliban, it is useless to impose sanctions and criticize them. The best way to eliminate them is to cut the supply of arms and money from their source, i.e., Pakistan. The U.N. must first impose sanction on Pakistan so she abstains from helping any more the Taliban.

It is then that the Taliban would immediately be diminished and disappear.

## B.G.

1. The coming of the Jihadi and then their brethren the Taliban to power made the life for the people of Afghanistan disastrous. I lost my husband in an explosion in the market when the rat race for power was going on between Ahmad Shah Massoud and Gulbuddin Hekmatyar in Kabul. I then lived with two brothers. When the Taliban captured Kabul city, the force of Massoud fired more than 100 rockets in Kabul city. My two brothers, two small daughters and elder sons were killed when a rocket hit directly on our house. I was left with my two young children who are four and five years old. I had no other relatives to go and live with them. My father and mother died 10 years ago. I had a brother-in-law who is living in Mazar-e-Sharif and it was too far away to go to Mazar-e-Sharif and we had no money to go there. Our whole house was destroyed. I then decided to sell the whole house possession and go to Pakistan. I did it. I with two young children went to Peshawar. I didn't know where to go. I asked the people in bus station and they told me that most of the Afghan refugees live in Kacha Gali. I went there and rented a tent for 200 rupee. I could not do anything but start begging. I used to go early in morning with my children to the Board area. I did begging and my children sold water at the bus station.

   A few months later my younger child became sick. I took him to hospital but the doctor diagnosed her that she had kidney problems and must be operated upon. I had no money to buy the items and medicine for the operation. I asked the manager of the hospital to make the medicine free for me but he told me that the hospital itself does not have any pharmacy. I sat all the day at the front gate of hospital with my child in my bosom and begged everyone to give money for my child. One day a handsome Pakistani gentleman came and asked me many questions about my life. I told him everything that was correct. He then promised me to give me money but he asked me to go with him and leave my child in the hospital. I agreed though I was a bit anxious that he might have a wrong thing in his mind. I went with him; he was living alone in his house. Suddenly he gave me 1,000 rupees from his pocket and asked me to let him do anything with me. My heart was beating strongly and my whole body was burning in pain. But I didn't care because I knew that there was no other way and my child would die. Caring for my child I was ready for everything. Within minutes I was dishonored. He told me that I should come every day and he would pay 100 rupee per day. The next day when I went there I saw five young men in his house. In this way I earned money for the treatment of my child but at the expense of my honor....

2. I told you everything now. I know it is an immoral thing but there is no other way out. Though I am young, I am ill and I can't do begging all the day. My children are too small to work. I don't care about the Taliban, I have no honor in society. I am alive just for my children and I want them to live like normal people. When they become young adults, I don't want to be alive even for a minute. Death is much better than this dirty life I have.

3. Before the Jihadi and Taliban we led a good life in Kabul. My husband was a carpenter and with my brother made furniture and many other wood items.

4. If the Taliban were no longer in power, the life of whole people of Afghanistan would be better. They committed such crimes that neither the history nor the people would forget. It was the Taliban who made life for me a torture. In fact, it was the Taliban and their rivals who dishonored me.

5. My country was destroyed by the Russians and Jiahdi and now Taliban. I wish that Allah place blessings on us and put an end to the misery of our people so that our people can return to their country and rebuild their houses and lands.

## MAHTAB

1. I am of the belief that the Taliban committed the greatest crime to the religion of Islam and that the pro–Russian regime revived Islam in Afghanistan. It might sound strange but it is a reality that I have observed and realized it in the course of 20 years of war. Khalqs and Parchams used "Communism" and "Democracy" as if they could take away Islam from the hearts of the people but the result they received was the revival of Islam. The people showed their opposition to those heinous acts by their Islamic slogans and soon started a countrywide Jihad (Holy war against those who are a danger to Islam) against them. During that 10 years of war for independence against the Russian and their servants, the Khalq and Purcham Islam, has achieved a greatest popularity among the masses. When the Jihadi grasped power the conditions got reversed. The various Jihadi groupings perpetrated thousands of crimes in the name of Islam and this was the time when

the people started distancing from the religion of Islam. They demonstrated their hatred to the Jihadi by opposing their harsh Islamic restriction. And when the Taliban gripped their clutches on the power, Islam was disgraced even more. The Taliban introduced such inhuman and harsh restrictions on our people that people began to refuse even to pray. I have seen many of such people who once were devoted followers of Islam but who now want to embrace another religion. This experience gives us some valuable pieces of advice and knowledge that while dealing with religion one should be very careful. Religion can neither be imposed on people nor can it take off from the people. This was the greatest mistake of previous rulers who intentionally used religion for their political goals and aims. The second experience that I have achieved from the war is that any effort for peace and stability would be doomed to fail if meddling by foreign countries is not cut out. And it has been proved throughout history that the nation of Afghanistan has never born the foreign interference in their country. Therefore if the U.N. or any other world body or country really wants an end to the misery of our innocent people, first and foremost exert pressure on those countries that continue to intervene in the internal affairs of Afghanistan.

2. The Taliban created a lot of hurdles in my work. For five years I was continuously traveling to Afghanistan. I had a clinic in a village with 10 nurses plus a mobile health team. We can't move to Afghanistan because my husband has worked with a company for the last 12 years and, most important, my children attend an English middle school in Pakistan. Therefore I found it better to stay in Afghanistan for two or three months and then have a visit in Pakistan for a week. In fact, the reason I chose Afghanistan for my work was that all my relatives live there and I wanted to serve my own people because they are really lacking medical care. There is no female doctor in the whole region. Women usually go for treatment to very distant places. The Taliban have threatened me many times and told me to be accompanied by a male while I was traveling and wear burqa all the time even when I am in the clinic. It is really difficult to work in that condition.

3. In fact, we have lived in Pakistan for the last 15 years, therefore the coming of the Taliban does not have any major impact on the life of my family.

4. Certainly the disappearance of the Taliban from the political scene would bring about good conditions for our people because they are committing the most inhuman atrocities against our people, and I

don't think there would exist elements more brutal than the Taliban. But I believe the wounds of our people would not be cured by the withdrawal of Taliban unless and until their masters are swept away.

5. Keeping in view the history of Afghanistan and the nine years of civil war, I am of the opinion that at present the practical way to solve the issue of Afghanistan is possible only if the U.N. takes the same decision as it did in Somalia, East Timor and Yugoslavia, i.e., the U.N. must send its peace-keeping force which would pave the way for the election by disarming all the warring factions. Sitting around tables or releasing resolutions are just prolonging the issue and going to do nothing with the solution.

## SAKENA

1. The Taliban are very harsh to women. They made our children uneducated. The previous ruler destroyed our houses and killed thousands of innocent people and now the Taliban want to kill the rest of us. The Taliban claim that they have brought peace and security, but I haven't seen any changes. The condition is as bad as it was when Jihadi had the power. Some weeks back, my nephew who was a driver took some passengers from Nemroze to Herat. On the way, the passengers threatened him with guns to give them all his money. He refused to give them money, then the passengers pulled him out of his car and shot him there on the spot and threw his dead body in a pool. After five days we were informed that he was killed by some unknown persons. We searched for the murderers and thanks God we found them after a month. We complained to the Taliban but they refused to take any action, and then we realized that those murderers were Taliban and belonged to the Taliban.

2. My husband was a teacher in a girls' school and had taught there for the last 18 years. When the Taliban closed the girls' school like others, he was sacked from his job. He then opened a small shop with his brother but it gives him nothing. Our life has really changed. When my husband was a teacher, we didn't have any problem. He went to school in the morning and I looked after the house. In the afternoon, he worked in the garden which gave us various vegetables such as potato, tomato, onion and some fruits, but now we buy them from the shop because my husband doesn't find time to work in the garden.

3. Before the Taliban, we led a normal life.

4. Yes, if the Taliban are removed from power our life would be much better, at least our children will get education. Now our children roam

about in the streets doing nothing. If they remain uneducated the whole nation will suffer. We wish a new government would replace the Taliban so that people could live in peace and security.

5. We have experienced the invasion of our country by the Russians and then by the Jihadi and Taliban. They are all responsible for the destruction of the country and killing of the people. I wish that new government would come and bring all those criminals and traitor who destroyed Afghanistan to court and trial according to the wish of the people.

## MASTORA

1. The Taliban are very harsh with the people. They whip people in the streets for petty things like not having a long beard or having long hair. They don't do anything to revive the economy of the country, which has collapsed due to the 20 years of war, but instead they insist on those things which bring them no positive results. At the beginning, we were very optimistic that the Taliban would put an end to all miseries and bring peace in the country because we had experienced a very bad life at the hand of criminal Jihadis. They killed thousands of people and even raped women. But the Taliban soon unveiled their real picture and proved themselves even worse than the Jihadi. They claim that they have closed the girls' schools because of the security problem and once peace comes in the country they will reopen the schools, but on the other hand they always praised their so-called Islamic Emirate because according to them it has established peace in the country.

2. The Taliban turned our life completely. We had a normal life in Kalakan (a city 50km away from Kabul). During the first fighting, in which the Taliban conquered the city and the opposition force ran away, our house received severe damage. A rocket hit directly in the middle of the house and destroyed two rooms with their contents which were our whole possessions. We were in our house when suddenly a group of Taliban entered and slapped and whipped my husband to give his weapons. My husband said that he is a simple farmer, he had no weapons and he had no link with opposition forces. But the criminal Taliban didn't hear any excuse and took my husband with them. I cried and begged them to release my husband but they kicked me with their feet. I didn't know what to do. I asked my brother-in-law and brother to go and search for my husband but they said if they go and ask about

my husband, the Taliban would arrest them also. I wait for two months but my husband didn't return and therefore I had no other option but to sell all my possessions and go to a safe place. I sold some of my house items and left some to my brothers and made my way to Kabul. But Kabul was even worse than Kalakan, therefore I came to Pakistan. I myself do begging and my children pick papers from the garbage. It is really difficult to live. I and my children earned 2,000 rupees per month, of which we pay 250 for the rent of a tent in Kacha Kagali.

3. We had a very good life before the Taliban. My husband was a farmer, working in a garden and earned plenty enough to meet our needs and I was looking after the house. We had two cows and ten sheep which provide us with sufficient milk and meat.

4. Yes, if the Taliban were out of power, our life would be better. The Taliban destroyed our house and lands and we live in constant fear that there might be again fighting between the Taliban and Massoud. We wish the Taliban would soon be withdrawn from power so that all the people from Pakistan and Iran and other countries could return to their motherland and start their life in their own land. Living in a foreign country is very difficult, especially for the poor people.

5. I have got that experience from my country that the current disaster is mainly due the interference of our neighbor countries (Pakistan and Iran) which provide their servants with money and arms for their political benefit and I want to tell the U.N. or any other country who really want to solve the problem the issue of Afghanistan that first they have to cut the supply of arms and money to the war factions then think about their negotiations or holding election.

## FATIMA

1. I am from Saria Khoja (a village situated in the north of Kabul). I had a very bad experience with the Taliban. Hundreds of people have lost their lives during last summer's fighting between Massoud and Taliban. A large number of people have been rounded up and arrested who were apparently suspected of cooperating with the former government or harboring arms to Massoud. Worse than that, scores of young girls and women have been drawn out from their houses by the Taliban and were taken to unknown destination. My 19 years daughter by the name of Simen was among those women. I shouted and begged for the Taliban to release her but the criminal gang dragged her body into the car and went away. I then with my three children went to Kabul by

foot. I asked the people over there if they have knowledge of the where-abouts of the lost women and some one told me that the Shomali women have been taken to Hilamand province (it is near Qandihar where the Taliban supreme leader Mullah Omar lives). I had some money and borrowed some more from my relative and went to Hil-mand. A shopkeeper told them that the Taliban bring women from Shomali and sell them to Arabs and Pakistani. I stayed two months in Hilmand but I could not find my daughter. I complained to the U.N. office in Kabul but they said that they are incapable of doing anything because the Taliban are so ignorant that they don't care about the com-plaints of the people.

2. The Taliban made life a misery for us. Now I am washing clothes of other people and earn a petty amount and my three children are sell-ing water in the bus stations. We live in a very ruined place with no clean water and electricity. My young child who is nine years old was ill and I didn't have money to buy drugs for him. Thanks to ICRC [International Committee of the Red Cross] that gives me free medi-cines. I don't know what will come of us.

3. We had relatively a normal life in Kalakan. My husband was killed five years ago when the Jihadi bombarded our village. I lived alone with my children and my mother-in-law and sister-in-law. I and my sister-in-law had sewing machines from which we could earned round about 200,000 ($32) Afghani per month. My children attended their school regularly. I also kept three cows and ten sheep, which provided us enough milk, oil and meat.

4. Definitely our life would be improved if the Taliban are sacked from power. They are so harsh and cruel to the people that there would exist hardly any other party worse than them.

5. Twenty years of war struck our country with such blows that it has left nothing for our country. The economy of the country has completely collapsed and its residents have been killed and those who remain alive lead a life of misery.

## BIBI KASHWAR

1. Although the forces loyal to Ahmed Shah Massoud brought lots of difficulties and miseries, with the coming of the Taliban our life really became a complete disaster. When the Taliban pushed back the Mas-soud forces in the last year, they stormed like wild animals in each and every house. We were all in our house when a group of Taliban entered

and told us that they had been ordered to take all the young girls and women to Jalalabad because the war will continue for a long time and there is possibility that they would be killed or raped. The Taliban pointed to my sister-in-law and told her to get in the car. My mother-in-law told the Taliban that we had planned to shift our house to Kabul and therefore we would take her with us, but the Taliban said that they were ordered to do so and took away my sister-in-law by force. We all cried and begged the Taliban to release her but they refused. I brought my golden ring and a large amount of money if they would release my sister-in-law, but the criminal gangs turned down any request.

We didn't know what to do. My mother-in-law asked my brothers-in-law to go and search for her and they went and complained to the Taliban authority. The reply we received was that it had been decided by the authority in Kabul and they are incapable of doing anything. My mother-in-law along with tens of other women whose daughter or sister had been taken by the Taliban went to Kabul to complain to the Taliban authority. My mother-in-law says that they had gone to the interior minister and they were advised to go to Jalalabad. When they went to Jalalabad, the authority over there denied having any information about the whereabouts of the women. My mother-in-law says that during her stay in Jalalabad, she met a young girl by the name of Ziba. Ziba told my mother-in-law that the Taliban had taken her from Ghorband and sold her for 100,000,000 ($2,000) to a man who already had two wives. Ziba said that she is now locked in a house and doesn't know where she is and her husband is so harsh and cruel that she can't say anything to him. People say that the Taliban take young girls and sell them to the Arabs for thousands of dollars.

2. The coming of the Taliban was a blow to our family. Since my sister-in-law was taken from us our whole family has been grieving and mourning, particularly my father-in-law. He weeps everyday. He had shut his shop for a week and within this time interval, robbers or it might be Taliban looted his shop. We felt it better to leave our village and go to safe place. We along with 10 more families who were our close relatives came to Kabul and here we rent a house for 300,000 Afghani. Now my father is selling vegetables and I wash clothes in other people's houses for a little amount of money but we plan to go to Pakistan. We sold out our whole possessions in Kabul. I am very worried about the education of my children.

3. Our life was not bad in Qara Bagh. I lost my husband 12 years ago. I lived with my father-in-law. Though he was old, he was the only breadwinner

of our family. With his small shop, he could provide us everything. My sister-in-law was very expert in weaving carpets and she weaved one carpet in two months.

4. Yes, if the Taliban are removed from power, the life of all people of Afghanistan would be improved. The Taliban made thousands of women widows and children orphans. The price is too high. The whole of Afghanistan has been laid into ruins. And we hope a new government would replace them and reconstruct our destroyed land and revive our collapsed economy.

5. I have that message to the whole world that they should do something to end our miseries. The U.N. and United States of America must remove the Taliban and the Jihadi from power.

## MARINA

1. When the Taliban came into our village, they burned the green garden and destroyed cultivated land because they said the force of Ahmed Shah Massoud had buried ammunitions in the gardens and lands and they wanted to set them off. It was really a bad time. You could see that your whole village was burning. Our village was very famous for its grapes and berries and the economy of the whole people depended on the exporting of fruits. As their gardens were turned into ashes, the whole village migrated to other places. Some went to northern provinces and some to the west but most of them went to Kabul and from there those who had money went to Pakistan. Our village that once was the most beautiful and rich in fruit village in the whole region now has turned into a desert and it is very difficult to rebuild it. All the people lost their hopes and even some decided to get the citizenship of other countries and never return to Afghanistan. Apart from burning our gardens, the most tragic event was that the Taliban took hundreds of beautiful young women and girls to unknown destination and the people say that those women were sold to Arabs and Pakistani businessmen for thousands of dollars.

    Fortunately, we had no such young girl in our family. I have only three sons and my age is 53. Instead they have taken my husband. The Taliban arrested hundreds of men because they suspected that those men were in the army of Ahmed Shah Massoud. All those men were taken to Pulcharkhi prison in Kabul. I went to Pulcharkhi to get information about my husband. At first, the police over there told me that my husband was not there but I then gave 200,000 Afghani to a Talib and asked him to go and find out if there is a man by the name of Zalmi. Thank God he brought good news and told me that my husband was in the prison. My husband told me that conditions in the prison are too horrible. There is not enough food or clean water. The Taliban treat the prisoners very harshly. One year has passed and my husband is still in the prison. People say that for every prisoner released, the judge over there wants 25 million ($500). I don't have that much money or any property to sell to be able to give to bribe to the judge and get my husband released. We left everything in Shomali.

2. The Taliban changed the life of all people. We now live with two other families in a small house and pay 350,000 Afghani ($7) for the rent. My elder son is selling fruits and I am working with a woman tailor.

3. We had a very good life in Shomali. We had a large grape yard and my husband and elder son were working all the day in that grape yard. This was our main source of income.

4. This is the wish of each and every Afghan that the Taliban should be thrown from the power, because except for misery and destruction and killing, they have brought nothing to the people. We hope a new government replaces them which could guarantee rights for each Afghan. We ask kindly from the U.N. to think a little about Afghanistan and do something to end our misery, I believe if the U.N. exerted a little effort the problem of Afghanistan would be solved.

5. I have reached the conclusion from 20 years of unprecedented war in Afghanistan that we shouldn't be very optimistic about the promises of the ruler. The Jihadi promised people that they would bring peace and security in Afghanistan and establish a true Islamic government, but instead they destroyed our country. Similarly, the Taliban accused the Jihadi of committing brutal crimes against the people and promised that they would put an end to all the misery, but now five years have passed since they took the power and our country declines more and more and the misery of our people was multiplied ten times. I want all countries that believe in peace for all human races to exert pressure on Pakistan and Iran to stop their servant from fighting anymore and let the people of Afghanistan to decide their future.

PARWANA

1. The Taliban are the most cruel and brutal rulers who don't have a similar example in the history of any country. In the four years of their rule, people got fed up with them and everyone wants them to be

removed from power. In our village, I don't remember a person who praised the Taliban. In the last year of fighting, they killed hundreds of innocent people and burned the whole cultivated land and green gardens. I remember that when I was in 5th grade, our teacher told us about the cruelty of [Genghis] Khan who, when he conquered the northern part of Afghanistan, destroyed all living things including the plants and livestock. The same was done by the Taliban when they conquered Shomali. I myself saw dead bodies lying over the roads. I can't tell you what happened to my husband. A group of Taliban came into our house and immediately took my husband. They accused my husband of having links with the opposition force and ordered him to give his gun to the Taliban. My husband told them that he had no gun but the traitor Taliban shot my husband and killed him there in front of us. We all cried over the dead body of my husband. I myself believed when we buried him that this was the end of the story. After killing my husband, they took my daughter with them. Believe me it was really difficult to bear all those disasters.

We had no other elder male in our house to go and search for my lost daughter, therefore we decided to leave the place and go to another place. I sold my whole possessions and we all, including my mother-in-law, went to Kabul. In Kabul, there was no house to live in, the rent of every house was over 300,000. We stayed three nights in a bus station and then went to the former Russian embassy where there were thousands of other women who were all from Shomali and had fled from the fighting. We are given very little food by the U.N. in the embassy but the condition over here is really unbearable. Here is no proper food nor clean water. More than 300 families live in this embassy. The crying of the children and the weeping of their mothers make everyone mad. My younger child is ill now and I don't know where I should find medicine for him. I asked the man in charge of that embassy who is a Talib but he cursed us and doesn't listen to our problem. The U.N. aid all goes in the pocket of the Taliban.

2.  What I have told you now is our present condition and I don't know what will be our future. I have lost hope and sometimes I think about committing suicide, but when I look at my children I pause a little.

3.  We had a good life in Istalif. My husband was a farmer and working in a garden of the landlord which gave him plenty enough to meet all of our needs. We were also given free fruits and firewood. We had a cow in our house which provided us about three liters of milk a day and I kept 10 hens.

4. Yes, certainly the life of the people would be improved but our life is now finished. I don't have any hope for the future, but my children would be living in a safe country if the Taliban are thrown out of power.

5. Except for war and killing and destruction and misery, I don't have any other experience in my life. Our country has been burning in the flame of fighting for the last 20 years. Thousands of people have lost their lives, all of Afghanistan has been turned into ruins. People migrated to other countries and those who are inside Afghanistan are in a constant fear that someday they would be the victim of the Taliban and Jihadi fighting.

## HASINA

1. The emergence of the Taliban meant a collapse of our life. The fighting between them and Ahmed Shah Massoud caused the death of hundreds of innocent people. The wild Taliban burned all the cultivated land and gardens and took with them hundreds of young women and girls. Thank God we had a Pushtun relative in our village. When the Taliban entered the village we all went to our relative's houses therefore my daughter remained safe but unfortunately my elder son who was working in a workshop was arrested by the Taliban. That day we didn't know that he has been taken by Taliban, but the next day someone told us that the Taliban took many people who were in the market. I asked my relative to go ask the Taliban to release my son. They went to different Taliban authorities but all their efforts were in vain, and my relative told me that my son and many other people had been taken to Kabul.

   Our house was destroyed completely by rocket shelling, therefore I found it better to go to Kabul. In Kabul we stayed one week in a ruined place and someone came there and offered us work. I accepted and went with him. It was a big house, which was owned by a rich businessman. The businessman was alone in his house with 10 servants. We were given a small room in the corner of the house and told to fill almonds in plastic. We worked in this house for one month and he gave us food and clothes but no salary. One day my daughter told me that the businessman proposed marriage with him. My daughter is 15 and the businessman is 69. I told my daughter to not marry that man but he promised me that if I give my daughter to him he would pay around $1,000. I agreed because we had no other place to live or anyone to feed us. A month later the businessman's wife came from Pakistan.

When she found out that her husband wanted to marry with my daughter, she got angry and expelled us from the house. Now we live in ruined school where five other families also live.

2. The Taliban destroyed our safe life. We were among our relatives and people and knew of each other but now one has gone to the west, one to the east and I don't think we will gather again and restart our life.

3. I lost my husband during the Afghan-Russian war and then I lived with three children and mother-in-law in a house, which had been left to us by my grand father-in-law. I had a sewing machine and had a kind of tailoring shop. I sewed dresses for women. We had a small garden at the back of our house from which we could get fruits and vegetables.

4. Yes, if the Taliban remain no longer in power, the life of whole people of Afghanistan would be improved. They brought misery to each and every Afghan life.

5. I have a lot of experience from my country. Our country was destroyed by war and thousands of people have lost their lives. I want from the U.N. and other world powers to exert pressure on those countries that are interfering in Afghanistan to stop supplying arms and money to the Taliban and their opposition.

## Conclusions

Some sadness rests within my soul because I can only record the voices, but not the names of most of the women interviewees. Nevertheless, the regret is quickly replaced with the knowledge that these women are part of a larger group that will move into the majority in Afghanistan. They will move because the war killed many men. Their voices will continue to be heard as they mold their country. They will address all issues facing Afghanistan, because as U.S. Senator Barbara Mikulski (D-MD) says of issues within the United States, "every issue is a woman's issue."[3] So every issue is a woman's issue for the women in Afghanistan.

Sometimes the poets say it best. RAWA's founding leader, Meena, wrote that her voice had mingled with those of thousands of women to break the sufferings, and the fetters of slavery. Zieba Shorish-Shamley, co-founder and director of Women's Alliance for Peace and Human Rights in Afghanistan, traces the Afghan woman's long journey in poetry. She writes,

I Remember You...
Dedicated to My Suffering Afghan Sisters
*by Zieba Shorish-Shamley*[4]

I remember you...
>    when you have no choice, no voice, no rights, no existence
>    when you have no laughs, no joy, no freedom, no resistance
>    your pain, your agony, your silence, your loneliness
>    your anger, your frustration, your cries, your unhappiness

I remember you...
>    when you are abused, attacked, beaten and veiled
>    when you are tortured, strangled, choked and almost killed
>    you feel numbness, nothingness, lifelessness and tears
>    you are a shadow, a ghost, a creature with many fears

I remember you...
>    when you in the darkness, stillness of a star-less night
>    lift your arms to the sky, with sadness and fright
>    and ask the universe with eyes full of tears and pain
>    why all these crimes? for what reason? can anyone explain?

I remember you...
>    when you finally will rise and stand on your feet!
>    and say "No! I will not stand for any more defeat!"
>    you will break the chains, burn the veil and destroy the walls!
>    you will scream with all your might "Damn you all!"

I remember you...
>    when you take the solemn oath that you will struggle, resist and fight
>    that you will gain your freedom with all your might
>    that you will never give up, no matter how heavy the cost
>    never again will you be confused, pitiful and lost

I remember you...
>    when you gain your rights, reach your goals and hope(s)
>    but the path is hard, full of obstacles; you must learn how to cope
>    to cope while struggling for your ultimate goal
>    a-reborn woman, free, independent and whole

# Hope for the Future

*RAWA is firmly of the opinion that knowledge is a great power that raises the awareness of women and the new generation of their rights and place in society and enables them to understand social and political problems of the country, therefore we focus our activities mainly in the field of education.[1]*
Shabana, RAWA Cultural Committee Member

The Taliban policy on women dictates that Afghan women are to "bring up the next generation of Muslims,"[2] yet women are not to be seen in public without a male escort and proper attire. They cannot work or go to school, and do not receive proper medical attention. For the most part, urban women must remain within the home behind windows painted black. Women have been beaten or lost their lives for infractions of the Taliban's extreme rules. Hundreds of thousands have fled their country and have to face new definitions of home, yet those women fortunate enough to have escaped with their lives, whether they are inside or outside of Afghanistan, will provide the strength and continuity of a culture that has not known peace for over 20 years. The hope is that a once beautiful life can return through the efforts of Afghan women, through political and diplomatic efforts and through people and organizations who are working for a better life for Afghan women.

## Political and Diplomatic Efforts for Peace

### THE UNITED NATIONS

#### The Six Plus Two

One of the many efforts the U.N. has to promote peace in Afghanistan is the Six Plus Two. Under the U.N. auspices, the Six Plus Two bring together the main countries with influence. The group consists of the six countries bordering Afghanistan: Pakistan, Iran, Turkmenistan, Uzbekistan, Tajikistan and China, plus the United States and Russia. In 1998, in the group's first ministerial session, the Six Plus Two addressed the grave situation both inside Afghanistan and along its borders. The international community, through the U.N. General Assembly, the Security Council, and the Six Plus Two called on all parties to declare a cease-fire and negotiate a political settlement.[3] In April 2000, the Security Council welcomed the renewed commitment of members of the Six Plus Two to contribute to a peaceful resolution of the Afghan conflict. It also urged them and the Afghan parties to implement the group's 1999 Tashkent Declaration on Fundamental Principles for a Peaceful Settlement of the Conflict, particularly the agreement of members of the group not to provide military support to any Afghan party and to prevent the use of their territories for such purposes.[4]

*Other Diplomatic Initiatives*

In September 1999, the report of the Secretary-General outlined efforts by different countries to bring about peace in Afghanistan. Uzbekistan invited officials including the two Afghan warring sides, the United Front and the Taliban, to meet in Tashkent. Both sides agreed to refrain from initiating new military offensives, but one week later, the Taliban began a major offensive against the United Front in the Shomali Plains. Pakistan announced that it was initiating an effort to facilitate reconciliation between the parties. The United Front believes that Pakistan can do little when it provides military and political support to the Taliban. The Taliban, according to the report, show little interest in Pakistan's efforts to facilitate reconciliation.[5]

The United States imposed financial and economic sanctions against the Taliban until the terrorist, Osama bin Laden, is expelled. The sanctions are not aimed at the people, and the U.S. continues to be one of the largest providers of humanitarian assistance. The former king of Afghanistan, Zahir Shah, met with a group of Afghan intellectuals and political leaders which decided to form a preparatory council to convene an emergency grand assembly.[6]

Specifically, as a result of the Taliban offensive, the U.N. continued to supply food assistance to 10,000 people, 90 percent of whom were women and children. According to the report,

> Deplorable socio-economic conditions coupled with the direct and indirect impact of the war makes Afghanistan one of the most deadly places on earth, particularly for women, children and others made vulnerable by years of unceasing conflict and growing impoverishment.... The separation of men from families, their arbitrary detention, violence against

women, the use of child soldiers, indiscriminate bombing and the use of landmines continue to add to the dismal human rights record of Afghanistan.[7]

U.N. Special Rapporteur on violence against women, Radhika Coomaraswamy, has met with the appropriate parties to stress the ending of the policy and practice of discrimination against women, and says sadly that she has never seen suffering like what she found in Afghanistan.[8] She has noted some improvements in women's access to health care, but systematic violations of women's rights continue.

## HUMANITARIAN INITIATIVES

In October 1999, the president of the U.N. Security Council reaffirmed its "commitment to the sovereignty, independence, territorial integrity and national unity of Afghanistan, and its respect for Afghanistan's cultural and historical heritage," and reiterated that among the council's deep concerns were "the continuing violations of international humanitarian law and of human rights, particularly discrimination against women and girls."[9] In October 1999, the U.N. Security Council also made a similar statement deploring the worsening human rights situation in Afghanistan.[10]

In April 2000, the president of the Security Council again issued a statement reiterating grave concern that the continuing and serious Afghan conflict is a growing threat to regional and international peace. Strongly condemning the Taliban for their latest offensives in March, the council issued a plea for all parties to discontinue the conflict. The council condemned the continuing grave violations of the human rights of women and girls, particularly in areas under the control of the Taliban. The council said that the recent reports of modest progress regarding the access of women and girls to certain services is incremental improvement and welcome, but the council believes that women's lives in Afghanistan "still fall far short of the minimum expectations of the international community, and calls upon all parties, particularly the Taliban, to take measures to end all violations of human rights of women and girls."[11]

In 2000, Angela King, special advisor to the secretary-general on gender issues and advancement of women, said, "Further progress was likely to be as slow as the modest progress achieved over the past two years, unless there was a strong negotiated peace. Unfortunately the issue of gender was usually very low on the list of priorities, or often not even a factor."[12] The council must continue to press for the full enjoyment of the human rights of women in Afghanistan, she said. Specifically, at the community level and in rural areas, some projects have involved both men and women, such as deciding where to place wells or what types of seeds to plant. Some mullahs in Herat were open to and often sought the opinions of women.

King says U.N. agencies could set an example by having more women, including at a high level, in their dealings with Afghanistan. The U.N. Drug Control Programme to transform a drug-producing factory into a wool manufacturing plant could be used as a model in that it stipulated that 200 of the 1,300 people employed must be women.

King suggests a strategy for how women might seek employment by more ministries opening up to women, for example, with a ministry for social affairs. The policy could be expanded to include ministries governing health and education. Establishing machinery for the advancement of women could serve as the focal point within the existing authorities for the U.N. agencies.

In July 2000, the Economic and Social Council passed resolutions condemning the continuing grave violations of the human rights of women and girls in all areas of Afghanistan, particularly in areas under control of the Taliban. The Council urged States to continue to give special attention to the promotion and protection of human rights, and to mainstream a gender perspective in all aspects of their policies and actions.[13]

In spite of the efforts of the U.N., according to the Physicians for Human Rights, Afghanistan remains "a monument to the avarice of the warring parties that brought it to this point, to the international and Afghan actors who promoted the Taliban and to the United Nations' failure."[14] PHR recommends action that would lead to a representative government committed to international human rights that include equal rights for women. The governments that support the Taliban, Pakistan in particular, would publicly end their assistance. An effective arms embargo and system of international human rights monitors need to be established, and the U.N.'s memorandum of understanding with the Taliban that acknowledges women's access to health care and education must be "gradual" requires rescinding and renegotiation. If the U.N. fails to reach an agreement, then there would be no assurance of the end of restrictions.

The United Nations is not without criticism. In 1998, Christine Aziz wrote that Equality Now, a pressure group, reported that U.N. officials in Afghanistan have consistently failed to address the issue of women's rights with Taliban leaders. Several U.N. agencies in Jalalabad suspended all women Afghan employees under pressure from government and rebel forces. Some non-governmental organization agencies refused to work with the Taliban's request to stop treating female patients and to transfer them to a partially destroyed health center, Rabia Balkhi, where they were to be treated separately. The World Health Organization offered funds to refurbish the center. About 75 percent of women's programs have been affected because skilled Afghan women are needed to make them succeed.

Charles Norchi, New York human rights attorney, reminds us that even though over half a century ago the U.N. adopted the Universal Declaration of Human Rights, the international human rights system has "failed the Afghans more than any other population.... In the last two decades, every human rights standard codified by the international community has been violated in Afghanistan."[15] Afghanistan does not fit the Western human rights model because the system revolves around states. The "state" has been important only to invaders, but not to the greater population. Norchi emphasizes, "The Universal Declaration of Human Rights was mostly drafted in Eleanor Roosevelt's New York City apartment. For ordinary Afghans these are more aspirational than real."[16] Human rights standards, moreover, are mostly Western. Afghanistan has always been "a land on everyone's way to somewhere else," but it was the Soviet Army, maintains Norchi, that set the stage for the long downward spiral of human rights. Norchi tells of one U.N. rapporteur at the time of the Mujahedin who referred to Afghanistan's status as "a country in which the power struggle creates more of an equilibrium of anarchy than an equilibrium of people's government." The new government did not respect the Afghan people, thus, the Taliban entered to correct the situation, but as they gained more control they inflicted their version of rigid Islam. Afghanistan's changes in regimes do not affect its obligations under international law, human rights law and humanitarian law. The problem is that there is no "state" or governmental authority to guarantee the human rights defined in international instruments. "The most serious infraction of human rights has been the loss of the Afghan culture, but its human rights future lies with its people rather than with the U.N. The tragedy is that Afghan lives will continue to be nasty, brutish and brief," concludes Norchi.

## THE UNITED STATES

Zalmay Khalilzad believes that "the level of American effort has been lower than its interests and values require."[17] As a world power, the United States has assisted Afghanistan, but not without criticism. President Clinton acknowledged the double edge on Dec. 6, 1999:

In Afghanistan, we have strongly condemned the Taliban's despicable treatment of women and girls. We have worked with the United Nations to impose sanctions against the Taliban, while ensuring that the Afghan people continue to receive humanitarian assistance. We are Afghanistan's strongest critic, but also its largest humanitarian donor.[18]

Clinton announced that in the year 2000 the United States would spend at least $2 million to educate and improve the health of Afghan women and child refugees, make an additional $1.5 million available in emergency aid for those displaced by the recent Taliban offensive, and expand the U.S. resettlement program for women and children who were not safe where they were. Clinton also acknowledged that the humanitarian aid of the United States is not the long-range solution, but that an Afghanistan government representative of the people is. On Dec. 6, 1999, on Human Rights Day, he described humanitarian aid programs as "but temporary solutions. The Taliban must stop violating the rights of women, and respect the human rights of all people. And we must continue to work until the day when Afghanistan has a government that reflects the wisdom of its people."

Three months earlier, in October 1999, Clinton acknowledged the difficult status of Afghan women:

Perhaps the most difficult place in the world for women today is still Afghanistan. And I hope that the fact that we have had two Afghan women here in one of our human rights events, and the fact that we continue to push for changes in the lives of those people and to take as many in as we can here, will someday lead to a change in that country— because no women should have to undergo what those women have experienced.[19]

Hillary Rodham Clinton led the way for global support of women in Afghanistan. In March 1999, at the United Nations International Women's Day, she stated,

There probably is no more egregious and systematic trampling of fundamental rights of women today than what is happening in Afghanistan under the iron rule of the Taliban. Just stop for a minute and think about how women used to make up almost half of Afghan doctors, and now they are forbidden to practice medicine. They used to be half the teachers; now they are barred from teaching. The girls used to go regularly to school; now the doors of those schools are slammed shut. And we've heard, all of us, the stories of women being flogged with metal cables because a bit of ankle would be showing. We've heard of women being taken to hospital after hospital and finally dying because no care could be given because there were no women doctors and no male doctor could be permitted to treat the woman. Now that is the most extreme example we can point to, but clearly it is an example that we must carefully examine because it is being justified in the name of culture and tradition. It is, as the Secretary of State, Madeline Albright, often says, "no longer acceptable to say that the abuse and mistreatment of women is cultural—it should be called what it is: criminal." And it should be addressed by individual leaders in societies and by all of us through the United Nations and other multi-lateral efforts. I am pleased that a campaign started here in the United States is aimed at improving educational opportunities for Afghan girls, primarily in refugee camps outside the borders of that country.[20]

Hillary Clinton's campaign for the women in Afghanistan has been persistent. In April 1999 she spoke out again. "When women are savagely beaten by so-called religious police for not being fully covered by the burqa or for making noises while they walk, we know that it is not just the physical beating that is the objective.... It is the destruction of the spirit of those women as well.... The women of Afghanistan, while other women are moving forward, are being pushed brutally backward in time."[21]

Peter Tomsen and Abdul Raheem Yaseer are familiar with the complexity of global government and are among those who are convinced that answers to address Afghanistan's problems are not easy. Putting control of the country's government in the hands of the Afghan people is not likely with the approach of the United States, primarily due to the U.S. support of Pakistan. In 1998, William O. Beeman wrote, "It is no secret that the United States, Pakistan and Saudi Arabia have been supporting the fundamentalist Taliban in their war for control of Afghanistan."[22]

In 1999, Colum Lynch wrote that the Taliban as part of their scorched-earth military campaign burned entire villages in the Shomali plain and Panjshir valley.[23] Beeman says that the U.S. support of the Taliban has nothing to do with religion or ethnicity, it has only to do with the economics of oil. The simplest and cheapest route to transport oil is by pipeline through Iran, and the U.S. desire to deny Iran this pipeline is to get the Taliban to agree to a pipeline through their territory. The Osama bin Laden bombing of two American Embassies in East Africa was a message to the United States to get out of "Islamic countries," and, Beeman says, bin Laden meant specifically Afghanistan.

Pakistan is a supporter or enabler of the Taliban militia. The United States, then, by supporting Pakistan, is supporting the Taliban militia. Peter Tomsen said in March 2000 that the U.S. needs to downsize its foreign assistance to all Afghan groups in order to force Afghans to search for an internal consensus regarding their leadership. Tomsen concludes,

Giving another U.S. green light to Pakistan to mediate the Afghan conflict will only further postpone the day when the United States must adopt a more effective policy to deal with the international Islamist extremist network centered in war-torn Afghanistan, but also well entrenched in Pakistan. The network includes the Taliban; the Pakistan government's military intelligence arm, the Interservices Intelligence Bureau (ISI); a number of Pakistani religious parties and their paramilitary forces are engaged with ISI support in Afghanistan alongside the Taliban; Osama bin Laden's terrorist web; and a growing medley of militant extremist groups operating in North Africa, the Middle East, the Northern Caucasus, and Central Asia.[24]

Further, Tomsen said that CIA Director George Tenet testified before Congress on Feb. 2, 2000, of the possibility that "the Islamist threat based on Afghan territory would likely escalate from bombings to chemical and biological attacks."

In testimony before the U.S. Congress, Assistant Secretary Karl F. Inderfurth said, "The U.S. does not now support and has never supported the Taliban."[25] On human rights, the United States has publicly recognized occasional local improvements, but the central authorities in Kabul have regressed. Inderfurth testified that the Taliban detained and then expelled Mary MacMakin, a U.S. citizen who had long lived in Afghanistan and had devoted herself for over four decades to humanitarian service. A new Taliban edict forbids women from working in international human itarian activities.

Inderfurth explained that the U.S. strategy is to first exert pressure on the Taliban in the areas of terrorism, narcotics and human rights. Executive Order 13129 imposed unilateral sanctions on the Taliban regime, but not on the Afghan people, to prevent them from deriving revenue or benefit from interaction with the United States. The U.N. followed up in October 1999 with Resolution 1267 placing sanctions against Taliban-controlled assets and international airline flights until bin Laden is brought to justice. Other options such as an arms embargo are being explored. Secondly, the United States is committed to the greatest possible involvement of Afghans in the search for peace, followed by the involvement of the United States and the international community in rebuilding Afghanistan.

## THE INTERNATIONAL COMMUNITY

International organizations work both inside and outside of Afghanistan. Some concentrate on effecting change within, while others concentrate their efforts outside. High profile private individuals help by bringing about a much needed collective consciousness.

Great controversy lies with the positions of various members of the international community. Nancy Hatch Dupree explains the Taliban reasoning on the issue. The community withdraws assistance, for example, in education, and the Taliban insist that "the movement considers it an Islamic duty to provide education for all, including women, as long as Islamic rules and regulations are properly followed."[26] In the case of education, the rules emphasize separate facilities and security in the streets. Adequate educational facilities and security for women are not to be found. The Taliban say that providing for women takes time. They criticize the international sources of aid for linking the availability of aid to women's issues. The Taliban do not recognize or believe in human rights. They believe only in, and rule by, their interpretation of the Sharia. In 1996 Madeleine Albright, the U.S. ambassador to the United Nations, said the Taliban rules were "medieval and impossible to justify or defend," and Maulana Fazlur Rahman, Chief of Jamiat-e Ulema-i Islam and an alleged supporter of the Taliban, said the Taliban's attitude toward women was unrealistic, and threatened international assistance. Despite this, the Taliban policy makers were not motivated to change.

Marsden concludes it is unlikely that all parties involved in the conflict will agree and that there are no easy answers for the international community. The permanent solution will be affected as much by the results of longstanding interference from the outside as it will be by Afghanistan's own traditions. Humanitarian assistance at best can only help ease the burden of war on the Afghan people. Assistance will always be fraught with value system problems from Islamic factions and from the West and Islamic groups. Marsden suggests that author Nira Yuval-Davis's observations in her book, *Gender and Nation*, could be applicable to dialogue between humanitarian agencies and those exercising power where the agencies work. Women who share a common concern over their disadvantaged position deny their own values to find elements within other groups that might be compatible with their own. Marsden argues that the need to combat poverty, for example, might be a compatible value that can cross "cultural divides."[27]

## INDIVIDUALS

### Mavis Leno

Individuals who are recognized as celebrities often raise money for political and charitable causes. In October of 1998 Mavis and Jay Leno held a meeting in their home to raise $500,000 and plan early strategy for a publicity campaign to end "gender apartheid in Afghanistan," according to *Time*. Their purpose is to "stop corporate investment and to cease recognition by any nation of the Taliban government." Soon after Mavis Leno's appearance at a "UNOCAL shareholders' meeting to demand that the oil company drop plans to build a $4.5 billion pipeline in Afghanistan," UNOCAL temporarily ceased the pipeline operations.[28] The Taliban would have received $50 to $100 million per year in revenue from the pipeline. The spokesperson for UNOCAL said there was no unilateral agreement with the Taliban, they had no contact with the Taliban, and the pipeline was a low-priority project.[29] Mavis and Jay Leno contributed $100,000 to the Feminist Majority Foundation's campaign to stop gender apartheid.[30] Mavis Leno and the Feminist Majority are a significant force in making U.S. citizens aware of the conditions of Afghan women under the Taliban.[31]

In March 1999 as a National Board Member of the Feminist Majority, Mavis Leno testified before the Senate on gender apartheid in Afghanistan, and outlined the basic human rights denied women: "Under Taliban's rule, women and girls have been stripped of their basic human rights and women have been held under virtual 'house arrest.'"[32] The goal of the Feminist Majority and the 130 women's rights and human rights organizations that have joined their effort is to restore the human rights of women and girls in Afghanistan. To realize this goal, the organization led demonstrations in 1997 at the Afghanistan and Pakistan embassies in Washington, D.C. Shortly after the demonstrations, the U.S. State Department closed the Afghanistan embassy. In addition, Leno testified that the Feminist Majority has urged President Clinton, Secretary of State Albright, and the U.N. Secretary General "not to recognize the Taliban as the official government of Afghanistan and to do everything in their power to restore the human rights of Afghan women."

Mavis Leno describes the ways in which the Feminist Majority believes the United States could do more. First, the United States bears some of the responsibility for the conditions of women in Afghanistan by providing weapons and other military resources to the Taliban. Second, the United States should urge its allies, Saudi Arabia and Pakistan, to discontinue arming and funding the Taliban. The United States provides assistance and military equipment to these two allies that in turn provide support and arms to the Taliban. Third, the United States should lift the quotas on the number of Afghan refugees. Fourth, the United States should not support UNOCAL or any other company that will be to the Taliban's gain. U.S. corporations should not be allowed to operate in Afghanistan until women's and girls' human rights are restored. Fifth, the United States should not contribute to programs that support the Taliban, such as the programs to counter opium production by creating economic and agricultural alternatives for Afghan people.

When I asked Leno what thought she would like to express for this book, she responded much the same way as other experts in the field have:

> Every person ... should go to their government and tell their government to go to the leaders of Pakistan and tell them to stop funding the Taliban, and this will end tomorrow. The Taliban will either sit down at the table and agree to treat the people in their country according to the same standards that the rest of the world uses or they would simply no longer be able to hold on to power. And our country in particular is well able to do this. We give millions, and millions and millions of dollars to Pakistan. We give them guns. We give them training. I'm not saying it will be easy or uncomplicated, but I am saying that it can be done and it must be done. Because it's all very fine posturing, deploring, and all that stuff makes you look good, and it's free, but this is the deal—it's within our power to do it. People have to tell their governmental officials to do it, and if their governmental officials won't do it, make them say why because we deserve to know who benefits from having these guys in power.[33]

## ORGANIZATIONS

Many organizations work to aid the people of Afghanistan in their struggle. Many of them have always worked for human rights, but now devote specific effort to campaign for women's rights there.

### Defense of Afghan Women's Rights (NEGAR)

This Paris-based group, led by Shoukria Haidar, organized the "Conference for Women of Afghanistan" held in Dushanbe, Tajikistan, on June 27 and 28, 2000. The conference was the culmination of the Women on the Road for Afghanistan initiative.

A trip to Afghanistan on June 29 coincided with the latest summer Taliban offensive north of Kabul, between June 30 and July 1. On July 2, part of the group met with Ahmad Shah Massoud, commander of the Mujahedin resistance forces in Afghanistan. Afghan Radio reported Massoud's position:

> There is no doubt that we have also had our share of internal problems, and that part of this crisis stems from internal causes. But I see the main cause in Pakistan and in foreign aggression. I repeat that as long as the international community does not exert the necessary pressure on Pakistan, and as long as it does not stop the hand of Pakistani interference

in Afghan affairs, it is certain that the flames of war in this country will never be extinguished. On the other hand, we have announced on numerous occasions that the only solution to the Afghan problem is through a peaceful settlement, through negotiations and talks.... And in these talks, the best way is to go toward elections, to go toward a democracy and to allow the people to determine their destiny.[34]

Massoud believes it unfortunate that as a result of misunderstandings, some of our writers and scholars do not realize the depth of the issue of Pakistan's interference.

Women, Massoud says, can play the same effective role as they did during the anti-communist struggle of the Jihad period. Afghan women on the outside can assist women inside the country financially and morally. "There are no problems, you can visit these areas, open schools for girls, establish a college and in so many other ways establish your links and assist them."

Activists from five continents attended the Dushanbe conference to speak out in solidarity with Afghan women against cruel and discriminatory treatment. A charter was drafted "as a basic declaration of rights of Afghan women for all and any governments in power."[35] Afghan women activists and 30 refugees who were leaders in their communities participated in the writing, review and amendment of the first draft of the Declaration of the Essential Rights of Afghan Women (see Appendix B). The declaration did not have signatures, but "was presented to the general assembly of the conference consisting of all the participants, about 250–300 persons. The long standing ovation that followed the reading of the Declaration, filled with cheers, tears streaming from every cheek, hugs, jubilation, applause and in some cases dancing represented the resounding ratification of this Declaration."[36] The non–Afghan group, the Women on the Road for Afghanistan (WORFA), composed a communiqué, condemning the Taliban practices and the silence of the world about it. WORFA is part of the Worldwide March of Women taking place five years after the Beijing Conference on Women.[37] (For a more complete list of participants see Appendix C.)

One very important organization was the Afghan Women's Council (AWC). Other active organizations include the Feminist Majority Foundation; Refugee Women in Development, Inc. (RefWID); Co-operation Centre for Afghanistan (CCA); Educators and the Human Rights Commission in Pakistan; Afghan Women's Network (AWN); Relief Organization for Afghan Orphans and Widows (ROAOW); Revolutionary Association of the Women of Afghanistan (RAWA); and Women's Alliance for Peace and Human Rights in Afghanistan(WAPHA). Three of these groups, CCA, RAWA and ROAOW, publish magazines that "are smuggled back into Afghanistan, a few at a time, under the burqas of women. They are taken secretly from house to house, often whole communities of women sharing one issue" providing "a desperately needed stimulus for discussion and tool for education."[38] Other groups that work vigilantly are the International Centre for Human Rights and Democratic Development (ICHRDD); Amnesty International; the Red Cross; Doctors Without Borders; and Physicians for Human Rights. (See Appendix 1.)

### The Afghan Women's Council (AWC)

The AWC was directed by Massouma Esmaty-Wardak in 1989. Wardak was appointed minister of education in 1990. In its beginnings, AWC was more political and less social and service oriented than it was under previous direction of Dr. Anahita Ratebzad. Social services provided to women included literacy, vocational training, income generating activities, assistance to mothers and widows and legal advice.[39] Wardak wrote a book, *The Position and Role of Afghan Women in Afghan Society: From the Late 18th to the Late 19th Century.*[40]

### The Feminist Majority Foundation

This global organization has a strong agenda for women's rights. It has organized women's rights groups in the United States to campaign on behalf of the women in Afghanistan. Their campaign is patterned after the worldwide effort that helped defeat the system of racial apartheid in South Africa. The foundation's president, Eleanor Smeal, says of the situation of the Afghan women,

> It's so horrific. We thought that as a group if we could not arouse the public on this, then what are we talking about when we say that women are going forward? We have to care about this. I mean, to what level can women be reduced? What's O.K.? If this is O.K., it means we become this class of people that you can do anything to.[41]

The Feminist Majority has raised society's level of consciousness of women's rights issues.

### Refugee Women in Development Inc. (RefWID)

RefWID is an international nonprofit, nongovernmental agency focusing on women caught in conflict and post-conflict reintegration. Established in 1982, RefWID has since pioneered in the field of incorporating refugee women in development. Over the years, RefWID has received several awards and citations for innovative programs and leadership.

"Empowerment of refugee women-led agencies lies at the heart of RefWID's mandate."[42]

In April 1992, RefWID produced *Leadership Development Model for Refugee Women: A Replication Guide*, a manual to help refugee women through workshops share their experiences. RefWID also promotes forums to define women's needs; skills-building workshops; and local and regional networks.[43]

### Co-operation Centre for Afghanistan (CCA)

The CCA produces the women's magazine, *Sadaf*, edited by journalist Homa Zafar. Zafar writes about human rights issues using photographs smuggled out of Afghanistan. The CCA also produces a newsletter.[44] The center is directed by Dr. Amir S. Hassanyar.[45] Nancy Hatch Dupree notes that "Afghan women are fortunate in enjoying" the CCA's "staunch support" of the male-directed agency.[46]

### Women's Alliance for Peace and Human Rights in Afghanistan (WAPHA)

WAPHA was cofounded by Zieba Shorish-Shamley, who is also its executive director. WAPHA works to promote peace and advocate rights for Afghan people with special emphasis on women and children. It also publishes a newsletter and other related materials.[47]

### The Human Rights Commission in Pakistan

*The Chronicle of Higher Education* reported that when Afghanistan's universities closed to women, some female students left Kabul for the Pakistani border city of Peshawar hoping to complete their training. In 1998, the Pakistani government closed all four universities that the exiled academics established for the refugees, alleging "that the institutions were operating illegally, and that they were providing substandard education."[48] The Pakistan government is one of three governments that recognize the Taliban as the legitimate government of Afghanistan. The Taliban and most Pakistanis belong to the same Pushtun ethnic group. The Taliban are mostly from Islamic religious schools, and do not have the same interpretation as those academics in refugee universities. Afrasyab Khattak, regional coordinator of the Human Rights Commission in Pakistan says that Afghan universities are where resistance groups form, but the commission presses the Pakistani government to reopen the refugee universities that serve about 5,000 students, 1,000 of whom are female.

In the past groups of educators attempted to persuade the Taliban leadership to reopen the universities. The male students received instructions to return to Afghanistan and help fight for the remaining five percent of the country that remained under Mujahedin control, and to obtain military training at camps in Khowst run by Osama bin Laden, the Saudi dissident suspected of financing international terrorism. The official position of the Taliban is that the camps were actually religious schools. Human-rights leaders and educators realize these offers may become students' only alternative if the universities do not reopen. Some female students, however, understand that the Taliban realize the desperate need for women doctors, and believe opportunity will eventually occur.

*Afghan Women's Network (AWN)*

In 1996, Pamela Collett, consultant for Save the Children, wrote that, because of 17 years of war, many Afghans have never known peace. One of the most beautiful efforts of Afghan women is their work to reconstruct a vision of peace for themselves, their families and their country. Collett says that, although tradition dictates that women are not major decision makers, "the shredding of their culture and the devastation of their country have pushed them to take steps for peace."[49] In 1995, after a few Afghan women attended the U.N.'s Fourth World Conference on Women, they returned and organized the Afghan Women's Network (AWN). Soon they took steps to try to bring women into the peace process when the then newly formed U.N. Advisory Group on Gender Issues in Afghanistan declined to endorse the idea that Afghan women should be involved in the process. In 1996, the network wrote to Ambassador Mahmoud Mestiri, special envoy of the U.N. Secretary General. Collett reported that the women explained peace "as something built up slowly in communities, based on mutual respect, cooperation and human rights ... complementary to the political process of stopping the fighting." They went on to ask, "Why is the U.N. talking to the warlords about peace? Their lives are based on making money and getting power from war. They don't want peace." Women are not occupied with war the way most men are in that women experience only war's deprivations.

The network was practical in its plan for advocating peace. It requested that Mestiri add a woman to his team because women could not meet with strange men. If he did not add a woman, women would not be participating in the peace process. Afghan women could be organized by a female representative of the U.N. Special Mission, who could in turn work through the shuras (councils) inside Afghanistan and through the refugee camps outside of the country. In 1998, AWN said that it had received verbal assurances from U.N. officials that there should be a woman on the special mission.[50] Meanwhile, the women could visit shrines to pray, and they gathered in front of a famous shrine in Mazar-i-sharif. In addition, they circulated a peace questionnaire to start a grassroots discussion about the topic. Network members who were teachers asked students to write and draw about peace to put into a booklet and to display.

### Relief Organization for Afghan Orphans and Widows (ROAOW)

ROAOW publishes the *Khaharan Women's Journal*, a magazine for Afghan women. A poet, Sajeda Milad, is largely responsible for the production. It covers a wide range of topics from embroidery to women's rights and the war.[51]

### The Revolutionary Association of the Women of Afghanistan (RAWA)

RAWA was established in 1977 "as an independent political organization of Afghan women fighting for human rights and for social justice in Afghanistan."[52] In 1987, RAWA's leading founder, Meena, was assassinated by KGB agents and their fundamentalist accomplices in Quetta, Pakistan.[53] Before the Soviet invasion in 1978, RAWA worked for women's rights and democracy. After the Soviets occupied Afghanistan, RAWA became involved in the war of resistance of Islamic fundamentalists committed to democracy and secularism. During this time, RAWA began working among refugee women in Pakistan, establishing schools, a hospital, and courses for nursing, reading and vocations.

Since the overthrow of the Soviets in 1992 and the fundamentalist factions of the Mujahedin until 1994, RAWA has been waging a political campaign against the Taliban-supported regime. The main goals and objectives of RAWA are:

> To struggle against the Taliban and Jehadi types of the fundamentalists and their foreign masters.
> To establish freedom, democracy, peace and women's rights in Afghanistan.
> To establish an elected secularist government based on democratic values.
> To unite all freedom-loving and democratic forces and to struggle against all those who collaborate with the fundamentalists.
> To struggle against those traitors who want to disintegrate Afghanistan by causing tribal and religious wars.
> To launch educational, health care and income generation projects in and outside the country.
> To support the freedom-loving movements all over the world.[54]

RAWA, now based in the refugee areas of Northwest Pakistan, operates secret schools for girls inside Afghanistan and schools for both boys and girls in refugee camps. RAWA also manages mobile healthcare teams and income-generating projects. Their work is not without risks, which they bravely take. In November 1999, the Taliban summoned women of Kabul to witness the city's first public execution of a woman. A RAWA member attended with a camcorder under her burqa to tape the "grisly proceedings."[55]

Political activism is another aspect of RAWA's work. Campaigns and demonstrations are not uncommon. On December 7, 1999, RAWA headed a letter writing campaign to Hillary Clinton in response to President Clinton's condemnation of human rights abuses in Afghanistan. RAWA urged Mrs. Clinton to involve RAWA and other Afghan women's organizations in policy making and that funding be given directly to the organizations rather than through a U.S. and Pakistan-based organization.[56] On December 11, 1999, International Human Rights Day, RAWA staged protest demonstrations and submitted an 11 point document for a free Afghanistan and a restoration of women's rights.[57] April 28, 1992, is Black Day, the day criminal fundamentalists entered Kabul. RAWA held protest rallies at Islamabad, Washington D.C., Rome and Milan, Italy, against Taliban and Jehadi forces.[58]

RAWA activism is sometimes noted by governments. Earlier in April 1992, the prime minister of France through the National Advisory Commission on Human Rights awarded RAWA the French Republic's Liberty, Equality, Fraternity Human Rights Prize. The honor was among the first presented by a country in the West. Prime Minister Laurent Fabius wrote, "This distinction is to reward your concrete, necessary and courageous action in Pakistan."[59]

Sally Ingalls says of RAWA, "Despite the overwhelming forces of repression against them, Afghan women do have a voice, albeit one that is largely ignored by the international community and the United Nations. Risking death threats and other intimidation tactics, RAWA bravely stand their ground."[60] Other scholars echo research by Ingalls on RAWA's courage and ensuing results. Nancy Hatch Dupree writes of RAWA's demonstrations, "from which they inevitably emerge bloodied." Hafizullah Emadi believes that their work is so worthwhile that individuals using their material should make a donation to their cause.[61]

## Rebuilding a Society

Some experts on Afghanistan are uncertain what leadership potential is available that will contribute to an Afghanistan that would be independent and reflect the wishes of its citizenry. Most believe that the international community led by the United States will play a critical part. Afghan women represent about half the population, but their participation in rebuilding their society presents unanswered questions for a culture seeking to rebuild. Changing women's roles will cause a political response. One hopes that women can participate in the transition to help insure the permanence of positive change.

## WOMEN'S MOVEMENT

Post World War II development gave impetus to women's movements in Afghanistan. As women worked outside of the home, they became more aware that they did not have equal rights with males. Effective organized women's movements occurred after the enactment of the 1964 constitution.[62] Hahzullah Emadi says that development of Afghanistan's political economy, social, cultural and educational arenas is uneven. The unevenness is reflected in the women's movement. Women of the upper and middle classes have led the struggle for equality, since women from low income families must focus on survival. The women's movements lacked unity from within and the Soviet occupation in 1979 hurt them.[63] For women in rural areas, employment and education are not issues because they always work on the land and parent. In urban areas women gradually entered the workforce in traditional roles, with a minority in the professions. Peter Marsden believes that tradition held because of "a fear that, if women were educated or worked, they would be influenced by Western and secular ideas and would instill these into their children."[64]

Afghan women have a remarkably strong history of working to improve their status, and have continued their efforts through many regimes, including the Soviet invasion and occupation and the Taliban supported government. Organizations play a critical role in women's movements. The Afghan Women's Network and the Revolutionary Association of the Women of Afghanistan are but two of the organizations that have remained active during the Taliban era.

Some groups, whether they be organizations, refugee women or a minority of educated Afghan women, will bear the brunt of rebuilding their country. These groups have fueled the ire of structural forces and challenged prevailing cultural roles. Their courage is based in a respect and love for their country. In 1996, the Afghan Women's Network described women and girls as being under siege by the Taliban, leading one woman to call Kabul "the biggest prison for women in the world."[65]

## CHANGE AND REBUILDING WOMEN'S ROLES

In 1992, Nancy Hatch Dupree believed Afghanistan stood on the threshold of peace, ready to rebuild. Repair of physical damage appeared to be the most "manageable," the political structure "vexing" and rebonding social institutions "fraught" with problems, with women's voices barely heard.[66] The future role of women will depend on the composition of the leadership, a factor that remains uncertain. Women's issues are highly politicized. Rules perceived as violated by women often involve punishment for their male protectors. On the leadership level, moderates did not speak out in the early 1990s for fear of being assassinated. Subsequent events did not permit the peace rebuilding. In fact, continued conflict, killings and destruction have plagued Afghanistan since then.

Sue Emmott believes that the strength of women's networks in the way they help their members through trauma comes from the women themselves.[67] Dupree saw the active and outspoken refugee women as a meaningful signal for the future, a beginning of the politicization of Afghan women. However, these women must move carefully. Their needs are great, implementation is difficult, and support minimal. They have a most difficult task of convincing assistance communities, motivating traditional women in their own groups, and combatting the perception that Western motives are to destroy Islam through aid programs, and that the unsuccessful Afghan governments were helped by Western forces in creating the current chaos and suffering. When the female refugee leaders of all classes return home, many members of their families will have no concept of the "refugee mentality," including such ideas as women producing items for sale, working outside the home, implementing programs where benefits do not fall solely to men and extending other traditional boundaries. Dupree believes the refugee women are aware of the problems and that their involvement in program planning is necessary. Their pragmatic pleas focus on more security, cultural tolerance toward the hejab, and support for Islamic education focused on women's rights within Islam.

If women are to be involved in their development after repatriation, new attitudes toward responsibility and commitment need to be included. The family will remain the single most important institution of Afghanistan, and motherhood will remain the primary option for most women. Thus, for some women, a conflict will not arise, but others will face challenges. The Afghan society as a whole, rather than specific segments, needs to debate human rights. A just legal system must be developed and women's voices should be heard.

In 1996, as Afghanistan stood in the context of past Soviet occupation and Taliban-supported control, Audrey C. Shalinsky proposed that the Afghans "live a complex existence that forces them to confront, draw upon, and rework different identity constructs—national, ethnic, racial, class and religious."[68] She examines the life of one young Afghan woman, Nadia, who migrated to the United States after the Soviet occupation. Afghans who are refugees, diasporic, without territorial homelands, and immigrants are "culturally displaced." Gender roles are renegotiated. In migration, a woman may gain autonomy but lose emotional support from others. In the Afghan culture, a woman may live surrounded by other women, family and friends, and when she becomes a part of a culture in which she is alone for most of the day, she may grow profoundly ambivalent. The ambivalence is displayed, for example, in veiling behavior. In the United States, a woman is not required to veil, but she will veil at prayer times in the home, the very place she was not restricted before. As most researchers must conclude, Shalinsky says her research is conducted on an evolving axis and presented without knowing the ending to Nadia's existence. An Iranian native and researcher who did want to be identified by name compares the movements in the two societies:

> In the Iranian situation, because the society is more developed than Afghanistan, it [oppression of women] was obvious (at least in my mind) that it would not last for long. And, as you may have heard from the reports, Iranian women are very much involved in the current reform/ opposition movement. In fact, along with the youth and university students, Iranian women constitute one of the key social forces demanding the reforms and changes. The process of reform and change in Iran will, I think, influence many other Islamic-theocratic movements/governments around the world, including Afghanistan. In a way, I would say, the women's situation in Iran (the degree of their oppression and the subsequent mobilization and demand for reform and change) can be used as a rough analogy for the future of Afghan women. The big question is what is the time horizon? That is to say, the question is not one of "if," but "when"? Given the fact that Afghanistan, in comparison to Iran, is somewhat less developed, it may take more time,... but one can only keep human spirit and aspirations chained for some time, certainly not for as long as the oppressors would wish to do despite their monopoly of the means of violence.

## The Role of the International Community

In 1994, Sima Wali wrote that repatriation depends on two elements: internal security and financial commitment from the international community. The United States must lead the way in working for peace by involving the moderate and politically unaligned Afghans from existing factions who have been left out of the process. She writes:

> If the international community is to make a difference in ending the prolonged suffering of the Afghan people, especially its women, it must commit to supporting a process to create a popularly elected platform of leadership committed to democratic values and principles, as well as respect for human rights and equity. Neither politics nor shifting global economics should be used to capitulate to oppression, nor should they dictate and drive humanitarian intervention.[69]

Wali says that women and children are affected the worst whether they are located inside Afghanistan or in the refugee camps. Most refugee camps are composed of at least 75 percent women and children. In 1994, there were more than three million refugees in Pakistan and 2.5 million in Iran. Wali estimates that "equivalent numbers of the internally displaced are female." She advocates that women from the international community work for "direct communication, linkage and partnership with Afghan women."

Because the United States has formed an alliance with Russia and China to block the growing threat of global terrorism, other issues may have an opportunity to be resolved. The countries who joined together in 2001, the United States, Russia, China, Turkey, Israel, India and Iran, want the Taliban's present leadership undermined, bin Laden extradited to the United States and an end to the 20-year conflict. Ahmed Rashid prophesized that this unprecedented and surprising alliance may force the world to return to Afghanistan.[70]

In 2000, Peter Tomsen wrote that the Taliban movement is on the decline, but the challenge lies in who will take their place.[71] In an interview Tomsen said:

> My idea would be there has to be a broad based responsible regime which replaces the Taliban, and only then will you be able to address not only gender discrimination, human rights, but also the huge opium problem, security, terrorism that Afghanistan is in a situation now where there has to be a stable regime which is supported by most Afghans. It will never be supported by all Afghans. Then when you get a government like that, you can address all of these issues. It can't be a government like the Taliban which is imposed from the outside. If change is going to come in these problem areas, it's going to come with a new regime which is supported by Afghans and is stable. You can't deal with the Talibans to reverse them on human rights or gender rights or terrorism, giving us [Osama] bin Laden, it's not going to work.[72]

Ansar Rahel has argued that promising to "work with" the militant Taliban in exchange for terrorist bin Laden translates into treating the

Taliban as if they constituted Afghanistan's lawful government, and is not likely to restore human rights or bring peace in 1999.[73]

The Feminist Majority leads the Campaign to Stop Gender Apartheid, bringing together over 180 human rights and women's organizations in the United States and from around the world. Their demand is that the human rights abuses against women and girls end. "Their campaign has helped stop the U.S. and the United Nations from officially recognizing the Taliban until human rights have been restored."[74] The organizations in the campaign include Amnesty International USA, Human Rights Watch, the International Women's Human Rights Law Clinic, the National Alliance for Peace and Human Rights in Afghanistan, and the World Council of Muslim Women Foundation.

Mavis Leno became interested in women in Afghanistan within the Feminist Majority she says,

> ...because I wanted an organization which was paying some attention to the situation of women in other countries besides this one, because I felt that the most important thing that feminists could do right now were two things: 1) consolidate our own position, very important and 2) help other women follow the same road in other countries by establishing a situation in their society where they can have an equal voice in the affairs of the society and so, ultimately in their own fate, and, really, pretty much every country in the world has a feminist organization. And their goals in each country differ according to the culture, the religious beliefs and so forth of that country. So, by that, I certainly don't mean that how women live in the United States has anything to do with how women should live in other countries. Simply that however people live in other countries should be equally decided by the men and women of that country.[75]

When Leno learned of the Afghan situation, she said that "everything just fell into place for me," because their circumstance was exactly the kind of human rights issue that was a very strong interest of hers.

The Feminist Majority Foundation President Eleanor Smeal and other organization leaders met with President Bill Clinton in March of 1999.[76] Leno says her organization presented the president with "a list, almost a little position paper" of issues they believed he would be able to address. The Feminist Majority learned through Afghan contacts that it couldn't get relatives into the United States. Leno says, "We decided to see if we could find what the numbers were for the number of people that were being allowed in, and we discovered that no people had been allowed in from Afghanistan." Ultimately the State Department decided to let appreciably more Afghans into the United States, because of the imminent danger to their lives.

Leno says in addition to increasing the number of Afghan immigrants allowed in the United States, the State Department agreed that "for every scholarship we could get at a college for a girl from Afghanistan, they would bring the girl in to the United States." The Feminist Majority Foundation launched its Afghan Women's Scholarship Program at the Expo 2000 in Baltimore, introducing the first Afghan scholarship awardee.

Leno says that these are some of the issues the Feminist Majority has been able to address to lighten the load a little bit. One of the first aims the organization has succeeded in very dramatically is to let people know what was happening to Afghan women, and motivate them to exert "unrelenting pressure on the government to act on it in any way that was possible." Leno says, "We have really gotten the word out and we have really seen to it that there is now absolutely no chance that the Taliban is going to be recognized as the legal government of Afghanistan by our country or any other Western country."

In 2000, while the overall situation in Afghanistan remained unacceptable, small improvements were noted by U.N. official John Renninger. In 1999, about 40 female medical students were allowed to finish their education. A nursing school had been opened in Kandahar for 50 female and 50 male nurses. Community-based schools for boys and girls had been established in some communities. Home-based crafts offered the only opportunities for women's employment. Women had no access to markets, due to their confinement. Although the Taliban policy basically remains unchanged, Richard Holbrooke told the Security Council, "Due to the efforts of the United Nations and the non-governmental organization community, there were signs of modest improvement, at least in terms of informal educational opportunities for girls and a trend towards improved access to medical treatment for women and girls."[77] Yet, Lloyd Axworthy, the minister for foreign affairs of Canada, noted that overall literacy rates were estimated at 30 percent, and for women, 13 percent. Maternal mortality rates in Afghanistan were the second highest in the world.

Zieba Shorish-Shamley, co-founder and executive director of the Women's Alliance for Peace and Human Rights in Afghanistan, in 1998 spoke of her efforts for the return of a group of 8,000 rare books to the city of Herat, once Afghanistan's cultural capital. These books, she said, were for sale in the United States, and were illegally acquired or stolen from Herat's libraries and homes under the Taliban's rule.[78]

In 1998, Nancy Hatch Dupree reported some progress regarding women's employment. An estimated 40,000 to 150,000 women were affected by prohibition on employment. The Taliban said that it would continue to pay female government employees, but women could not work in government offices in the future. Dupree believes that harsh realities forced modifications. Internally displaced persons and homeless returning refugees crowded into Kabul and were faced with limited earning opportunities. Neither government services nor family networks survived. Thus, she reports that in January 1997, the International Committee of the Red Cross (ICRC) estimated 50,000 widows, averaging seven to nine children each in Kabul.[79]

## Health Care

There are credible reports that by the end of 1999 restrictions on health care for women were not applied in practice, and that some improvement existed in access to health care. Kabul hospitals were reported to treat women, but there is only one maternity hospital in the country.[80]

"Women and children form the great majority of refugee populations all over the world and are especially vulnerable to violence and exploitation,"[81] according to the United Nations. In refugee camps, they are raped, abused and forced into prostitution by military and immigration personnel, bandit groups, male refugees and rival ethnic groups. The special rapporteur proposes improvement of refugee camp security, deployment of trained female officers at all points of the refugees' journey, participation of women in organizational structures of the camps and prosecution of government and military personnel responsible for abuse against refugee women.

Author Geraldine Brooks reminds us that cultural relativism should not allow the local despot to define human rights. Are human rights the fight of Westerners? As a mental test Brooks reverses the gender: "If some ninety million little boys were having their penises amputated, would the world have acted to prevent it by now? You bet."[82] Mutilation of any kind is not cultural relativism. It is a violation of human rights.

## A Human Rights Issue

The plight of Afghan women is indeed a human rights issue. Celebrities often help create a milieu for change and help influence policy makers. When the serious press failed to adequately cover the plight of the women of Afghanistan, In 2000, in an interview with the author, Mavis Leno said, "You know what? We're going to fly under their radar, because Jay and I are going to give a big lump sum to this cause, and then we are going to put Jay's publicist on it, who's a show business publicist, and we're not going to go through the serious press. We're going to put it on *Entertainment Tonight.* We're going to get it in *People Magazine.* We're going to go with the popular press." To Leno, the women's story was "a very remarkable and horrifying story and even in terms of human rights, it was unique in a lot of ways, and I could not believe that other people, especially other women, hearing this, would not have that same reaction. And that was exactly it. It hit everybody exactly the way that it hit me, that these women are benign, hard working women." Leno told *People Weekly* that she spoke out because "the silence is killing these women.... The bravery of these women is stunning. I firmly believe we are their last hope."

## *Conclusion*

As out attention turns to a new era in Afghanistan with the Taliban no longer ruling, we must also focus on the role Afghan women must play in reconstructing their society and its government. On October 12, 2001, president Eleanor Smeal stated on the Feminist Majority web site:

> A democratic, civil society cannot exist in Afghanistan if women—a large portion of its healthcare workers and educators—are not utilized. The restoration of a broad-based democracy, representative of both ethnic minorities and women, with women at the table, is necessary to break the back of a terrorist and a war-torn existence.

If the Taliban fall from power, they must be replaced with a government that restores women to their rightful place in Afghan society. Such a government must be democratically elected and not be controlled by external forces.

The Afghan women know that their hope for a peaceful, prosperous and happy life depends on having a government that respects and empowers them. Until then, they continue to show their strength as they do what is necessary to survive another day.

# Appendix A: Selected Organizations That Provide Information on Afghanistan*

**Afghan Radio**
e-mail: azadi@afghanradio.com; web site: http://www.afghanradio.com

**Afghan Web**
e-mail: qazi@afghan-web.com; web site: http://www.afghan-web.com

**Afghanistan Foundation**
209 Pennsylvania Avenue, SE, Suite 700, Washington, D.C. 20003; tel.: (202) 543-1177; fax: (202) 543-7931; e-mail: dyaqub@afghanistanfoundation.org; web site: http://www.afghanistanfoundation.org.

**Amnesty International**
322 8th Ave., New York, N. Y., 10001; tel.: (212) 807-8400; fax: (212) 463-9193/(212) 627-1451; or 600 Pennsylvania Ave. SE, 5th floor, Washington, D.C. 20003; tel.: (202) 544-0200; fax: (202) 546-7142; email: admin-us@aiusa.org; web site: www.amnesty.org. (See web site for specific country addresses.)

**Co-operation Centre for Afghanistan**
GPO, P.O. Box 1378 Peshawar, Pakistan; tel: 92-091-816386/815647; fax: 92-091-816386; e-mail: hussaini@pes.comsats.net.pk; web site: http://www.ccamata.com.

*Information on organizations came from: "Advocacy Work Is Essential for Safeguarding the Human Rights That Are Guaranteed to All People Through the U.N. Universal Declaration of Human Rights," Lifting the Veil of Silence Bulletin, Women for Women in Afghanistan, sent via e-mail by Janice Eisenhauer, Women for Women in Afghanistan, Calgary, Jan. 9, 2000; Haron Amin, (Afghan diplomat, first secretary, Islamic State of Afghanistan, United Nations), interview by the author, Feb. 3, 2000; and Abdul Raheem Yaseer (coordinator of International Exchange Programs, and deputy director of the Center for Afghanistan Studies at the University of Nebraska at Omaha), interview by the author, Apr. 13, 2000. See also: Diane Birrell and Stephen Hunt, "Afghanistan," Emporia State University, Kansas: School of Library and Information Management. Available: http://slim2.emporia.edu/globenet/audits/afghanistan/afghan.htm, Jun. 19, 2000.

**Defense of Afghan Women's Rights (NEGAR)**
Ms. Shoukria Haidar, B.P. 10, 25770 Franois, France; tel. 01-48-350-756.

**Doctors Without Borders**
6 East 39th Street, 8th Floor, New York, NY 10016; tel: (212) 679-6800, fax: (212) 679-7016, e-mail: doctors@newyork.msf.org; web site: www.dwb.org or see: http://www.msf.org/intweb99/going/projects/afghani3.htm. (See web site for specific country addresses.)

**Feminist Majority Foundation**
Afghanistan Campaign, 1600 Wilson Boulevard, Suite 801, Arlington, VA 22209; tel: (703) 522-2214; e-mail: hghaus@feminist.org; web site: www.feminist.org or see: http://www.feminist.org/afghan/intro.html.

**Help the Afghan Children**
8133 Leesburg Pike, Suite 310, Vienna, VA 22182; tel: (703) 848-0407; fax: (703) 848-0408; email: htaci@msn.com or suraya@helptheafghanchildren.org; web site: www.htaci.com.

**International Centre for Human Rights and Democratic Development Centre**
63, Rue de Bresoles, Montreal, Que. Canada, H2Y1V7; tel: (514) 283-6073; fax: (514) 283-3792; e-mail: ichrdd@ichrdd.ca; web site: www.ichrdd.ca.

**Islamic Center of Southern California**
434 S. Vermont Ave., Los Angeles, CA. 90020; tel: (213) 382-9200; fax (213) 384-4572; e-mail: icsc@islamctr.org; web site: http://www.islamctr.org/icsc.

**National Afghanistan Women's Organization and the Afghan Women's Counseling and Integration Community Support Organization**
2333 Dundas Street West, Suite 205A, Toronto, ON, Canada. M6R3A6; (416) 588-3585.

**Physicians for Human Rights (PHR)**
100 Boylston Street, Suite 702, Boston, MA 02116, tel: (617) 695-0041; web site: www.phrusa.org/.

**Refugee Women in Development, Inc.**
5225 Wisconsin Avenue, NW, Suite 502, Washington, D.C. 20015; tel: (703) 931-6442; e-mail: refwid@erols.com.

**Revolutionary Association of the Women of Afghanistan**
P.O. Box 374, Quetta, Pakistan; mobile: 092-300-551638; fax: 001-760-2819855; e-mails: rawa@rawa.org, rawa@geocities.com; web site: http://www.rawa.org; mirror site: http://members.xoom.com/ra_wa.

**Women for Women in Afghanistan**
Bankview P.O. Box 32014, 2619-14 Street SW, Calgary, AB, Canada T2T5X6; tel: (403) 228-4622; fax (403) 229-3037; email: eisenhauer@praxis.ca; web site: www. womenasia.com/w4wafghan.

**Women Living Under Muslim Laws**
International Coordination Office, WLUML, BP 20023, 34791 Grabels Cedex, France; web site: http://wluml.org/ENGblurb.html.

**Women on the Road for Afghanistan**
email: info@worfa.org; web site: http://worfa.free.fr/.

**Women's Alliance for Peace and Human Rights in Afghanistan**
P.O. Box 77057, Washington, D.C. 20013-7057; tel: (202) 882-1432; web site: http://www.wapha.org.

# Appendix B: Notes from the 2000 Conference for Women of Afghanistan*

The Conference for Women of Afghanistan took place in Dushanbe, Tajikistan, June 27 and 28, 2000. This appendix contains the text of the "Declaration of the Essential Rights of Afghan Women" as well as some information on the conference participants.

## Declaration of the Essential Rights of Afghan Women

### SECTION I

Considering that the Universal Declaration of Human Rights, as well as the international statements addressing the rights of women listed in Section II of this document, are systematically trampled in Afghanistan today.

---

*"The second day of the conference [in Dushanbe] was chaired by Nasrine Gross. The task of the day was for the Afghan women to draft a charter of the fundamental rights of Afghan women and for the non–Afghans to draw up a communique of their stand. The charter was prepared as first draft by Shoukria Haidar and Nasrine Gross mostly from UN documents but with consultation with two of the non–Afghans, Annie Sugier (who has a lot of experience having started with Simone de Beauvoir, mother of Feminism) and Mary Quin, a representative of Feminist Majority and president of 100 Heroines. Then, in a closed session, the charter was reviewed, edited and amended with a solely Afghan group composed of all those from the United States and France and about 25 women representing major groups of refugees. Finally, the resulting document, 'Declaration of the Essential Rights of Afghan Women' was presented to the general assembly of the conference consisting of all the participants, about 250–300 persons. The long standing ovation that followed the reading of the Declaration, filled with cheers, tears streaming from every cheek, hugs, jubilation, applause and in some cases dancing represented the resounding ratification of this Declaration." (Nasrine Abou-Bakre Gross, "Conference in Dushanbe for Women of Afghanistan," report based on eyewitness knowledge as attendee of the conference, Aug. 2, 2000, email to the author, Aug. 2, 2000.)*

Considering that all the rules imposed by the Taliban concerning women are in total opposition to the international conventions cited in Section II of this document.

Considering that torture and inhumane and degrading treatment imposed by the Taliban on women, as active members of society, have put Afghan society in danger.

Considering that the daily violence directed against the women of Afghanistan causes, for each one of them, a state of profound distress.

Considering that, under conditions devoid of their rights, women find themselves and their children in a situation of permanent danger.

Considering that discrimination on the basis of gender, race, religion, ethnicity and language is the source of insults, beatings, stoning and other forms of violence.

Considering that poverty and the lack of freedom of movement pushes women into prostitution, involuntary exile, forced marriages, and the selling and trafficking of their daughters.

Considering the severe and tragic conditions of more than twenty years of war in Afghanistan.


## Section II

The Declaration which follows is derived from the following documents:

- United Nations Charter
- Universal Declaration of Human Rights
- International Covenant on Economic, Social and Cultural Rights
- International Covenant on Civil and Political Rights
- Convention on the Rights of the Child
- Convention on the Elimination of All Forms of Discrimination Against Women
- Declaration on the Elimination of Violence Against Women
- The Human Rights of Women
- The Beijing Declaration
- The Afghan Constitution of 1964
- The Afghan Constitution of 1977

## SECTION III

The fundamental right of Afghan women, as for all human beings, is life with dignity, which includes the following rights:

1. The right to equality between men and women and the right to the elimination of all forms of discrimination and segregation, based on gender, race or religion.
2. The right to personal safety and to freedom from torture or inhumane or degrading treatment.
3. The right to physical and mental health for women and their children.
4. The right to equal protection under the law.
5. The right to institutional education in all the intellectual and physical disciplines.
6. The right to just and favorable conditions of work.
7. The right to move about freely and independently.
8. The right to freedom of thought, speech, assembly and political participation.
9. The right to wear or not to wear the veil or the scarf.
10. The right to participate in cultural activities including theatre, music and sports.

## SECTION IV

This Declaration developed by Afghan women is a statement, affirmation and emphasis of those essential rights that we Afghan women own for ourselves and for all other Afghan women. It is a document that the State of Afghanistan must respect and implement.

This document, at this moment in time, is a draft that, in the course of time, will be amended and completed by Afghan women.

For further information, please contact:

Ms. Shoukria Haidar
NEGAR Organization
B.P. 10
25770 Franois, France
Tel. 01 48 350 756

## Participants

The conference was attended by a number of Afghan women from the United States and Europe, more than 250 Afghan refugee women in Dushanbe and by more than 40 women and two men, from France, England, Spain, Algeria and the United States. The participants from the West are activists in their own countries.

> The Afghans consisted of Shoukria Haidar, the president of NEGAR, Shekeba Hashemi, Manilla Khaled, Dr. Maliha Zulfacar, Hassina Sherjan Samad and Nasrine Gross. Some of the non–Afghans were Patricia Lalonde, Constance Borde, Mary Quin, Juliette Mince, Annie Sugier, Francoise Causse, Gerard Cardeau, Chantal Veron, Lucette and Roland Fremont, Elizabeth Cazeau, Khalida Messaoudi and others. The conference and its Women on the Road for Afghanistan initiative, some of whose main supporters and organizers, from the inception, were Patricia Lalonde, Constance Borde, Ellie Shaetter and Mary Quin, were advertised through the internet and other media for about five months and admission was open. Thanks to the effort of these women, a large number of women's organizations had joined in solidarity with the women of Afghanistan, such as the Feminist Caucus, Femmes Solidaires, International Women's Rights, Iranian Women's League, RACHDA (Algeria), RTV-21 Prishtina (Kosovo), Women's Network Angola, Feminist Majority Foundation, etc.(*) Many of the non–Afghans in the conference were representatives of these organizations.

# Appendix C: Some of the Restrictions and Decrees Imposed by the Taliban

## Some of the Restrictions*

1. Complete ban on women's work outside the home, which also applies to female teachers, engineers and most professionals. Only a few female doctors and nurses are allowed to work in some hospitals in Kabul.

2. Complete ban on women's activity outside the home unless accompanied by a mahram (close male relative such as a father, brother or husband).

3. Ban on women dealing with male shopkeepers.

4. Ban on women being treated by male doctors.

5. Ban on women studying at schools, universities or any other educational institution. (Taliban have converted girls' schools into religious seminaries.)

6. Requirement that women wear a long veil (Burqa), which covers them from head to toe.

7. Whipping, beating and verbal abuse of women not clothed in accordance with Taliban rules, or of women unaccompanied by a mahram.

8. Whipping of women in public for having non-covered ankles.

9. Public stoning of women accused of having sex outside marriage. (A number of lovers have been stoned to death under this rule.)

*Revolutionary Association of the Women of Afghanistan, "Some of the Restrictions Imposed by Taliban on Women in Afghanistan." Available: http://rawa.org/rules.htm, Apr. 3, 2000.

10. Ban on the use of cosmetics. (Many women with painted nails have had fingers cut off.)

11. Ban on women talking or shaking hands with non-mahram males.

12. Ban on women laughing loudly. (No stranger should hear a woman's voice.)

13. Ban on women wearing high heel shoes, which would produce sound while walking. (A man must not hear a woman's footsteps.)

14. Ban on women riding in a taxi without a mahram.

15. Ban on women's presence in radio, television or public gatherings of any kind.

16. Ban on women playing sports or entering a sport center or club.

17. Ban on women riding bicycles or motorcycles, even with their mahrams.

18. Ban on women's wearing brightly colored clothes. In Taliban terms, these are "sexually attracting colors."

19. Ban on women gathering for festive occasions such as the Eids, or for any recreational purpose.

20. Ban on women washing clothes next to rivers or in a public place.

21. Modification of all place names including the word "women." For example, "women's garden" has been renamed "spring garden."

22. Ban on women appearing on the balconies of their apartments or houses.

23. Compulsory painting of all windows, so women cannot be seen from outside their homes.

24. Ban on male tailors taking women's measurements or sewing women's clothes.

25. Ban on female public baths.

26. Ban on males and females traveling on the same bus. Public buses have now been designated "males only" (or "females only").

27. Ban on flared (wide) pant-legs, even under a burqa.

28. Ban on the photographing or filming of women.

29. Ban on women's pictures printed in newspapers and books, or hung on the walls of houses and shops.

In addition:

30. Ban on listening to music, not only for women but men as well.

31. Ban on the watching of movies, television and videos, for everyone.

32. Ban on celebrating the traditional new year (Nowroz) on March 21. The Taliban have proclaimed the holiday un–Islamic.

33. Disavowal of Labor Day (May 1st), because it is deemed a "communist" holiday.

34. Order that all people with non–Islamic names change them to Islamic ones.

35. Order that all Afghan youth will have their hair cut in a prescribed manner.

36. Order that men wear Islamic clothes and a cap.

37. Order that men not shave or trim their beards, which should grow long enough to protrude from a fist clasped at the point of the chin.

38. Order that all people attend prayers in mosques five times daily.

39. Ban on the keeping of pigeons and playing with the birds, describing it as un–Islamic. The violators will be imprisoned and the birds shall be killed. Kite flying has also been stopped.

40. Order that all onlookers, while encouraging sportsmen, will chant "Allah-o-Akbar" (God is great) and refrain from clapping.


## Summary of Taliban Decrees*

The following 16 decrees came from the office of Amr Bel Maruf wa Nai Az Munkar (Ministry for the Promotion of Virtue and the Prevention of Vice, also known as the Religious Police). The decrees, in a literal translation by the Agency Co-ordinating Body for Afghan Relief office on 6 January 1997, show a number of close parallels with the previously listed restrictions.

1. To prevent sedition and female uncovers. No drivers are allowed to pick up female who are using Iranian Burqa [chador]. In the case of violation the driver will be imprisoned. If such kind of female are observed in the street, their house will be found and their husbands punished.

2. To prevent music. In shops, hotels, vehicles and rickshaws cassettes and music are prohibited. If any music cassette is found in a shop, the shopkeeper should be imprisoned and the shop shut.

---

*Media Action International, "Tali-bans," Oct. 16, 1999, extract from the Essential Field Guide to Afghanistan. Available: http://www.mediaaction.org/pubcn/efgafghn/taliban.htm, Aug. 12, 2000.

3. To prevent beard shaving and its cutting. If anyone is observed with a shaved and/or cut beard, they should be arrested and imprisoned until their beard gets bushy.

4. To prevent not-praying and order gathering pray at the bazaar. Pray should be done on their due times in all districts. If young people are seen in the shops they will be immediately imprisoned. If five people guarantee their good character, the person should be released, otherwise the criminal will be imprisoned for ten days.

5. To prevent keeping pigeons and playing with birds. This habit/hobby should be stopped. After ten days this matter should be monitored and the pigeons and any other playing birds should be killed.

6. To eradicate the use of addiction and its user. Addicts should be imprisoned and investigation made to find the suppliers and the shops involved. The shop should be locked and both criminals (the owner and the user) should be imprisoned and punished.

7. To prevent kite flying. Advise the people of its useless consequences such as betting, death of children and their deprivation from education. The kite shops in the city should be abolished.

8. To prevent idolatry. In the vehicle, shops, room, hotels and any other places, pictures/portraits should be abolished. The monitors should tear up all pictures in the above places. The vehicle will be stopped if any idol is found in the vehicles.

9. To prevent gambling. The main centres should be found and the gamblers imprisoned for one month.

10. To prevent the British and American hair style. People with long hair should be arrested and taken to the Religious Police department to shave their hair. The criminal has to pay the barber.

11. To prevent interest charge on loans, charge on changing small denomination notes and charge on money orders. All money exchangers should be informed that the above three types of exchanging the money are prohibited in Islam. In the case of violation the criminal will be imprisoned for a long time.

12. To prevent washing cloth by young ladies along the water streams in the city. Violator ladies should be picked up with respectful Islamic manner, taken to their houses and their husbands severely punished.

13. To prevent music and dances in wedding parties. The above two things should be prevented. In the case of violation the head of the family will be arrested and punished.

14. To prevent the playing of music drum. If anybody does so, decision will be left to the religious elders.

15. To prevent sewing ladies cloth and taking female body measures by tailor. If women or fashion magazines are seen in the shop the tailor should be imprisoned.

16. To prevent sorcery. All the related books should be burnt and the magician should be imprisoned until his repentance.

# Glossary

*Note on spelling:* In general, I used the spellings reflecting the source cited.

| | |
|---|---|
| **burqa** | Arabic term for a large head-to-toe pleated garment designed to cover a woman's body completely |
| **chadari** | or chaadaree, or chadori, large head-to-toe pleated garment designed to cover a woman's body completely |
| **chader** | or chaadar or chadar, large shawl-like head scarf draped over the hair, leaving face exposed and covering about three fourths of the body; can be drawn over face when needed |
| **hejab** | or hejaab, general Arabic term for body covering |
| **Jihad** | or Jihaad, Islamic holy war |
| **Khalq** | one of the communist political parties whose founders believed that women belonged at home, and no women were followers |
| **madrassas** | religious (Islamic) schools in Pakistan |
| **mahr** | payment that the husband makes to the wife as part of the marriage contract |
| **mahram** | male family member |
| **mosques** | religious houses |
| **Mujahedin** | or Mujahideen, or Mujahedeen, freedom fighters (Pakistan-based Islamic party); any Muslim who fights a jihad, *singular* Mujahid or Mujahed |
| **mullahs** | religious leaders |

**paarda**      in Afghan *Dari*, known also as hejab, Islamic practice of covering one's head

**Parcham**     one of the communist political parties whose origins were progressive, with women serving on its councils

**purdah**      literal meaning, curtain; practice of secluding women inside their homes; includes veiling in public places

**Pushtun**     an ethnic group of Afghanistan

**shura**       council formed for a particular purpose

# Notes

## Preface

1. Revolutionary Association of the Women of Afghanistan, "Biography of Martyred Meena, Founding Leader of RAWA." Available: http://rawa.fancymarketing. net/meena.html, Oct. 8, 2001. Reprinted with permission from RAWA.

2. Peter Marsden, *The Taliban: War, Religion and the New Order in Afghanistan* (Karachi, Lahore, Islamabad: Oxford University Press, London and New York: Zed Books Ltd., 1998), 99–100.

## Introduction

1. Nasrine Abou-Bakre Gross, interview by the author, July 16, 2000.

2. Electric Library Presents Encylcopedia.com. "Afghanistan (History)" (New York: Columbia University Press, 1994). Available: http://www.encyclopedia.com/articles/00164.html, Apr. 24, 2000; Afghan-Info.com, "Afghan Politics," Jan. 30, 2000. Online. Internet. Available: http://www.afghan-info.com/afgpolitics. htm, Feb. 5, 2000; Online Center for Afghan Studies, "Yearly (Brief and Detailed) Chronology of Events in Afghanistan," 2000. Available: http://www.afghan-politics. or/Reference/Chronology/ChronoShort.htm, Jun. 12, 2000.

3. Ralph H. Magnus and Eden Naby, *Afghanistan: Mullah, Marx, and Mujahid* (Boulder, Colo.: Westview Press, 1998), 24.

4. Peter Hopkirk, *The Great Game: The Struggle for Empire in Central Asia* (New York, N.Y.: Kodansha International, 1992), xv.

5. Electric Library Presents Encyclopedia.com. "Afghanistan (History)"; Afghan-Info.com, "Afghan Politics," Jan. 30, 2000.

6. Haron Amin (Afghan diplomat, first secretary, Islamic State of Afghanistan, United Nations), interview by the author, Feb. 3, 2000.

7. Muslim Women's League, "Crisis in Afghanistan," Nov. 1996. Available: http://www.mwlusa.org/news_agghan.shtml, Apr. 26, 2000.

8. Hopkirk, xv, xviii.

9. Louis Dupree, *Afghanistan* (Princeton, N.J.: Princeton University Press, 1980), xx.

10. CIA, *The World Factbook 2001*—"Afghanistan," Jan. 1, 2001. Available: http://www.cia.gov/cia/publications/factbook/geos/af.html , Jan. 28, 2000 and Oct. 6, 2001; U.S. Department of State, Bureau of Democracy, Human Rights, and Labor, *1999 Country Reports on Human Rights Practices: Afghanistan*, Feb. 25, 2000. Available: http://www.state.gov/www/global/human_rights/1999_hrp_report/afghanis.html, Feb. 25, 2000.

11. Jan Goodwin, *Price of Honor: Muslim Women Lift the Veil of Silence on the Islamic World* (Boston: Little, Brown, 1994) 77.

12. Pam Constable, "Afghan Minefields Go to the Dogs," *Washington Post*, Mar. 6, 2000, A16.

13. CIA, Jan. 1, 1999 and 2001.

14. Barry Bearak, "An Afghan Mosaic of Misery: Hunger, War and Repression," *New York Times*, Feb. 25, 2000, A1.

15. CIA, 1999 and 2001.

16. *Ibid.*

17. Robin Banerji, "Books: the Agony of Afghanistan Robin Banerji Hears a Timely Warning," *The Daily Telegraph* [London], Mar. 18, 2000, 2.

18. Peter Tomsen (Ambassador-in-residence, University of Nebraska at Omaha and special envoy to the Afghan Resistance with the rank of ambassador, 1989–1992), interview by the author, Feb. 9, 2000.

19. Hafizullah Emadi, *Politics of Development and Women in Afghanistan* (New York: Paragon House, 1993), xvii, xviii.

20. Cecil Marie Cancel, "The Crisis of Afghan Women ... a Human Rights Issue." "Brief History of Afghan Women Struggle," Mar. 13, 1998. Available: http://women3rdworld.about.com/culture/women3rdworld/library/weekly/11031398.htm, Jan. 30, 2000.

21. Banerji, "Books: the Agony of Afghanistan..."

22. Bearak, "Afghanistan's Girls Fight...,"

23. Angela King, "Statement," *In* "No Reason for Optimism About Early Ceasefire in Afghanistan Security Council Told During Open Briefing," United Nations Press Release, SC/6840, Apr. 7, 2000. Available: http://www.un.org/News/Press/docs/2000/20000407.sc6840.doc.html, Oct. 8, 2001.

## Chapter 1

1. Jala al-Din Rumi, "Poem 208," In his *Mystical Poems of Rumi 1: Second Selection, Poems 201–400*, tr. A. J. Arberry, ed. Ehsan Yarshater (Boulder, Colo.: Westview Press, 1979; Chicago: University of Chicago Press, 1991). Copyright ©1979 Ehsan Yarshater. Used by permission of the University of Chicago Press.

2. Haron Amin (Afghan diplomat, first secretary, Islamic State of Afghanistan, United Nations), interview by the author, Feb. 3, 2000.

3. Christine Aziz, "Defiance and Oppression—the Situation of Women in Afghanistan," Oct. 16, 1999. extract from the *Essential* Field Guide to Afghanistan. Available: http://www.mediaaction.org/pubcn/efgafghn/defandopp.htm, May 13, 2000.

4. Valentine M. Moghadam, *Modernizing Women: Gender and Social Change in the Middle East* (Boulder, Colo.: Reinner, 1993), 216–221.

5. Rhea Talley Stewart, *Fire in Afghanistan, 1914–1929; Faith, Hope, and the British Empire* (Garden City, N.Y.: Doubleday, 1973), 377; Hafizullah Emadi, "State, Modernization and the Women's Movement in Afghanistan," *Review of Radical Political Economics* 23 no. 3–4 (Fall-Winter 1991), 227–228; Hafizullah Emadi, *Politics of Development and Women in Afghanistan* (New York: Paragon House, 1993), 37–60.

6. Moghadam, *Modernizing Women*, 217–218.

7. Amin, interview, Feb. 3, 2000.

8. Moghadam, *Modernizing Women*, 218–219.

9. Louis Dupree, *Afghanistan* (Princeton, N.J.: Princeton University Press, 1980), 466.

10. Emadi, "State, Modernization and…," 227–228.

11. *Ibid.*, 228–229.

12. Aziz, "Defiance and Oppression…."

13. Moghadam, "Revolution, Religion, and Gender Politics: Iran and Afghanistan Compared," *Journal of Women's History* 10 no. 4(Winter 1999), 177; Emadi, "State, Modernization and…," 228–229, 234–235.

14. Nancy Hatch Dupree, "Afghan Women under the Taliban," In William Maley, ed., *Fundamentalism Reborn? Afghanistan and the Taliban* (Washington Square, N.Y.: New York University Press, 1998), 152–153.

15. Moghadam, "Revolution, Religion, and Gender Politics," 177; Emadi, "State, Modernization and…," 228–229, 234–235.

16. Moghadam, "Revolution, Religion, and Gender Politics," 177.

17. Emadi, "State, Modernization and…," 234.

18. Louis Dupree, 532.

19. *Ibid.*, 578.

20. *Ibid.*, 590.

21. Jan Goodwin, *Price of Honor: Muslim Women Lift the Veil of Silence on the Islamic World* (Boston: Little, Brown, 1994), 89.

22. Emadi, "State, Modernization and…," 232.

23. *Ibid.*, 232–234.

24. Jan Goodwin, *Caught in the Crossfire* (New York: E.P. Dutton, 1987), 142–143.

25. Nancy Hatch Dupree, "Afghanistan: Women, Society and Development," *Journal of Developing Societies* 8 no. 1 (Jan.-Apr. 1992), 34–35.

26. Anthony Arnold, *Afghanistan's Two-Party Communism: Parcham Khalq* (Stanford, Calif.: Hoover Institution Press, 1983), 21.

27. Emadi, "State, Modernization and…," 237–240.

28. *Ibid.*, 235.

29. Goodwin, *Price of Honor*, 88; Arnold, 184–185.

30. "Women in Afghanistan." Mar. 13, 1998. Available: http://women3rdworld. miningco.com/culture/women3rdworld/library/weekly/aa031398.htm, Jan. 8, 2000.

31. "Afghan History." "The Communist Coup and the Soviet Invasion [The Darkest Hours]." "Noor Mohammad Taraki [Soviet Puppet]," The Online Center for Afghan Studies, Mar. 6, 2000. Available: http://www.afghan-politics.org/Reference/History/Taraki.htm, Mar. 19, 2000.

32. Moghadam, *Modernizing Women*, 210, 229–230.

33. Nancy Hatch Dupree, "Afghanistan: Women, Society and Development," 31.

34. Goodwin, *Price of Honor*, 88; Arnold, 184–185.

35. Aziz, "Defiance and Oppression...."

36. Emadi, "State, Modernization and...," 239.

37. Rahman Hashimi (U.S. resident who fled from Afghanistan in 1983), interview by the author, Feb. 16, 2000.

38. "Afghan History." "The Communist Coup and the Soviet Invasion [The Darkest Hours]," The Online Center for Afghan Studies, Mar. 6, 2000. Available: http://www.afghan-politics.org/Reference/History/Commi_Coup.htm, Mar. 19, 2000.

39. Morwarid (Mora) Hashimi (U.S. resident who fled from Afghanistan in 1983), interviews by the author, Feb. 16, 2000, Mar. 21, 2000.

40. Audrey C. Shalinsky, "Gender Issues in the Afghanistan Diaspora: Nadia's Story," *Frontiers* 17 no. 3 (1996) 120.

41. Goodwin, *Price of Honor*, 78, 84.

42. Louis Dupree, 531–533, 577–578, 589–590, 651.

43. Mavis Leno, "Prepared Testimony of Mavis Leno, National Board Member, Feminist Majority Before the Senate Appropriations Committee Foreign Operations Subcommittee, Subject—Gender Apartheid in Afghanistan," *Federal News Service*, Mar. 9, 1999.

44. Catherine Daly (Department of Textiles, Clothing and Design and Research Association for the Center of Afghanistan Studies, University of Nebraska at Omaha), interview by the author, Mar. 8, 2000.

45. Angela E.V. King, Office of the Special Adviser on Gender Issues and Advancement of Women, United Nations, New York, "Report of the United Nations Interagency Gender Mission to Afghanistan," Nov. 12–24, 1997, 13.

46. Moghadam, *Modernizing Women*, 9–10.

47. Nancy Hatch Dupree, "Afghan Women under the Taliban," In Maley, 161.

48. Lara Paul, "Women in Danger in Afghanistan," *Peace* (Sept.-Oct. 1997). Available: http://www.peacemagazine.org/9709/lara-afg.htm, Jan. 8, 2000.

49. Peter Marsden, *The Taliban: War, Religion and the New Order in Afghanistan* (Karachi Lahore Islamabad: Oxford University Press; London and New York: Zed Books Ltd., 1998), 98–99.

50. Mike Wallace and Christiane Amanpour, "Islamic Group Takes over Afghanistan Capital, Hangs Former Leaders and Brings Strict Rules to Men and Women," CBS News Transcripts, *60 Minutes*, Aug. 23, 1998.

51. William Maley, "Introduction: Interpreting the Taliban," In Maley, 1–2; Marsden, 1; Amin, interview, Feb. 3, 2000; Daly, interview, Mar. 8, 2000.

52. Bob Herbert, "Half a Nation, Condemned," *The New York Times* (Oct. 8, 1998) A31, A35.

53. Vincent Iacopino, et al. *The Taliban's War on Women: A Health and Human Rights Crisis in Afghanistan: A Report* (Boston: Physicians for Human Rights, 1998), 5, 10.

54. Moghadam, "Revolution, Religion, and Gender Politics," 190.

55. *Ibid.*, 190–191.

56. *Ibid.*, 177.

57. Emadi, "State, Modernization and...," 224–226.

58. Aziz, "Defiance and Oppression...."

59. Marsden, 92–93.

60. Nancy Hatch Dupree, in Maley, 163.

61. Pamela Collett, "Afghan Women in the Peace Process," *Peace-Review* 8 no. 3 (Sept. 1996), 399.

62. Sue Emmott, "'Dislocation', Shelter, and Crisis: Afghanistan's Refugees and Notions of Home," *Gender and Development* 4 no. 1 (February 1996), 31–38.

63. Emmott, 37.

64. Emmott, 38.

65. Marsden, 1; Nancy Hatch Dupree, "Afghan Women under the Taliban," In Maley, 165–166.

66. Emadi, "State, Modernization and...," 224–226.

67. U.S. Department of State. Bureau of Democracy, Human Rights, and Labor. *Annual Report on International Religious Freedom for 1999: Afghanistan.* "Section 3. Women," Washington, D.C., Sept. 9, 1999. Available: http://www.state.gov/www/global/human_rights/irf/irf_rpt/1999/irf_afghanis99.html, Apr. 23, 2000.

68. Paul Clarke, "Afghanistan Outlook." "Food Security in Afghanistan," U.N., May 9, 2000.

69. Women's Alliance for Peace and Human Rights in Afghanistan (WAPHA), "The Facts." n.d. Available: http://www.angelfire.com/on/wapha/facts.html, Apr. 30, 2000.

70. Emmott, 31–38.

71. Nasrine Abou Bakre Gross, interview by the author, July 16, 2000.

72. American Council of Voluntary Agencies for Foreign Service, Committee on Development Assistance, Subcommittee on Women in Development, *Criteria for Evaluation of Development Projects Involving Women* [New York]: American Council of Voluntary Agencies for Foreign Service, Technical Assistance Information Clearing House (Dec. 1975), 8.

73. U.S. Department of State, Annual Report...

74. Catherine Daly, "The 'Paarda' Expression of Heejab Among Afghan Women in a Non-Muslim Community," in L. Boyton Arthur, ed., *Body, Dress and Religion* (Oxford, England: Berg Publishers, 1999), 9, 10, 156–159.

75. Megan Reif, "Beyond the Veil—Bigger Issues," *The Christian Science Monitor* (May 3, 2000), 11.

76. Ansar Rahel, Laina Farhat-Holzman, Philip Dacey and Will Webster, "Treatment of Afghan Women Needs Attention," *The Christian Science Monitor* (May 9, 2000), 10.

77. Daly, "The 'Paarda'...," 147.

78. Anaga Dalal, "What?" *Ms.* (Apr./May 2000), 9.

79. Nancy Hatch Dupree, "Afghan Women under the Taliban," in Maley, 159–160.

80. Daly, interview, Mar. 8, 2000.

81. Abdul Raheem Yaseer (Coordinator of International Exchange Programs, and deputy director of the Center for Afghanistan Studies at the University of Nebraska at Omaha), interview by the author, Apr. 13, 2000.

82. Mavis Leno (Feminist Majority Board Member for Drive to End Gender Apartheid in Afghanistan), interview by the author, Apr. 19, 2000.

83. Leno, interview, Apr. 19, 2000.

84. Moghadam, "Revolution, Religion, and Gender Politics," 172, 190–191.

85. Angela E.V. King, Office of the Special Adviser on Gender Issues and Advancement of Women, United Nations, New York, "Report of the United Nations Interagency Gender Mission to Afghanistan," Nov. 12–24, 1997, 13.

86. Moghadam, *Modernizing Women*, 210–216, 249, 250.

## *Chapter 2*

1. Zieba Shorish-Shamley, Ph.D., Women's Alliance for Peace and Human Rights in Afghanistan, U.S. Congress. Senate. Committee on Foreign Relations, Near Eastern and South Asian Affairs Subcommittee. *Testimony*, Hearings, 106th Cong., 2d sess., Jul. 20, 2000.

2. Louis Dupree, *Afghanistan* (Princeton, N.J.: Princeton University Press, 1980), 531.

3. Emmanuel Todd, *The Explanation of Ideology: Family Structures and Social Systems* (Oxford, England: Basil Balckwell Ltd., 1985), 140–141.

4. Shorish-Shamley, *Testimony*, Hearings, Jul. 20, 2000.

5. Abdul Raheem Yaseer (Coordinator of International Exchange Programs, and deputy director of the Center for Afghanistan Studies at the University of Nebraska at Omaha),interview by the author, Apr. 13, 2000.

6. Zieba Shorish-Shamley, "Women's Position, Role, and Rights in Islam," Women's Alliance for Peace and Human Rights in Afghanistan, Available: http://www.angelfire.com/on/wapha/islam.html, Apr. 30, 2000.

7. William Maley, "Introduction: Interpreting the Taliban," in William Maley, ed., *Fundamentalism Reborn? Afghanistan and the Taliban* (Washington Square, N.Y.: New York University Press, 1998), 28.

8. Haron Amin (Afghan diplomat, first secretary, Islamic State of Afghanistan, United Nations), interview by the author, Feb. 3, 2000.

9. Hassan Hathout, "Islamic Intellectual Forum." "Plight of Women in Afghanistan," Nov. 5, 1996. Available: http://www.web.mit.edu/bilal/www/islam.html, Oct. 8, 2001.

10. Hassan Hathout, *Reading the Muslim Mind* (Plainfield, Ind.: American Trust Publications, 1995), Chapter 4.

11. Muslim Women's League, "Crisis in Afghanistan," Nov. 1996. Available: http://www.mwlusa.org/news_afghan.shtml, Apr. 26, 2000.

12. Women Living Under Muslim Laws, "Increased Structural Violence," *Off Our Backs* 27 no. 3 (Mar. 1997), 11.

13. *Ibid.* 11.

14. Catherine Daly (Department of Textiles, Clothing and Design and Research Association for the Center of Afghanistan Studies, University of Nebraska at Omaha), interview by the author, Mar. 8, 2000.

15. Michael Church, "Tuesday Book: Traumatised by the Tyranny of the Taliban" *The Independent* [London], Feb. 29, 2000, Comment, 5.

16. Yaseer, interview, Apr. 13, 2000.

17. U.S. Department of State, Bureau of Democracy, Human Rights, and Labor. *Annual Report on International Religious Freedom for 1999: Afghanistan.* "Section 1. Freedom of Religion," Washington, D.C., Sept. 9, 1999. Available: http://www.state.gov/www/global/human_rights/irf/irf_rpt/1999/irf_afghanis99.html, Apr. 23, 2000.

18. *Ibid.*

19. Vincent Iacopino, *The Taliban's War on Women: A Health and Human Rights Crisis in Afghanistan: A Report* (Boston: Physicians for Human Rights, 1998), 11.

20. U.S. Department of State, "Section 1. Freedom of Religion."

21. Peter Tomsen, "A Chance for Peace in Afghanistan: The Taliban's Days are Numbered," *Foreign Affairs* 79 no. 1 (Jan/Feb 2000), 179.

22. Amin, interview, Feb. 3, 2000.

23. Mike Wallace and Christiane Amanpour. "Islamic Group Takes over Afghanistan Capital, Hangs Former Leaders and Brings Strict Rules to Men and Women," CBS News Transcripts, *60 Minutes*, Aug. 23, 1998.

24. Ahmed Rashid, "Scourge of God: Strict Islamic Rules Imposed in Afghanistan by the Ruling Taliban Are Plunging That Strife-Torn Country Deeper Into Ruin," *Far Eastern Economic Review* 160 no. 32 (Aug. 7, 1997), 52–53.

25. *Ibid.*

26. Wallace and Amanpour, op. cit.

27. Hathout, *Reading the Muslim Mind*, Ch. 4.

28. *Ibid.*

29. Nancy Hatch Dupree, "Afghan Women under the Taliban," in Maley, 145.

30. "Hillary Clinton Hits Persecution of Women," *Milwaukee Journal Sentinel* wire report, Mar. 27, 1999.

31. Nathaniel Hawthorne, *The Best of Hawthorne: Edited with Introduction and Notes by Mark Van Doren* (New York: The Ronald Press, 1951), 428.

32. Amin, interview, Feb. 3, 2000.

33. Pamela Collett, "Afghan Women in the Peace Process," *Peace-Review* 8 no. 3 (Sept. 1996), 397.

34. Jan Goodwin, *Price of Honor: Muslim Women Lift the Veil of Silence on the Islamic World* (Boston: Little, Brown, 1994), 79, 85–86.

35. Human Rights Watch, "Asia Overview: Afghanistan." Available: http://www.hrw.org/wr2k/Asia.htm, Apr. 23, 2000.

## Chapter 3

1. Revolutionary Association of the Women of Afghanistan, "Patriotic Songs of RAWA: Grieving Mother," Tape No. 10, side B, song no. 3. Available: http://www.geocities.com/Nashville/8474/10khonen.htm, Aug. 18, 2000. Reprinted by permission of RAWA.

2. Jan Goodwin, *Price of Honor: Muslim Women Lift the Veil of Silence on the Islamic World* (Boston: Little, Brown, 1994), 82.

3. Farooka Gauhari, *Searching for Saleem: An Afghan Woman's Odyssey* (Lincoln: University of Nebraska Press, 1997), xviii, xix, 253.

4. Amnesty International, "Women in Afghanistan: A Human Rights Catastrophe." "RAWA from the Eye of Amnesty International," *The Burst of the "Islamic Government" Bubble in Afghanistan* (Quetta, Pakistan: RAWA, Jan. 1997), No. 2, 5.

5. Haron Amin, (Afghan diplomat, first secretary, Islamic State of Afghanistan, United Nations), interview by the author, Feb. 3, 2000.

6. Shabana (RAWA Activist), email to the author, Jul. 1, 2000.

7. See, for example: Anthony Davis, "How the Taliban Became a Military Force", in William Maley (ed.), *Fundamentalism Reborn? Afghanistan and the Taliban* (Washington Square, N.Y.: New York University Press, 1998), 43–71; Barnett R. Rubin, "Testimony, Oct. 8, 1998, Barnett R. Rubin, Director of the Center for Preventive Action and Senior Fellow Senate Foreign Relations Near Eastern and South Asian Affairs Events in Afghanistan," *Federal Document Clearing House*; Barnett R. Rubin, "Afghanistan: The Forgotten Crisis," February 1996, "Introduction." (*Writenet Country Papers*). Available: http://www.unhcr.ch/refworld/country/writenet/wriafg.htm, Apr. 24, 2000; William Maley, "Introduction: Interpreting the Taliban," in Maley, ed., *Fundamentalism Reborn?* 14, 37–38.

8. Barnett R. Rubin, "Conflict and Peace in Afghanistan," *Afghanistan Outlook*, UNSMA and the World Bank, Dec. 1999. Available: http://www.afghanistanvoice.org/ARTICLES/OUTLOOK_Conflict.shtml, Oct. 7, 2001.

9. Amin, interview by the author, Feb. 3, 2000.

10. Peter Tomsen (ambassador-in-residence, University of Nebraska at Omaha and special envoy to the Afghan Resistance with the rank of ambassador, 1989–1992), interview by the author, Feb. 9, 2000.

11. Amin, interview by the author, Feb. 3, 2000.

12. Abdul Raheem Yaseer (coordinator of International Exchange Programs, and deputy director of the Center for Afghanistan Studies at the University of Nebraska at Omaha), interview by the author, Apr. 13, 2000.

13. Maley, "Introduction: Interpreting the Taliban," in Maley, ed., *Fundamentalism Reborn* 23.

14. Peter Marsden, *The Taliban: War, Religion and the New Order in Afghanistan* (Karachi, Lahore, Islamabad: Oxford University Press; London and New York: Zed Books Ltd., 1998) 43–46.

15. U.S. Department of State, Bureau of Democracy, Human Rights, and Labor, *1999 Country Reports on Human Rights Practices: Afghanistan*, Section 3, "Respect for Political Rights: The Right of Citizens to Change Their Government," Washington, D.C., Feb. 25, 2000. Available: http://www.state.gov/www/global/human_rights/1999_hrp_report/afghanis.html, Feb. 25, 2000.

16. Rubin, "Testimony, Oct. 8, 1998."

17. Karl. F. Inderfurth, Assistant Secretary of State, Testimony, "Afghan Update: Signs of Change?" U.S. Congress, Senate. Committee on Foreign Relations, Near Eastern and South Asian Affairs Subcommittee. *The Taliban: Engagement or Confrontation?* Hearings, 106th Cong., 2d sess., Jul. 20, 2000.

18. Peter Tomsen, professor of International Studies and Programs, University of Nebraska at Omaha, former ambassador and special envoy to the Afghan Resistance, testimony, "Untying the Afghan Knot," Hearings, Jul. 20, 2000.

19. U.S. Department of State, *1999 Country Reports on Human Rights Practices: Afghanistan.* Section 3, Feb. 25, 2000.

20. Mike Wallace and Christiane Amanpour, "Islamic Group Takes Over Afghanistan Capital, Hangs Former Leaders and Brings Strict Rules to Men and Women," CBS News Transcripts, *60 Minutes,* Aug. 23, 1998.

21. Karl F. Inderfurth, "Prepared Statement.... Before the Senate Foreign Relations Committee, Subcommittee on Near Eastern and South Asian Affairs, *Federal News Service,* Oct. 8, 1998.

22. "The Cost of an Afghan 'Victory,'" *The Nation* 268 (Feb. 15, 1999), 16, 17.

23. Rubin, "Testimony, Oct. 8, 1998."

24. Peter Tomsen, "Beyond Marx and Mullahs," *The Washington Times,* May 23, 1999, B3.

25. Ahmed Rashid, "The Taliban: Exporting Extremism," *Foreign Affairs* 78 no. 6 (Nov/Dec 1999), 22, 35.

26. Rubin, "Testimony, Oct. 8, 1998."

27. Nasrine Abou-Bakre Gross, "Afghan Women and Education· Letter to the Washington Post," unpublished, Apr. 7, 1999. Available: http://users.erols. com/kabultec/letter.html, Jul. 16, 2000.

28. Nasrine Abou-Bakre Gross, interview by the author, July 16, 2000.

29. Nasrine Abou-Bakre Gross, *Qadam-ha-ye Awshti wa Massouliat-e Ma Afghan-ha (Steps of Peace and Our Responsibility as Afghans),* Falls Church, VA: Kabultec, 2000.

30. Sima Wali, "Ansima Wali: America's Debt to the People of Afghanistan," *The Boston Globe,* Dec. 4, 1999, A19.

31. Sima Wali, "Beyond Sanctions," *Ms.* (Apr./May 2000), 27.

32. Human Rights Watch. "Asia Overview: Afghanistan." Available: http://www.hrw.org/wr2k/Asia.htm, Apr. 23, 2000.

33. U.S. Department of State, Bureau of Democracy, Human Rights, and Labor, *1999 Country Reports on Human Rights Practices: Afghanistan,* Feb. 25, 2000.

34. Rubin, "Conflict and Peace in Afghanistan," Dec. 1999.

35. Sue Emmott, "'Dislocation', Shelter, and Crisis: Afghanistan's Refugees and Notions of Home," *Gender and Development* 4 no. 1(February 1996), 31–38.

36. Emmott, 31–38.

37. U.N., Daily Press Briefing of Office of Spokesman for Secretary-General, Jun. 2, 2000.

38. Jim Moret and Brent Sadler, "Afghanistan Ruled with Taliban Style of Islam," *The World Today,* Oct. 1, 1998; CNN transcript #98100108V23.

39. Jacki Lyden, *All Things Considered,* Aug. 22, 1998, NPR transcript #98082204-216.

40. Mike Wallace and Christiane Amanpour, op. cit.

41. Tomsen, interview by the author, Feb. 9, 2000.

42. Rubin, "Testimony, Oct. 8, 1998."

43. Marsden, 148.

44. Nancy Hatch Dupree, "Afghan Women under the Taliban," in Maley, *Fundamentalism Reborn?* 150.

45. Vincent Iacopino, et al. *The Taliban's War on Women: A Health and Human Rights Crisis in Afghanistan: A Report* (Boston: Physicians for Human, 1998), 1, 4.

46. Islamic Emirate of Afghanistan, "The Movement of the Taliban," *Homepage*, Feb. 2, 2000. Available: http://www.afghan-ie.com/taliban/tailimov.htm, Jun. 17, 2000.

47. Maulana Zahid-ur-Rashidy, "Osama bin Laden, Klashnikov and 'Uncle Sam,'" *Islamic Emirate of Afghanistan Homepage*, Feb. 2, 2000. Available: http://www.afghan-ie.com/jihad/osama.htm, Jun. 17, 2000.

48. AI, "Afghanistan. in: Amnesty International Report 2001," Oct. 1, 2001. Available: http://web.amnesty.org/web/ar2001.nsf/webasacountries/AFGHANISTAN?OpenDocument, Oct. 14, 2001.

49. CBS News, "Indepth Backgrounder: The Taliban," CBS Front Page, July 2001. Available: http://www.cbc.ca/news/indepth/background/taliban.html, Oct. 13, 2001.

50. PBS, "Frontline: Target America: The Evolution of Islamic Terrorism—An Overview," 2001. Available: http://www.pbs.org/wgbh/pages/frontline/shows/target/etc/modern.html, Oct. 14, 2001.

51. *Ibid.*

52. In Miles O'Brien, "Target: Terrorism—The U.S. and Afghanistan," CNN Live at Daybreak, Transcript #100215CN.V73, Oct. 2, 2001.

## *Chapter 4*

1. Haron Amin (Afghan diplomat, first secretary, Islamic State of Afghanistan, United Nations), interview by the author, Feb. 3, 2000.

2. Revolutionary Association of the Women of Afghanistan, "Some of the Restrictions Imposed by Taliban on Women in Afghanistan," Available: http://rawa.org/rules.htm, Apr. 3, 2000.

3. Media Action International. "Tali-bans," extract from the *Essential Field Guide to Afghanistan*, Oct. 16, 1999. Available: http://www.mediaaction.org/pubcn/efgafghn/taliban.htm, May 13, 2000.

4. "Stop the Violence," *Women's Health Journal* (October-December 1996), 4, 11.

5. Mavis Leno (Feminist Majority board member for Drive to End Gender Apartheid in Afghanistan), interview by the author, April 19, 2000.

6. United Nations Human Rights Commission, Center for Documentation and Research, "Update to the Background Paper on Refugees and Asylum Seekers from Afghanistan," Geneva, Jan. 1999. Available: http://www/unhcr.ch/refworld/country/cdr/cdrafg02.htm, Jun. 10, 2000.

7. Michael Church, "Tuesday Book: Traumatised by the Tyranny of the Taliban" [London], *The Independent*, Feb. 29, 2000, Comment, 5.

8. Human Rights Watch, "Asia Overview: Afghanistan." Available: http://www.hrw.org/wr2k/Asia.htm, Apr. 23, 2000.

9. Luisa Dillner, "Inequalities Cause Reproductive Deaths," *British Medical Journal* 311 (Clinical Research ed.) (Jul. 15, 1995), 148.

10. Angela E.V. King, Office of the Special Adviser on Gender Issues and

Advancement of Women, United Nations, New York, "Report of the United Nations Interagency Gender Mission to Afghanistan," Nov. 12–24, 1997, 13.

11. Vincent Iacopino, et al., *The Taliban's War on Women: A Health and Human Rights Crisis in Afghanistan*, Report (Boston: Physicians for Human Rights), 1998, 76.

12. *Ibid.*

13. *Ibid.*, 3.

14. U.S. Department of State, Bureau of Democracy, Human Rights, and Labor. *1999 Country Reports on Human Rights Practices: Afghanistan*, "Section 3 Respect for Political Rights: The Rights of Citizens to Change Their Government." "Children." Washington, D.C., Feb. 25, 2000. Available: http://www.state.gov/www/global/human_rights/1999_hrp_report/afghanis.html, Feb. 25, 2000.

15. Human Rights Watch, "Asia Overview: Afghanistan."

16. Nancy Hatch Dupree, "Afghan Women under the Taliban," in William Maley, ed., *Fundamentalism Reborn? Afghanistan and the Taliban* (Washington Square, N.Y.: New York University Press), 1998, 153–154.

17. U.S. Department of State, *Country Reports on Human Rights Practices for 1996*, 1415-1416, in Nancy Hatch Dupree, "Afghan Women . . ," 154.

18. U.S. Department of State, Bureau of Democracy, Human Rights, and Labor. *1999 Country Reports*, "Section 3." "Women," and "Children."

19. United Nations, Statistics Division, "Indicators on Literacy." Available: http://www.un.org/Depts/unsd/social/literacy.htm, Jun. 2, 2000.

20. Ahmed Rashid, "Scourge of God: Strict Islamic Rules Imposed in Afghanistan by the Ruling Taliban Are Plunging That Strife-Torn Country Deeper Into Ruin," *Far Eastern Economic Review* 160 no. 32 (Aug. 7, 1997), 52, 53.

21. Kate Clark, "Afghanistan Has One of the Worst Records on Education in the World," *BBC Worldnews Services*, Apr. 27, 2000.

22. Karen Mazurkewich, "Bringing Hope—and Homework—to the Girls," *Time* 156 (May 29, 2000), 21. Available: http://www.cnn.com/ASIANOW/time/magazine/2000/0529/afghanistan.womenduction.html, Jun. 6, 2000.

23. Co-operation Centre for Afghanistan, "Status of Girls' Education at the Beginning of 21st Century in Afghanistan," [Peshawar, Pakistan] VII no. 2, *CAA Newsletter* (Apr. 2000), 1.

24. *Reports from the Land of Savageries, Insults and Obscenities.* "Mariam Girl's [*sic*] High School Turned into a Market," *Payam-e-Zan* (*Women's Message*) No. 50, Dec. 1998. Available: http://rawa.org/50reports.htm, Aug. 14, 2000.

25. Mike Wallace and Christiane Amanpour, Islamic Group Takes Over Afghanistan Capital, Hangs Former Leaders and Brings Strict Rules to Men and Women," CBS News Transcripts, *60 Minutes*, Aug. 23, 1998.

26. Barry Bearak, "Afghanistan's Girls Fight to Read and Write," *New York Times*, Mar. 9, 2000, A9.

27. Iacopino, et al., 3.

28. Iacopino, et al., 74.

29. Co-Operation Centre for Afghanistan, "Prostitution," *Violence Against Women in Afghanistan Report*, Peshawar, Pakistan, Nov. 1999.

30. *Ibid.*, "Trafficking of Women," *Violence Against Women . . .*, Nov. 1999.

31. Zohra Rasekh, Heidei M. Bauer, Michele M. Manos and Vincent

Iacopino, "Women's Health and Human Rights in Afghanistan," *JAMA*, 280 no. 5, Aug. 5, 1998, 449–455.

32. Sheila Hotchkin, "Afghan Woman Decries Taliban" [Baltimore], *AP*. Available: http:www.afghanradio.com/azad.html, "News Archive," Apr. 3, 2000. Oct. 7, 2001.

33. Marion Lloyd, "Brutal Struggle Over Tradition; Taliban's Efforts to Achieve Islamic Purity in Afghanistan Sets Civilization back 1,000 years," *The Houston Chronicle*, Dec. 13, 1998, A1.

34. Iacopino, 6.

35. Iacopino, 8–10.

36. Abbas Faiz, "Health Care under the Taliban," *Lancet* 349 (Apr. 26, 1997), 1247–1248.

37. Iacopino, 6–13. See also Iacopino, "Afghanistan Campaign," "Methods of Investigation" and "Summary of Findings," 5, 6.

38. *Ibid.*, 7.

39. *Ibid.*, 66.

40. *Ibid.*, 68.

41. *Ibid.*, 70.

42. *Ibid.*, 70.

43. *Ibid.*, 10.

44. United States. Congress. Senate. Committee on Foreign Relations. Subcommittee on Near Eastern and South Asian Affairs, "Afghanistan, is there hope for peace? : Hearings before the Subcommittee on Near Eastern and South Asian Affairs of the Committee on Foreign Relations, United States Senate, One Hundred Fourth Congress, second session," Jun. 6, 25, 26, and 27, 1996, 27.

45. Amnesty International (AI) in U.S. Department of State, *1999 Country Reports on Human Rights Practices: Afghanistan*, Sections 1.b and 1.g.

46. Christiane Amanpour, CNN correspondent, "Newsroom Worldview for September 30, 1997," *News*; *International*, transcript #97093000V05.

47. RAWA, "Some of the Restrictions Imposed by Taliban."

48. Iacopino, et al., 1–4.

49. CNN.com, "AsiaNow." "Taliban Free 46 Prisoners in Afghanistan," Jul. 1, 2000. Available: http://www.cnn.com/2000/ASIANOW/central/06/30/afghanistan.prisoners.ap/index.html, Jul. 4, 2000.

50. Revolutionary Association of the Women of Afghanistan Activist, "A Report from the Pol-e-Charkhi Prison in Kabul," Dec. 1999. Email to the author, Jan. 19. 2000.

51. Amnesty International, "Women in Afghanistan: Pawns in Men's Power Struggles," *Report—ASA 11/11/99* (November 1999). Available: http://www.amnesty.org/alib/aipub/1999/ASA/31101199.htm, Jan. 8, 2000.

52. Robin Wright, "The Final Humiliation: Afghan Children Are Ignored," *LA Times*, April 30, 2000, 2. Available: http:///www.afghanradio.com/2000/april/apr30g2000.htm, "Archives," Oct. 7, 2000.

53. Co-Operation Centre for Afghanistan, "Women's Prisons," *Violence Against Women…*, Nov. 1999.

54. Amnesty International, "Refugees from Afghanistan: the World's Largest Single Refugee Group," *Report—ASA*, Nov. 16, 1999. Online. Internet. Available:

http://web.amnesty.org/ai.nsf/Index/ASA110161999?OpenDocument&of=COUNTRIES\
AFGHANISTAN, Oct. 8, 2001.

55. United Nations. Secretary General, Report of the Secretary-General, "The Situation in Afghanistan and Its Implications for International Peace and Security," Sept. 21, 1999. Available: http://www.un.org/documents/search.htm, No. S/1999/994, Oct. 8, 2001.

56. Robert Fisk, "Far from the Taliban, Where the Young Live in Fear of Overnight Shooting, Kidnapping and Theft" *The Independent* [London], Apr. 13, 2000, Foreign News, 18.

57. Don Krumm, U.S. Committee for Refugees, "Worldwide Refugee Information: Country Report: Afghanistan," 2000. http://www.refugees.org/world/countryrpt/scasia/1998/afghanistan.htm, Jun. 10, 2000; and "Report" 2000, http:www.refugees.org/world/countryrpt/scasia/afghanistan.htm, Oct. 7, 2001.

58. Zohra Rasekh, *et al.* "Women's Health and Human Rights," 449–455.

59. Barry Bearak, "Afghan Rulers Drive 130,000 from Homes" [Bazarak, Eastern Afghanistan], *The Guardian*, Oct. 20, 1999.

60. Peter Marsden, *The Taliban: War, Religion and the New Order in Afghanistan* (Karachi Lahore Islamabad: Oxford University Press; London; New York: Zed Books Ltd., 1998), 89, 91.

61. Revolutionary Association of the Women of Afghanistan Activist Shabana, email to the author, Jul. 1, 2000.

62. Katha Pollitt, "Tearing at the Veil," (Interview with Sajeda Hayat And Sehar Saba), *The New York Times Magazine*, May 14, 2000, 23.

63. Bill Lambrecht, "Afghan Woman Refugee Who Lives Here Denounces Taliban at White House Rights Event: She Says Situation for Women in Repressive Regime Is Worsening," *St. Louis Post-Dispatch*, Dec. 7, 1999, A10.

64. Humera Rahi, "Afghans Go to Battle with Poems Upon Their Lips by Ahmed Rashid [The Federal Capital Press of Australia], *The Canberra Times*, Mar. 8, 1998, A22.

65. Humera Rahi, "Afghans Go to Battle."

66. Christine Aziz, "Defiance and Oppression—The Situation of Women in Afghanistan," Oct. 16, 1999, extract from the *Essential Field Guide to Afghanistan*. Available: http://www.mediaaction.org/pubcn/efgafghn/defandopp.htm, May 13, 2000.

67. Penney Kome, "Lifting the Shroud," *WIN Magazine* no. 27 (Dec. 1999), B. Available: http://www.winmagazine.org/issues/issue27/win27d.htm, May 1, 2000.

68. Zohra Rasekh, *et al.*, "Women's Health and Human Rights," 449–455 in Kome.

69. Hafizullah Emadi, *Politics of Development and Women in Afghanistan* (New York: Paragon House, 1993), 30–33.

70. "Women's Self-Immolation Under the Taliban's Domination," *The Burst of the "Islamic Government," Bubble in Afghanistan* (Quetta, Pakistan: RAWA, Jan. 1997), No. 2, 9.

## Chapter 5

1. Ansima Wali (same as Sima Wali) (President, Refugee Women in Development (RefWID) Inc. Washington, D.C.), "Ansima Wali: America's Debt to the People of Afghanistan," *The Boston Globe*, Dec. 4, 1999, 3rd ed., A19.

2. Revolutionary Association of the Women of Afghanistan, Interviews with Afghan women provided to and translated for the author, Mar. 14, 2000, May 15, 2000, and Jul. 2, 2000.

3. *Larry King Live*, "The Women of the Senate Discuss 'The Women of the Senate,'" transcript #00072600V22, Jul. 26, 2000.

4. Zieba Shorish-Shamley, co-founder and executive director, Women's Alliance for Peace and Human Rights in Afghanistan, "I remember you...: Dedicated to My Suffering Afghan Sisters," Mar. 8, 1998. Available: http://www.angelfire.com/on/wapha/remember.html, July 22, 2000.

## *Chapter 6*

1. Shabana, email to the author, Jul. 1, 2000.

2. Peter Marsden, *The Taliban: War, Religion and the New Order in Afghanistan* (Karachi Lahore Islamabad: Oxford University Press; London and New York: Zed Books Ltd., 1998), 46.

3. Amnesty International. "Women in Afghanistan: Pawns in Men's Power Struggles." *Report—ASA 11/11/99*, Nov. 1999. Available: http://www.amnesty.org/ailib/aipub/1999/ASA/31101199.htm, Jan. 8, 2000; Karl F. Inderfurth, "Prepared Statement Karl F. Inderfurth Assistant Secretary of State for South Asian Affairs Before the Senate Foreign Relations Committee Subcommittee on Near Eastern and South Asian Affairs," *Federal News Service*, Oct. 8, 1998.

4. U.N., Security Council, Statement by the President of the Security Council, Apr. 7, 2000. Available: http://www.un.org/Docs/sc/statements/2000/prst12e.pdf, Jun. 20, 2000. See also: A/54/174-S/1999/812, annex for Declaration.

5. U.N. Secretary General, Report of the Secretary-General, "The Situation in Afghanistan and Its Implications for International Peace and Security." "Political Developments," Sept. 21, 1999. Available: http://www.un.org/Docs/sc/reports/1999/sgrep99.htm, Oct. 8, 2001.

6. *Ibid.*

7. *Ibid.*, Section V., A. and B., Humanitarian Activities and Human Rights, Nos. 23, 30, 32.

8. *Ibid.*, No. 33.

9. United Nations, Security Council, "Security Council Resolution 1267," S/RES/1267, Oct. 15, 1999. Available: http://www.un.org/Docs/scres/1999/99sc1267.htm, May 11, 2000.

10. *Ibid.*, Statement by the President of the Security Council, Oct. 22, 1999, No. S/PRST/1999/29. Available: http://www.un.org/Docs/SC/statements/1999/prst9929.htm, No. S/1999/994, May 11, 2000.

11. *Ibid.*, Statement by the President of the Security Council, Apr. 7, 2000 Available: http://www.un.org/Docs/sc/statements/2000/prst12e.pdf, Jun. 20, 2000.

12. Angela King, "Statement," in United Nations, "No Reason for Optimism About Early Ceasefire in Afghanistan Security Council Told During Open Briefing," United Nations Press Release, SC/6840, Apr. 7, 2000. Available: http://www.un.org/Presssc.htm, Jun. 20, 2000.

13. "U.N.: Council, Entering Final Phase of 2000 Substantive Session, Adopts

17 Draft Texts, Approves Three Resolutions," July 28, 2000. Available: http://worfa.free.fr/UN_council_28.07.2000.htm, Oct. 8, 2001.

14. Vincent Iacopino. *The Taliban's War on Women: A Health and Human Rights Crisis in Afghanistan: A Report* (Boston: Physicians for Human Rights, 1998), 14.

15. Charles Norchi, "Human Rights in Afghanistan: Two Decades of Abuse," Oct. 16, 1999. Available: http://www.mediaaction.org/pubcn/efgafghn/hum.htm, May 13, 2000.

16. *Ibid.*

17. Zalmay Khalilzad, "Anarchy in Afghanistan," *Journal of International Affairs* 51 no. 1 (Summer 1997), 38.

18. William Jefferson Clinton, "Remarks by the President at Human Rights Day/Eleanor Roosevelt Award Ceremony," The White House, Office of the Press Secretary, Dec. 6, 1999.

19. President Clinton, and Hillary Rodham Clinton, "Remarks by the President and the First Lady at *Vogue* Reception," Oct. 26, 1999.

20. Hillary Rodham Clinton, "Remarks by First Lady Hillary Rodham Clinton." United Nations International Women's Day Speech on Women's Rights, New York City, Mar. 4, 1999.

21. Cassandra Burrell, "Mrs. Clinton Cites Plight of Afghan Women," *The Boston Globe*, Apr. 29, 1999, A7.

22. William O. Beeman, "It's the Same Old Story," *The Plain Dealer*, Sept. 12, 1998, B6.

23. Colum Lynch, "Taliban Burns Rival Villages; Afghan Refugees Flood the Capital," *The Washington Post*, Aug. 18, 1999, A11.

24. Peter Tomsen, "Flawed Policy in Afghanistan," *Washington Times*, Mar. 17, 2000, A19.

25. Karl. F. Inderfurth, Assistant Secretary of State, Testimony, "Afghan Update: Signs of Change?" U.S. Congress, Senate. Committee on Foreign Relations, Near Eastern and South Asian Affairs Subcommittee. *The Taliban: Engagement or Confrontation?* Hearings, 106th Cong., 2d sess., Jul. 20, 2000.

26. Nancy Hatch Dupree,, "Afghan Women under the Taliban," in William Maley, ed., *Fundamentalism Reborn? Afghanistan and the Taliban* (Washington Square, N.Y.: New York University Press), 1998, 146–150.

27. Marsden, 149–153.

28. Elaine Lafferty, "Hollywood: Celebrities Weigh in Against the Taliban," *Time* (Oct. 19, 1998), 16, 40(1).

29. Deborah Prussel, "Feminists Take on UNOCAL," *The Progressive* 62 no. 10 (Oct. 1998) 14–15.

30. "Jay and Mavis Leno Donate $100,000 to Expand Campaign Against Gender Apartheid in Afghanistan," *Philanthropy News Digest* 4 (Oct. 28, 1998), 43.

31. Margaret Carlson, "May, 1999 Honorary Wild Wolf Woman of the Month." *Time* (Apr. 12, 1999), 14. Available: http://www.wildwolfwomen.com/honorary/may.htm, Jan. 1, 2000; Yahlin Chang, "Hollywood's Latest Cause," *Newsweek*, Dec. 6, 1999, International, 42.

32. Mavis Leno, "Prepared Testimony of Mavis Leno, National Board Member, Feminist Majority Before the Senate Appropriations Committee Foreign

Operations Subcommittee, Subject—Gender Apartheid in Afghanistan," *Federal News Service*, Mar. 9, 1999.

33. Mavis Leno (Feminist Majority Board Member for Drive to End Gender Apartheid in Afghanistan), interview by the author, Apr. 19, 2000.

34. Ahmad Shah Massoud, "Interview with Commander Ahmad Shah Massoud," 2000, Azadi Afghan Radio, Jul. 2, 2000. Available: http://www.afghanradio.com/interview/ahmadshahmasoud07082000.htm, Jul. 27, 2000.

35. Shoukria Haidar (NEGAR), "Conference in Dushanbe for Women of Afghanistan," Announcement, Women on the Road for Afghanistan, Feb. 2000. Available: http://www.worfa.org, Feb. 2000.

36. Nasrine Abou-Bakre Gross, "Conference in Dushanbe for Women of Afghanistan," report based on eyewitness knowledge as attendee of the Conference, Aug. 2, 2000, email to the author, Aug. 2, 2000.

37. Women on the Road for Afghanistan, "Call for Action by the Women on the Road for Afghanistan," Dushanbe, Tadjikistan, Jun. 28, 2000. Available: http://www.worfa.org, Aug. 2, 2000.

38. Deb Ellis, "Women's Journalism in Afghanistan," *NGO Coalition on Women's Human Rights in Conflict Situations Newsletter*, (Aug. 1999), 3:2. Available: http://www.ichrdd.ca/111/english/commdoc/publications/women/bulletin/vol3no2e.html, Jun. 14, 2000.

39. Valentine M. Moghadam, *Modernizing Women: Gender and Social Change in the Middle East* (Boulder, Colo.: Reinner, 1993), 234–235.

40. Massouma Esmaty Wardak, *The Position and Role of Afghan Women in Afghan Society: From the Late 18th to the Late 19th Century*, Kabul, Afghanistan: [Dawlati Matba'ah], 1991.

41. Bob Herbert, "Half a Nation, Condemned," *The New York Times* (Oct. 8, 1998) A31, A35.

42. United Nations Development Programme, "Gender Sensitive Institutional Capacity—Building of Afghan NGOs for Civil Society," Project Proposal, 1999. Available: http://www.reliefweb.int/library/appeals/afg99/pro_adv_human/rwd.htm, Aug. 17, 2000.

43. Sisterhood Is Global Institute, "Human Rights Bibliography," Dec. 30, 1999. Available: http://www.sigi.org/Resource/hr_bib.htm, Aug. 17, 2000.

44. Ellis, "Women's Journalism in Afghanistan."

45. Amir S. Hassanyar, email to the author, Jun. 6, 2000.

46. Nancy Hatch Dupree, "Afghan Women under the Taliban," in Maley, 162.

47. Women's Alliance for Peace and Human Rights in Afghanistan (WAPHA), "Zieba Shorish-Shamley." Available: http://www.wapha.org/zieba.html, Oct. 8, 2001; WAPHA, "Our Mission." Available: http://www.wapha.org/mission.html, Oct. 8, 2001.

48. Marion Lloyd, "In Pakistan, Afghan Academics Struggle to Maintain Universities for Refugees," *The Chronicle of Higher Education* 45 no. 11 (Nov. 6, 1998), A65.

49. Pamela Collett, "Afghan Women in the Peace Process," *Peace-Review* 8 no. 3 (Sept. 1996), 397, 400–402.

50. Edward Girardet and Jonathon Walter, *Zanweb*: "Widows," 1998. Excerpted from The CrossLines *Essential Field Guide to Afghanistan*. Available: http://www.mediaaction.org/zanweb/briefswdw.htm, May 12, 2000.

51. Ellis, "Women's Journalism in Afghanistan."

52. RAWA, "About RAWA…." Available: http://rawa.fancymarketing.net/rawa. html, Oct. 8, 2001.

53. RAWA, "Biography of Martyred Meena, Founding Leader of RAWA." Available: http://rawa.fancymarketing.net/meena.html, Oct. 8, 2001.

54. RAWA, "Our Main Goals and Objectives," Available: http://rawa.fancy-marketing.net/goals.html, Oct. 8, 2001.

55. Katha Pollitt, "Underground Against the Taliban," *The Nation*, May 29, 2000, 10. Available: http://www.thenation.com/issue/000529/0529pollitt.shtml, Jun. 3, 2000.

56. Inger Brinck, Letter to Mrs. Clinton, Dec. 7, 1999. Email to author Dec. 11, 1999.

57. RAWA correspondent, "Afghan Women Hold Demonstration for Rights," *DAWN*, Dec. 11, 1999; News Network International, "Afghans Demo in Front of U.N. Office," Islamabad, Dec. 11, 1999.

58. RAWA, "RAWA Observes Black Day of April 28 in Islamabad and Washington, D.C.," email to author Apr. 29, 2000.

59. RAWA, "France Grants RAWA a Human Rights Prize,"; Laurent Fabius letter to RAWA, English Translation, Nov. 1999. Email to author Apr. 16, 2000.

60. Sally Ingalls, "War Against Women and Children." "Taliban." "Afghani Women Speak Out Against Human Rights Violations," Change Links, Jun. 2000. Available: http://www.change-links.org/Afghani.htm, Oct. 8, 2001.

61. Nancy Hatch Dupree, 162; Hafizullah Emadi, *Politics of Development and Women in Afghanistan* (New York: Paragon House, 1993), 114–115.

62. Emadi, 65.

63. Emadi, 114–115.

64. Marsden, 88.

65. Afghan Women's Network, Statement, Oct. 15, 1996 in "Afghanistan: 'The Biggest Prison for Women in the World,'" *Off Our Backs* 27 no. 3 (Mar. 1997) 12.

66. Nancy Hatch Dupree, "Afghanistan: Women, Society and Development," *Journal of Developing Societies* 8 no. 1 (Jan.-Apr. 1992), 30, 35, 37–41.

67. Sue Emmott, "'Dislocation', Shelter, and Crisis: Afghanistan's Refugees and Notions of Home," *Gender and Development* 4 no. 1 (February 1996), 32.

68. Audrey C. Shalinsky, "Gender Issues in the Afghanistan Diaspora: Nadia's Story," *Frontiers* 17 no. 3 (1996), 102–103, 120.

69. Sima Wali, "Repatriation and the Reconstruction of Afghanistan: The Role of Women, *Migration World Magazine* 22 no. 4 (1994), 28.

70. Ahmed Rashid, "Epicentre of Terror," *Far Eastern Economic Review* 160 (May 11, 2000), 16–18.

71. Peter Tomsen, "A Chance for Peace in Afghanistan: The Taliban's Days Are Numbered," 79 no. 1 *Foreign Affairs* (Jan/Feb 2000), 179.

72. *Ibid.* (Ambassador-in-residence, University of Nebraska at Omaha and special envoy to the Afghan Resistance with the rank of ambassador, 1989–1992), interview by the author, Feb. 9, 2000.

73. Ansar Rahel, "State Department Dances with Terrorists," *San Francisco Chronicle*, Nov. 4, 1999, A31.

74. The Feminist Majority Foundation, "Stop Gender Apartheid in Afghanistan," 1999. Available: http://www.feminist.org/afghan/facts.html, Apr. 23, 2000.

75. Leno, interview by the author, April 19, 2000.

76. *Ibid.* Feminist Majority Foundation, "Stop Gender Apartheid in Afghanistan: Afghan Women's Scholarship Program," 1998. Available: http://www.feminist. org/afghan/scholarship.html, Apr. 23, 2000.

77. John Renninger, officer-in-charge of the Asia and Pacific Division of the Department of Political Affairs, "Statement," in United Nations, "No Reason for Optimism About Early Ceasefire in Afghanistan Security Council Told During Open Briefing," press release, SC/6840, Apr. 7, 2000. Available: http://www.un.org/ News/Press/docs/2000/20000407.sc6840.doc.html, Oct. 8, 2001.

78. Jacki Lyden, *All Things Considered*, Washington, D.C.: NPR transcript #98082204-216, Aug. 22, 1998.

79. Report of the Senior Coordinator for Refugee Women on Mission to Afghanistan and Pakistan 30th April 9th to May 1997 (Peshawar, UNHCR, May 1997) in Nancy Hatch Dupree, 155.

80. U.S. Department of State, Bureau of Democracy, Human Rights, and Labor. *Annual Report on International Religious Freedom for 1999: Afghanistan.* "Section 3: Women," Washington, D.C., Sept. 9, 1999. Available: http://www.state. gov/www/global/human_rights/irf/irf_rpt/1999/irf_afghanis99.html, Apr. 23, 2000.

81. United Nations Department of Public Information DPI/1772/HR "Women and Violence," Feb. 1996. Available: http://www.un.org/rights/dpi1772e. htm, Oct. 8, 2001.

82. Geraldine Brooks, *Nine Parts of Desire: The Hidden World of Islamic Women* (New York: Anchor Books, 1995), 237.

# Bibliography

Afghan Women's Network. Statement, Oct. 15, 1996 in "Afghanistan: 'The Biggest Prison for Women in the World.'" *Off Our Backs* 27 no. 3 (Mar. 1997) 12.

American Council of Voluntary Agencies for Foreign Service. Committee on Development Assistance. Subcommittee on Women in Development. *Criteria for Evaluation of Development Projects Involving Women*. [New York]: Technical Assistance Information Clearing House, Dec. 1975.

Amin, Haron (Afghan diplomat, first secretary, Islamic State of Afghanistan, United Nations), interview by the author, Feb. 3, 2000.

Amnesty International. "Refugees from Afghanistan: The World's Largest Single Refugee Group." *Report—ASA*, Nov. 16, 1999. Available: http://web.amnesty.org/ai.nsf/Index/ASA110161999?OpenDocument&of=COUNTRIES/AFGHANISTAN\AFGH, Oct. 8, 2001.

_____. "Women in Afghanistan: A Human Rights Catastrophe." "RAWA from the Eye of Amnesty International," in *The Burst of the "Islamic Government" Bubble in Afghanistan* (Quetta, Pakistan: RAWA, Jan. 1997), No. 2, 5.

_____. "Women in Afghanistan: Pawns in Men's Power Struggles." *Report—ASA 11/11/99*, Nov. 1999. Available: http://www.amnesty.org/ailib/aipub/1999/ASA/31101199.htm, Jan. 8, 2000.

Arnold, Anthony. *Afghanistan's Two-Party Communism: Parcham Khalq*. Stanford, Calif.: Hoover Institution Press, 1983.

Aziz, Christine. "Defiance and Oppression—The Situation of Women in Afghanistan," Oct. 16, 1999, extract from the *Essential Field Guide to Afghanistan*. Available: http://www.mediaaction.org/pubcn/efgafghn/defandopp.htm, May 13, 2000.

Brooks, Geraldine. *Nine Parts of Desire: The Hidden World of Islamic Women*. New York: Anchor Books, 1995.

CIA. *The World Factbook 1999 and 2001*—"Afghanistan." Jan. 1, 1999 and Jan. 1, 2001. Available: http://www.cia.gov/cia/publications/factbook/geos/af.html, Jan. 28, 2000 and Oct. 6, 2001.

Clark, Kate. "Afghanistan Has One of the Worst Records on Education in the World." *BBC Worldnews Services*, Apr. 27, 2000.

Clarke, Paul. "Afghanistan Outlook." "Food Security in Afghanistan," U.N.: The U.N. Office of the Co-ordinator for Afghanistan, UNSMA and the World Bank, Dec. 1999. Available: http://www.pcpafg.org/news/week/i/update/#1999, Oct. 8, 2001.

"The Cost of an Afghan 'Victory.'" *The Nation* 268(Feb. 15, 1999), 17–20.

Clinton, Hillary Rodham. "Remarks by First Lady Hillary Rodham Clinton," New York City, in her United Nations International Women's Day speech on women's rights, Mar. 4, 1999.

Clinton, William Jefferson. "Remarks by the President at Human Rights Day/ Eleanor Roosevelt Award Ceremony." The White House, Office of the Press Secretary, Dec. 6, 1999.

_____ and Hillary Rodham Clinton. "Remarks by the President and the First Lady at *Vogue* Reception." The White House, Office of the Press Secretary, Oct. 26, 1999.

Collett, Pamela. "Afghan Women in the Peace Process," *Peace-Review* 8 no. 3, (Sept. 1996), 397–402.

Co-operation Centre for Afghanistan. "Status of Girls' Education at the Beginning of 21st Century in Afghanistan" [Peshawar, Pakistan], *CAA Newsletter* VII no. 2 (Apr. 2000), 1.

_____. *Violence Against Women in Afghanistan Report* [Peshawar, Pakistan], Nov. 1999.

Dalal, Anaga. "What?" *Ms.* (Apr./May 2000), 9.

Daly, Catherine. (Department of Textiles, Clothing and Design and Research Association for the Center of Afghanistan Studies, University of Nebraska at Omaha), interview by the author, Mar. 8, 2000.

_____. "The 'Paarda' Expression of Hejaab Among Afghan Women in a Non-Muslim Community." In L. Boyton Arthur, ed., *Body, Dress and Religion*. Oxford, UK: Berg Publishers, 1999, 147–161.

Davis, Anthony. "How the Taliban Became a Military Force," in Maley (ed.), *Fundamentalism Reborn?* 43–71.

Dillner, Luisa. "Inequalities Cause Reproductive Deaths." *British Medical Journal* (Clinical Research ed.) 311 (Jul. 15, 1995), 147–148.

Dupree, Louis. *Afghanistan*. Princeton, N.J.: Princeton University Press, 1980.

Dupree, Nancy Hatch. "Afghan Women under the Taliban," In William Maley, ed., *Fundamentalism Reborn?* 145–166.

_____. "Afghanistan: Women, Society and Development." *Journal of Developing Societies* 8 no. 1 (Jan.-Apr. 1992), 30–42.

Eckhard, Fred. "Daily Press Briefing of Office of Spokesman for Secretary-General." June 2, 2000.

Electric Library Presents Encyclopedia.com. "Afghanistan (History)." (New York: Columbia University Press, 1994). Available: http://www.encyclopedia.com/articles/00164.html, Apr. 24, 2000.

Ellis, Deb. "Women's Journalism in Afghanistan." *NGO Coalition on Women's Human Rights in Conflict Situations Newsletter*, (Aug. 1999), 3:2. Available: http://www.ichrdd.ca/111/english/commdoc/publications/women/bulletin/vol3no2e.html, Jun. 14, 2000.

Emadi, Hafizullah. *Politics of Development and Women in Afghanistan*. New York: Paragon House, 1993.

_____. "State, Modernization and the Women's Movement in Afghanistan." *Review of Radical Political Economics* 23 no. 3–4 (Fall-Winter 1991), 224–243.

Emmott, Sue. "'Dislocation', Shelter, and Crisis: Afghanistan's Refugees and Notions of Home." *Gender and Development* 4 no. 1 (February 1996), 31–38.

Faiz, Abbas. "Health Care under the Taliban." *Lancet* 349 (Apr. 26, 1997), 1247–1248.

Feminist Majority Foundation. 1999. "Stop Gender Apartheid in Afghanistan." Available: http://www.feminist.org/afghan/facts.html, Apr. 23, 2000.

_____. "Stop Gender Apartheid in Afghanistan!" "Afghan Women's Scholarship Program." 1998. Available: http://www.feminist.org/afghan/scholarship.html, Apr. 23, 2000.

Fields-Meyer, Thomas. "Speaking Out: Mavis Leno Speaks Out Against the Taliban's Treatment of Women." *People Weekly* (Nov. 16, 1998), 232–234.

Gauhari, Farooka. *Searching for Saleem: An Afghan Woman's Odyssey*. Lincoln: University of Nebraska Press, 1997.

Goodwin, Jan. *Caught in the Crossfire*. New York: E.P. Dutton, 1987.

_____. *Price of Honor: Muslim Women Lift the Veil of Silence on the Islamic World*. Boston: Little, Brown, 1994.

Gross, Nasrine Abou-Bakre. "Afghan Women and Education: Letter to the *Washington Post*," unpublished, Apr. 7, 1999. Available: http://users.erols.com/kabultec/letter.html, Jul. 16, 2000.

_____. "Conference in Dushanbe for Women of Afghanistan." Report based on eyewitness knowledge as attendee of the conference, Aug. 2, 2000. Email to author, Aug. 2, 2000.

_____. Interview by the author, July 16, 2000.

_____. *Qadam-ha-ye Awshti wa Massouliat-e Ma Afghan-ha* (*Steps of Peace and Our Responsibility as Afghans*). Falls Church, VA: Kabultec, 2000.

_____. *Qassarikh-e Malay: Memories of the First Girls' High School in Afghanistan*. Falls Church, VA: Kabultec, June 1998 at "Afghan Women and Education." "Translation of the First Three Pages." Available: http://users.erols.com/kabultec/firstbk.html, Oct. 8, 2001.

Haidar, Shoukria. NEGAR Organization, "Declaration of the Essential Rights of Afghan Women." Dushanbe, Tajikistan, Jun. 28, 2000.

Hanifi, M. Jamil. *Historical and Cultural Dictionary of Afghanistan*. Metuchen, N.J.: Scarecrow Press, 1976.

Hashimi, Morwarid (Mora). (U.S. resident who fled from Afghanistan in 1983), interviews by the author, Feb. 16, 2000, Mar. 21, 2000.

Hashimi, Rahman. (U.S. resident who fled from Afghanistan in 1983), interview by the author, Feb. 16, 2000.

Hassanyar, Amir S. (Director, Co-operation Centre for Afghanistan, Peshawar), email to the author, Jun. 6, 2000.

Hathout, Hassan. *Reading the Muslim Mind*. Plainfield, Ind.: American Trust Publications, 1995.

Hawthorne, Nathaniel. *The Best of Hawthorne: Edited with Introduction and Notes by Mark Van Doren*. New York: Ronald Press, 1951.

Hopkirk, Peter. *The Great Game: The Struggle for Empire in Central Asia*. New York: Kodansha International, 1992.

Human Rights Watch. "Asia Overview: Afghanistan." Available: http://www.hrw.org/wr2k/Asia.htm, Apr. 23, 2000.

Iacopino, Vincent, et al. *The Taliban's War on Women: A Health and Human Rights Crisis in Afghanistan: A Report*. Boston: Physicians for Human Rights, 1998, 1–119.

Inderfurth, Karl F. "Prepared Statement Karl F. Inderfurth Assistant Secretary of State for South Asian Affairs Before the Senate Foreign Relations Committee Subcommittee on Near Eastern and South Asian Affairs." *Federal News Service*, Oct. 8, 1998.

Islamic Emirate of Afghanistan. "The Movement of the Taliban," *Homepage*, Feb. 2, 2000. Available: http://www.afghan-ie.com/taliban/tailimov.htm, Jun. 17, 2000.

"Jay and Mavis Leno Donate $100,000 to Expand Campaign Against Gender Apartheid in Afghanistan." *Philanthropy News Digest* 4 (Oct. 28, 1998), 43.

Khalilzad, Zalmay. "Anarchy in Afghanistan." *Journal of International Affairs* 51 no. 1 (Summer 1997), 37–38.

King, Angela E.V. Office of the Special Adviser on Gender Issues and Advancement of Women, United Nations, New York. "Report of the United Nations Interagency Gender Mission to Afghanistan." Nov. 12–24, 1997, 1–42.

_____. "Statement," in "No Reason for Optimism About Early Ceasefire in Afghanistan Security Council Told During Open Briefing." United Nations Press Release, SC/6840, Apr. 7, 2000. http://www.un.org/News/Press/docs/2000/20000407.sc6840.doc.html, Oct. 8, 2001.

Kome, Penney. "Lifting the Shroud." *WIN Magazine* no. 27 (Dec. 1999), Part B. Available: http://www.winmagazine.org/issues/issue27/win27d.htm, May 1, 2000.

Larry King Live. "The Women of the Senate Discuss 'The Women of the Senate.'" CNN transcript #00072600V22, Jul. 26, 2000.

Leno, Mavis. (Feminist Majority board member for Drive to End Gender Apartheid in Afghanistan), interview by the author, April 19, 2000.

_____. "Prepared Testimony of Mavis Leno, National Board Member, Feminist Majority Before the Senate Appropriations Committee Foreign Operations Subcommittee, Subject—Gender Apartheid in Afghanistan." *Federal News Service*, Mar. 9, 1999.

Lloyd, Marion. "In Pakistan, Afghan Academics Struggle to Maintain Universities for Refugees." *The Chronicle of Higher Education* 45 no. 11 (Nov. 6, 1998), A65.

Lyden, Jacki. "*All Things Considered*." Aug. 22, 1998, NPR transcript #98082204-216.

Magnus, Ralph H. and Eden Naby. *Afghanistan: Mullah, Marx, and Mujahid*. Boulder, Colo.: Westview Press, 1998.

Maley, William, ed. *Fundamentalism Reborn? Afghanistan and the Taliban*. Washington Square, N.Y.: New York University Press, 1998.

_____. "Introduction: Interpreting the Taliban," in William Maley, ed., *Fundamentalism Reborn? Afghanistan and the Taliban*. Washington Square, N.Y.: New York University Press, 1998, 1–28.

Marsden, Peter. *The Taliban: War, Religion and the New Order in Afghanistan*. Karachi, Lahore, Islamabad: Oxford University Press; London and New York: Zed Books Ltd., 1998.

Massoud, Commander Ahmad Shah. Interview by Azadi Afghan Radio, July 2, 2000. Available: http://www.afghanradio.com/interview/ahmadshahmasoud07082000.htm, July 27, 2000.

Mazurkewich, Karen. "Bringing Hope—and Homework—to the Girls." *Time* 156 (May 29, 2000), 21. Available: http://www.cnn.com/ASIANOW/time/magazine/2000/0529/afghanistan.womenduction.html, Jun. 6, 2000.

Media Action International. "Tali-bans." Oct. 16, 1999, extract from the *Essential Field Guide to Afghanistan*. Available: http://www.mediaaction.org/pubcn/efgafghn/taliban.htm, Aug. 12, 2000.

Moghadam, Valentine M. *Modernizing Women: Gender and Social Change in the Middle East*. Boulder, Colo.: Reinner, 1993.

_____. "Revolution, Religion, and Gender Politics: Iran and Afghanistan Compared." *Journal of Women's History* 10 no. 4 (Winter 1999), 172–195.

Moret, Jim and Brent Sadler. "Afghanistan Ruled with Taliban Style of Islam." The World Today, Oct. 1, 1998; CNN transcript #98100108V23.

Norchi, Charles. "Human Rights in Afghanistan: Two Decades of Abuse." Oct. 16, 1999. Available: http://www.mediaaction.org/pubcn/efgafghn/hum.htm, May 13, 2000.

Paul, Lara. "Women in Danger in Afghanistan." *Peace* (Sept.-Oct. 1997). Available: http://www.peacemagazine.org/9709/lara-afg.htm, Jan. 8, 2000.

Pollitt, Katha. "Tearing at the Veil." (Interview with Sajeda Hayat and Sehar Saba.) *The New York Times Magazine* (May 14, 2000), 23.

Prussel, Deborah. "Feminists Take on UNOCAL." *The Progressive* 62 no. 10 (Oct. 1998) 14–15.

Rahel, Ansar, Laina Farhat-Holzman, Philip Dacey and Will Webster. "Treatment of Afghan Women Needs Attention." *The Christian Science Monitor* (May 9, 2000), 10.

Rahi, Humera. In "Afghans Go to Battle with Poems Upon Their Lips" by Ahmed Rashid [The Federal Capital Press of Australia], *The Canberra Times*, Mar. 8, 1998, A22.

Rasekh, Zohra, Heidei M. Bauer, Michele M. Manos and Vincent Iacopino. "Women's Health and Human Rights in Afghanistan." *JAMA* 280 no. 5, (Aug. 5, 1998), 449–455.

Rashid, Ahmed. "Epicentre of Terror." *Far Eastern Economic Review* 160 (May 11, 2000), 16–18.

_____. "Scourge of God: Strict Islamic Rules Imposed in Afghanistan by the Ruling Taliban Are Plunging That Strife-Torn Country Deeper Into Ruin." *Far Eastern Economic Review* 160 no. 32 (Aug. 7, 1997), 52–53.

_____. "The Taliban: Exporting Extremism." *Foreign Affairs* 78 no. 6 (Nov/Dec 1999), 22–35.

_____. *Taliban: Militant Islam, Oil and Fundamentalism in Central Asia*. New Haven: Yale University Press, 2000.

Reif, Megan. "Beyond the Veil—Bigger Issues." *The Christian Science Monitor* (May 3, 2000), 11.

*Reports from the Land of Savageries, Insults and Obscenities*. "Mariam Girl's [*sic*] High School Turned into a Market." Available: http://rawa.org/50reports.htm, Aug. 14, 2000.

Revolutionary Association of the Women of Afghanistan. Activist. "A Report from the Pol-e-Charkhi Prison in Kabul." Dec. 1999. Email to the author, Jan. 19. 2000.

_____. "Biography of Martyred Meena, Founding Leader of RAWA." Available: http://rawa.fancymarketing.net/meena.html, Oct. 8, 2001.

_____. "About RAWA." Available: http://rawa.fancymarketing.net/rawa.html, Oct. 8, 2001.

_____. "France Grants RAWA a Human Rights Prize." Email to author Apr. 16, 2000.

_____. Interviews with Afghan women provided to and translated for the author, Mar. 14, 2000, May 15, 2000, and Jul. 2, 2000.

_____. "RAWA Observes Black Day of April 28 in Islamabad and Washington, D.C." Email to author Apr. 29, 2000.

_____. Shabana (RAWA Activist), email to the author, Jul. 1, 2000.

Rubin, Barnett R. "Afghanistan: The Forgotten Crisis (February 1996)." *WRITENET Country Papers.* Available: http://www.unhcr.ch/refworld/country/writenet/ wriafg.htm, Apr. 24, 2000.

_____. "Conflict and Peace in Afghanistan." *Afghanistan Outlook.* U.N.: The U.N. Office of the Co-ordinator for Afghanistan, UNSMA and the World Bank, Dec. 1999. Available: http://www.afghanistanvoice.org/ARTICLES/OUTLOOK_ Conflict.shtml, Oct. 7, 2001.

_____. "Testimony, Oct. 8, 1998, Barnett R. Rubin, Director of the Center for Preventive Action and Senior Fellow, Senate Foreign Relations, Near Eastern and South Asian Affairs Events in Afghanistan." *Federal Document Clearing House.*

Rumi, Jelaluddin. "Poem 208." In his *Mystical Poems of Rumi.* Tr. A. J. Arberry: Boulder, Colo.: Westview Press, 1979.

Shalinsky, Audrey C. "Gender Issues in the Afghanistan Diaspora: Nadia's Story." *Frontiers* 17 no. 3 (1996), 102–123.

Skaine, Rosemarie. *Power and Gender: Issues in Sexual Dominance and Harassment.* McFarland & Co., 1996.

Shorish-Shamley, Zieba (Co-founder and executive director, Women's Alliance for Peace and Human Rights in Afghanistan). "I remember you…: Dedicated to My Suffering Afghan Sisters." Mar. 8, 1998. Available: http://www.angelfire. com/on/wapha/remember.html, July 22, 2000.

_____. "Women's Position, Role, and Rights in Islam." Women's Alliance for Peace and Human Rights in Afghanistan, Available: http://www.angelfire.com/on/ wapha/islam.html. Apr. 30, 2000.

Stewart, Rhea Talley. *Fire in Afghanistan, 1914–1929; Faith, Hope, and the British Empire.* Garden City, N.Y.: Doubleday, 1973.

"Stop the Violence." *Women's Health Journal* no. 4 (October-December 1996), 11.

"Taliban Appeal to UNSC Not to Slap More Curbs on Afghanistan." *Afghan News,* Jun. 12, 2000. Accessed at *Afghan News* website, Jun. 12, 2000.

Todd, Emmanuel. *The Explanation of Ideology: Family Structures and Social Systems.* Oxford, England: Basil Blackwell, 1985.

Tomsen, Peter (Ambassador-in-residence, University of Nebraska at Omaha and special envoy to the Afghan Resistance with the rank of ambassador, 1989–1992), interview by the author, Feb. 9, 2000.

_____. "Beyond Marx and Mullahs." *Washington Times,* May 23, 1999, B3.

_____. "A Chance for Peace in Afghanistan: The Taliban's Days Are Numbered." *Foreign Affairs* 79 no. 1 (Jan/Feb 2000), 179–182.

_____. "East of the Oder Afghan Peace Is Finally Within Reach." *The Wall Street Journal Europe,* Jun. 2, 2000, 9.

_____. "Flawed Policy in Afghanistan." *Washington Times,* Mar. 17, 2000, A19.

United Nations. Development Programme. "Gender Sensitive Institutional Capacity—Building of Afghan NGOs for Civil Society." Project Proposal, 1999. Available: http://www.reliefweb.int/library/appeals/afg99/pro_adv_human/rwd. htm, Aug. 17, 2000.

_____. Department of Public Information DPI/1772/HR "Women and Violence." Feb. 1996. Available: http://www.un.org/rights/dpi1772e.htm, Oct. 8, 2001.

_____. High Commissioner for Refugees Centre for Documentation and Research. "Update to the Background Paper on Refugees and Asylum Seekers from Afghanistan." Geneva, Jan. 1999. Available: http://www/unhcr.ch/refworld/country/cdr/cdrafg02.htm. Jul. 9, 2000.

_____. Secretary General, Report of the Secretary-General: "The Situation in Afghanistan and its Implications for International Peace and Security." Sept. 21, 1999. Available: http://www.un.org/documents/search.html, No. S/1999/994, Oct. 8, 2001.

_____. Security Council. "Security Council Resolution 1267." Oct. 15, 1999. Available: http://www.un.org/Docs/scres/1999/99sc1267.htm, S/RES/1267, Oct. 8, 2001.

_____ Statement by the President of the Security Council, Oct. 22, 1999. Available: http://www.un.org/Docs/sc/statements/1999/prst9929.htm, S/PRST/1999/29, Oct. 8, 2001.

_____. Statement by the President of the Security Council, Apr. 7, 2000 Available: http://www.un.org/Docs/sc/statements/2000/prst12e.pdf, Jun. 20, 2000.

_____. Statistics Division. "Indicators on Literacy." Available: http://www.un.org/Depts/unsd/social/literacy.htm, Jun. 2, 2000.

U.S. Committee for Refugees. "Worldwide Refugee Information: Country Report for Afghanistan." 2000. Available: http://www.refugees.org/world/countryindex/afghanistan.htm, Jun. 10, 2000.

U.S. Congress. Senate. Committee on Foreign Relations. Subcommittee on Near Eastern and South Asian Affairs. *Afghanistan, Is There Hope for Peace?* Hearings, 104th Cong., 2d sess., June 6, 25, 26, and 27, 1996.

_____. *The Taliban: Engagement or Confrontation?* Hearings, 106th Cong., 2d sess., July 20, 2000.

U.S. Department of State. Bureau of Democracy, Human Rights, and Labor. *Annual Report on International Religious Freedom for 1999: Afghanistan.* "Section 1: Freedom of Religion" and "Section 3: Women." Washington, D.C., Sept. 9, 1999. Available: http://www.state.gov/www/global/human_rights/irf/irf_rpt/1999/irf_afghanis99.html, Apr. 23, 2000.

_____. *1999 Country Reports on Human Rights Practices: Afghanistan.* Washington, D.C., Feb. 25, 2000. Available: http://www.state.gov/www/global/human_rights/1999_hrp_report/afghanis.html, Feb. 25, 2000.

Wali, Sima. "Beyond Sanctions." *Ms.* (Apr./May 2000), 27.

_____. "Repatriation and the Reconstruction of Afghanistan: The Role of Women." *Migration World Magazine* 22 no. 4 (1994), 26–28.

Wallace, Mike and Christiane Amanpour. "Islamic Group Takes over Afghanistan Capital, Hangs Former Leaders and Brings Strict Rules to Men and Women." CBS News Transcripts, *60 Minutes*, Aug. 23, 1998.

Wardak, Massouma Esmaty. *The Position and Role of Afghan Women in Afghan*

*Society: From the Late 18th to the Late 19th Century.* Kabul, Afghanistan: [Dawlati Matba'ah], 1991.

Women for Women in Afghanistan. "Advocacy Work Is Essential for Safeguarding the Human Rights That Are Guaranteed to All People Through the U.N. Universal Declaration of Human Rights." *Lifting the Veil of Silence Bulletin,* email from Janice Eisenhauer, Women for Women in Afghanistan, Calgary, Jan. 9, 2000.

"Women in Afghanistan." Mar. 13, 1998. Online. Internet. Available: http:// women3rdworld.miningco.com/culture/women3rdworld/library/weekly/aa0313 98.htm, Jan. 8, 2000.

Women Living Under Muslim Laws. "Increased Structural Violence." *Off Our Backs* 27 no. 3. (Mar. 1997) 11.

Women on the Road for Afghanistan, "Call for Action by the Women on the Road for Afghanistan." Dushanbe, Tadjikistan, Jun. 28, 2000. Available: http:// www.worfa.org, Aug. 2, 2000.

Women's Alliance for Peace and Human Rights in Afghanistan. "The Facts." n.d. Available: http://www.wapha.org/facts.html, Oct. 8, 2001.

"Women's Self-Immolation Under the Taliban's Domination." *The Burst of the "Islamic Government" Bubble in Afghanistan* (Quetta, Pakistan: RAWA, Jan. 1997), No. 2, 8–23.

Yaseer, Abdul Raheem (Coordinator of International Exchange Programs, and deputy director of the Center for Afghanistan Studies at the University of Nebraska at Omaha), interview by the author, Apr. 13, 2000.

# Index